Alice Paul,
the National Woman's
Party and the Vote

Alice Paul, the National Woman's Party and the Vote

The First Civil Rights Struggle of the 20th Century

BERNADETTE CAHILL

McFarland & Company, Inc., Publishers
Jefferson, North Carolina

Library of Congress Cataloguing-in-Publication Data

Cahill, Bernadette.
　　Alice Paul, the National Woman's Party and the vote : the first civil
rights struggle of the 20th century / Bernadette Cahill.
　　　　p.　cm.
　　Includes bibliographical references and index.

　　ISBN 978-0-7864-6979-6 (softcover : acid free paper) ∞
　　ISBN 978-1-4766-1978-1 (ebook)

　　1. Paul, Alice, 1885–1977.　2. Suffragists—United States—
Biography.　3. Women's rights—United States—History.
4. National Woman's Party—History.　I. Title.

JK1899.P38C35　2015
324.2732—dc23
[B]　　　　　　　　　　　　　　　　　　　　　　2015004454

British Library cataloguing data are available

On the cover: Alice Paul, leader of the National Woman's Party,
unfurls the completed Ratification Flag in Washington, D.C.,
in August 1920 (Library of Congress)

Printed in the United States of America

McFarland & Company, Inc., Publishers
　Box 611, Jefferson, North Carolina 28640
　www.mcfarlandpub.com

To
Miss McCann
and to
Thomas Peter Cahill

Table of Contents

Preface

The civil rights movement in the United States was about African Americans in the 1960s. That, at least, is how the term is defined in modern times. Whenever the "civil rights movement" is recalled, visions of marches, police dogs attacking protesters and Martin Luther King, Jr.'s "I have a dream" speech reverberating around the Reflecting Pool in Washington, D.C., are what come to mind.

Yet, such a definition distorts the real history of civil rights. The fact is that campaigns for civil rights in the United States lasted much longer than a period in the middle of the twentieth century. Of equal importance, civil rights in the United States were never about only race: they also involved women and have included women's campaigns for equality under the law, which women have failed to win. They have included struggles for equality of education, of pay, for jobs and in countless other aspects of life—all the same goals for which blacks have also struggled. Women's campaigns have included, specifically, the struggle for the right to vote. Yet these simple facts are today generally ignored. It was not always the case that women were excluded from the concept of civil rights; their exclusion from that concept seems to be a phenomenon of the past fifty years.[1]

Another key fact in the history of these two struggles has also been lost. While they have had a direct impact on each other at key moments in their respective histories and the impact of the black movement on women has been recognized, the equally important influence of women's rights on blacks has largely been ignored. In particular, it is virtually unheard of that the black civil rights movement in the 1960s could not have achieved what it did when it did without the pivotal event of the victory of women's suffrage forty years earlier, specifically the campaign of Alice Paul and the National Woman's Party. Yet the strategy of this group to bring the issue of votes by women right

1

to the gates of the president in the teen years of the twentieth century established the model for succeeding sustained political activism and secured important precedents and rights that African Americans were able to utilize in their own struggle against racial inequality and discrimination.

The travails of the two movements may have been different in many details, but the movements had the same origin at the founding of the nation and they both have worked towards making the nation established on liberty and equality live up in practice to its principles. As such, the black civil rights movement and the woman civil rights movement are equal in import, as are their histories and influence on U.S. history. Yet today, the Civil Rights Movement—capitalized—is the name given to the sixties struggle for African American rights, while the still-incomplete struggle for the emancipation of women is referred to as women's rights—often not capitalized—as if it is only a side issue. The former long ago won the goal of equality, in theory at least, in United States fundamental law. By contrast, the campaigns for women's civil rights a century after women won the vote have still not achieved that same basic goal. Further, the African American movement is constantly honored and recognized. Women's long struggle receives considerably less recognition in United States history and its significance is subordinated to that of black rights. The recognition that the women's struggle receives hardly accords with the percentage of women in the population. Further, there are distinct practical results for women and their history because of this second-class status in civil rights.

This book aims to rebalance this situation. It looks at these issues and examines the pivotal role of Alice Paul and the National Woman's Party in helping to establish civil rights for all in the United States.

Introduction

This book is ultimately about place. It is about particular places in a key development in United States history and specifically about Alice Paul, the National Woman's Party (NWP) and the significance of each in that history. It is about neglected civil rights sites—the places where Paul and the NWP struggled to win and guarantee the primary civil right of this nation, the right to vote, for 50 percent of the population.

This book grew out of two events in my own life: finding the *Iron Jawed Angels* movie and a visit to the nation's capital in 2010. *Iron Jawed Angels* tells how a group of young women went to Washington, D.C., in late 1912 and until 1920 faced down the president of the United States in order to force a successful conclusion to the campaign for votes for women, which had been ongoing since 1848. A remarkable story of determination and unbounded courage, the victory of these women was so unquestionable that many people in the twenty-first century are unaware that the struggle took place.

My mother's work with Lilian Lenton in Britain for equal rights for women helped to spark my own lifelong interest in women's past. By spring 2008, in Boone, North Carolina, I was writing many articles for the local newspaper and magazine about women's history, particularly the Equal Rights Amendment. *Iron Jawed Angels* and further researches raised my knowledge level. Then in August 2010 a long-planned trip to Washington, D.C., turned out to coincide with a 90th anniversary demonstration at the White House for ratification of the Equal Rights Amendment. This triggered the idea of going to see for myself the places where the major scenes in *Iron Jawed Angels* had occurred. In particular, I wanted to know the actual location of the building with the balcony where Alice Paul had displayed the star-spangled NWP flag when the Nineteenth Amendment was promulgated. I assumed that not only would the building be marked clearly, but also that many other locations in Washington would be similarly marked. I also expected to find books easily on this specific subject.

I had expected a lot. During my few days in the area, I found that, apart from the White House and the Capitol, the Sewall-Belmont House Museum was the only building I could easily locate that was associated in some way with the NWP's campaign. Further afield, I did find the Occoquan museum in Lorton, about twenty miles to the south in Virginia, and Alice Paul's family home in Moorestown, New Jersey. Multiple searches on the Web while I was in Washington produced a brochure of women's history sites from the National Woman's History Museum (NWHM). This raised my hopes, but, although it contained a useful summary of the suffrage struggle, it was empty of the kind of detail I wanted. My curiosity unsatisfied by this particular trip, I now immediately began a month of solid research on the Web while I also hunted for places and events through every book I could get my hands on about the final suffrage campaign in D.C. This period ended in another quick trip to Washington to locate and photograph the places I had found. My tour saddened me: so little of the city remained the way it was a century ago that pinning down specific locations was almost impossible.

This second trip to Washington also raised my ire, for I found a brochure about civil rights in the city. Unlike the NWHM brochure, however, it contained nothing to help me in my hunt for the places where Alice Paul and the NWP fought for the vote. Worse, the brochure was a guide to several clearly marked walking tours that contained virtually nothing about women. I now found myself wondering how anything to do with civil rights could include scarce a mention of women's campaign for the vote. I concluded that if women were all but excluded from civil rights, then the official history was wrong and it needed to be corrected. Within another month, I had compiled a slide show of my discoveries to that date, calling it "Forgotten Civil Rights Sites in Washington, D.C.," with the subtitle "Where Women Fought for Equal Rights." The reactions were interesting. Women gaped and wistfully wanted to know why they had never heard about the subject. On the other hand, many people turning up for my talks were often put out to find that my subject was not about African Americans.

Soon, with a move to Little Rock, Arkansas, I spent a year there researching suffrage history and unraveling the history of who did what when and where. What was especially fascinating in this work, new as my D.C. research seemed to be, was to find out how the paths of national and local stories crossed, while knowledge of the national history both enhanced and corrected local history. This Little Rock research led to several invitations to speak on the suffrage struggle, for which I compiled slide presentations demonstrating how the local and national campaigns intertwined. Whenever possible, I included the words "civil rights" in the title and found the same reactions: women were astounded at the tale and fascinated with the history, while those who came to hear a talk about civil rights were taken aback to hear about women. If I left "civil rights" out of the title, attendances dropped. Had I needed any confirmation that the current presentation of the true history of civil rights in the United States is at best incomplete, this was it. It was gratifying, therefore, to attract a full house at the Clinton School of Public Service when I was asked to talk about suffrage there during a brief display of the actual Nineteenth Amendment in the Clinton Presidential Library in October 2012.

That presentation was about how the amendment came to be. Its final, required ratification occurred on August 18, 1920, when Tennessee concluded a successful cliff-hanging vote. Promulgation took place on August 26, when the secretary of state of the United States signed the amendment, which successfully concluded a struggle that spanned 72 years. But the ideas of that struggle extended much further back in history. All along, it was a hard-fought campaign and during the long struggle women used every tool they could devise within the bounds of the law to win the same voting privileges that over time authorities had conferred on almost all male citizens. The result was to nearly double the total vote. When Alice Paul celebrated Tennessee's vote, therefore, she commemorated the most momentous civil rights victory in the history of the nation.

In 1920 the vote was the first, and so far only, successful reform of those that women called for in the Declaration of Sentiments published at the Seneca Falls Convention in New York in 1848. Those other reforms amounted essentially to equality and equal justice. With victory, therefore, Paul was only closing the first act in the long tale of equal rights for women. An intermission of several years followed, but soon the National Woman's Party picked the story up and began its campaign to secure the rest of the Seneca Falls goals. With suffrage now settled, however, other issues could rise and one of those was civil rights for black Americans, whose rights under the Fourteenth and Fifteenth amendments had been severely truncated since Reconstruction. And for African Americans, in August 1920, thanks to the women's victory, the issues were suddenly reinforced for a renewed struggle against racial injustice.

While the victory of suffrage was, therefore, pivotal for civil rights in the United States, the irony is that woman suffrage is more or less excluded from the term "civil rights" and sidelined to the category of "women's rights."

Further, where "civil rights" automatically evokes images of mass meetings of African Americans in Washington in the 1960s, the precursors of this process, and the first of their kind in Washington and across the country, that Alice Paul orchestrated nearly fifty years before are known by only a tiny number of people. And while the Civil Rights Act aimed at the most egregious examples of legally based racism across the nation and also began to tackle racial discriminations through social and other conventions, today the female half of the population still do not have equality under the fundamental law of the land.

The purpose of this book, therefore, is to commemorate the triumphs of Alice Paul, the National Woman's Party and the countless other women who worked to win the vote, to place their work squarely in the context of civil rights and to restore them to their rightful place in the nation's history and consciousness. It is also to pin those events to specific locations, just as any momentous contributions to a nation's history are. The book begins with a history of what happened when two young women headed to Washington, D.C., at the end of 1912 determined to secure votes for women. It continues with an analysis of what the Nineteenth Amendment was and what it was not. It looks at what women did after ratification and examines the pivotal role of woman suffrage in United States history for civil rights generally and its effect on the black civil rights movement in particular. It concludes with a tour of Washington's places where those young women fought and won the battle to amend the Constitution. Throughout, as the term "suffrage" a century ago by definition meant "woman suffrage," this is what appears here.

From the first presentation of my Washington, D.C., slide show, I was encouraged to write a book of this work, for which I have to thank Virginia Roseman of Boone, North Carolina. I must also thank the countless librarians and researchers across the nation who have helped me pin down facts and articles.

As I am an independent scholar, this volume is the result of what I have researched and written in my own time with the financial help only of my husband, Ron Davis, and my sister, Dr. Catherine Smith, and her husband, Cairns Mason, both of Stirling, Scotland. For their help, I am very grateful. This generosity has allowed me intellectual freedom while applying rigorous standards of history and journalism to the work. Unfortunately, absolute perfection is hard to achieve, even if only because of wayward fingers on the keyboard. For those wayward fingers and anything that I have entered with error, or for anything that I have inadvertently omitted or unintentionally misrepresented, I apologize.

For emotional support and constant encouragement I once again must thank my sister and her husband. For being my full-time, unpaid caregiver during my long recovery from a broken leg, during which I finally managed to complete this task, I extend my most heartfelt thanks to my husband, Ron Davis, who was with me at the start, walking through D.C. and taking photographs. He has listened to me, moved books countless times, assisted me into and out of bathtubs and showers, wheeled me to the car, helped me hobble around the house, and is now enabling me to walk again, in spite of his own physical challenges. Without him, this book would not have made it into print.

CHAPTER 1

What Alice Paul Did
for Suffrage Between
1912 and 1920

On March 3, 1913, throngs of women, estimated by various sources to be between five thousand and eight thousand, assembled near the United States Capitol. Around three o'clock, with a woman on a white horse at their head, they began to march along Pennsylvania Avenue. A horse-drawn cart with a huge banner followed immediately behind the white horse. Then in close formation, succeeding sections in the parade represented contrasting groups—women of industry, social workers, teachers, opera celebrities, government clerks and many others. In one group of university graduates the instigator of the event also marched: Alice Paul of New Jersey, a recent PhD graduate of the University of Pennsylvania in Philadelphia. Nearby also walked Paul's second-in-command, Lucy Burns of Brooklyn, New York, a graduate of Vassar. The woman on the white horse, also a New Yorker and a Vassar graduate, was Inez Milholland. A group in brown capes, looking the worse for wear, brought up the rear.

This march in Washington more than a century ago was an event the like of which the United States had never before witnessed. In fact, ever since Paul and Burns had announced the coming event that January, America's newspapers had avidly followed it. Their office had instantly become a focus for newsmen, noses twitching for the latest scoop. Almost on their own, Paul and Burns had pulled together in a matter of months a publicity coup with inestimable potential.

The banner on the cart that followed immediately behind Milholland gave the reason for the march:

WE DEMAND AN AMENDMENT TO THE CONSTITUTION
OF THE UNITED STATES ENFRANCHISING
THE WOMEN OF THE COUNTRY.

The purpose of this parade was to jump-start a campaign for a federal amendment to the Constitution to ban discrimination in voting on account of sex. Paul and Burns, acting through the Congressional Committee of the largest woman suffrage organization in the nation—the National American Woman Suffrage Association (NAWSA)—were picking up where the parent organization's strategy had fizzled out long ago. Years earlier, the National had begun to concentrate on campaigning to win suffrage through the several states, to the neglect of a long-established federal amendment campaign. Already the revived federal activity had provoked opposition: on February 19, a month after the opening of the Congressional Committee office, the National Association Opposed to Woman Suffrage had opened a branch nearby, presenting journalists with the kind of conflict they thrive on.

Paul and Burns had planned the grand parade on March 3, 1913, for maximum impact. It took place the day before the inauguration of Woodrow Wilson as president, gaining advantage in presenting its message to the large, celebrating crowds, at that point a captive audience in the nation's capital waiting for the inauguration. With the parade routed along highly decorated Pennsylvania Avenue, the women's march would benefit from aligning with the theme of the festivities, identifying suffrage as being as patriotic an idea as all the partisan and nationalistic sentiments celebrated during the inauguration of a new chief executive, of whatever party. By marching along the same route that the nation's men had used for decades for national celebrations and commemorations, the women asserted the equality of the female half of the nation with that of males, even if the message they wanted attended to was an end to the exclusion of women from equal participation in government.

As the planning of the parade attested, Paul and Burns were no neophytes in such work. They had received the best training in the world with the militant suffragettes of the United Kingdom, which by 1913 had been setting the pace for agitation for woman suffrage for nearly ten years. Paul and Burns had met when they were arrested in a suffrage protest in London in June 1909 as members of the militant Pankhurst family's Women's Social and Political Union (WSPU). As suffragettes in Britain, they had sold newspapers on the street, held street meetings, chalked sidewalks and been central to the organization of major parades, such as the great pageant of Scottish suffragettes in Edinburgh in October 1909. They had both been imprisoned and on hunger

Alice Paul began her work in Washington, D.C., as leader of the Congressional Committee of the National American Woman Suffrage Association (NAWSA). She then became national chairman of the Congressional Union for Woman Suffrage and finally leader of the National Woman's Party (Library of Congress Prints and Photographs Division, Washington, D.C., Harris & Ewing Collection, 1915, Digital ID: http://www.loc.gov/pictures/item/hec2008004840/).

Lucy Burns was originally vice chairman of the Congressional Committee of the National American Woman Suffrage Association, then vice chairman of the Congressional Union for Woman Suffrage, which she founded with Paul. She took on varied roles within the NWP and was an instigator of the picketing campaign. She spent more time in prison than any other suffragist (Library of Congress Prints and Photographs Division, Washington, D.C., Harris & Ewing Collection, 1913, Digital ID: http://www.loc.gov/pictures/item/hec2008002755/).

strike for the cause and Paul had been forcibly fed while serving and protesting during one of several jail sentences.

The route of the march was to be from the Capitol, round the White House and thence to a grand rally; but when the marchers finally converged there, they were ragged, cold and enraged, for very early in the parade a mob had laid in on them and the initial mêlée had degenerated along the route into a full-scale riot with no police action protecting either the women from their largely male attackers or the women's right to march peacefully. The riot demonstrated clearly that the idea of votes for women—even in 1913 and after a campaign for American female enfranchisement that had begun sixty-five years before with Elizabeth Cady Stanton's call at Seneca Falls for the inclusion of women in the polity—was still as disturbing and revolutionary as a practical proposal for the national government as was the idea in the Deep South that black men should be allowed to exercise their constitutional right to vote, which they were granted in 1870 in the Fifteenth Amendment to the Consti-

The Great Suffrage March of March 3, 1913, on the eve of President Wilson's inauguration ended in a riot when the crowd attacked the women and the police did virtually nothing to stop it. The event began eight years of pageantry, petitions and parades across the United States and delegations to the president and Congress from all over the country. This deluge of attention from American women focused on the amendment that would finally win them the vote (Library of Congress Prints and Photographs Division, Washington, D.C., National Photo Company Collection, Digital ID: http://www.loc.gov/pictures/item/npc2008000733/).

tution. Paul and Burns had experienced similar deranged behavior against women during their work with the Pankhursts in Britain. Yet Paul, on returning home in 1910, said she believed the like would not occur in the United States.[1] Now she and Burns saw the reality of pressing for votes for women in their home country.

President Wilson's arrival in Washington, D.C., for his inauguration, according to the reports of the time, was quiet because the cheering crowds for him were instead jeering crowds attacking women on Pennsylvania Avenue. Reports and images of men attacking women in the processional thoroughfare of the nation's capital now began to compete with his presidency. As well-seasoned publicists for the cause, Paul and Burns knew that, with the public outraged against the mob attack on the march, they held the public relations advantage. They did not hesitate to press it. Within a week, Paul testified at a Senate investigation into the riot. Ultimately, the D.C. chief of police would lose his job in the fallout. Then, that March 17, Paul led a delegation to meet with President Wilson to canvass the inclusion of the proposed federal suffrage amendment in his message to the new Congress.

Again this was a new departure. At that time, the capital and president were poised only to assume the central role in the nation's life that they now hold, but Paul and Burns had begun to apply yet another lesson from their experience with the suffragettes in Britain. There, where only one center of political power existed, it had been logical and natural for the WSPU to focus on the king and Parliament in London for its campaign. In the United States, where up to this point in national life the several states had been the place where political power had mostly resided, it had not been automatic to think of Washington, D.C., or the president as the focus of a political campaign such as this. In fact, the president had no role in amending the Constitution under any of its provisions: that was for Congress and the states to do under Article V. Nevertheless, Paul and Burns planned to win the president's support, aiming for him to use his *political* influence to vault suffrage to victory. The new president was known to advocate increased executive and centralized powers. Yet, when the suffrage delegation met with him, this former president of Princeton University and governor of New Jersey looked askance: he had more important issues to consider, such as his campaign promises of currency and tariff reform. Paul's point that his focus on such reforms would, without enfranchisement for women, be legislating without the consent of the governed went over this intellectual's head.

Wilson stonewalled in two more meetings, following which, on April 3, 1913, Paul and Burns organized a second suffrage march with representatives

Alice Paul and Lucy Burns opened their first office in the basement of 1420 F Street in January 1913. By early 1914, the Congressional Committee had become the Congressional Union, completely separate from the NAWSA, occupying two more floors of this same building and having expanded into 1416 F Street, where the editorial offices of the new publication, *Suffragist,* were located (Library of Congress, Prints and Photographs Division, Washington, D.C., Harris & Ewing Collection, 1913, Digital ID: http://www.loc.gov/pictures/item/hec2008001390/).

from every state and congressional district. This time the marchers—again with banners flying—headed to Congress, where they submitted petitions for the same federal suffrage amendment that Susan B. Anthony had first submitted in 1878 and which the U.S. Senate had rejected sixteen to thirty-four when it finally came up for vote in 1887. In 1913, the amendment, then called the Bristow-Mondell Amendment after the two Republicans who introduced it in their respective houses, read:

> The right of citizens of the United States to vote shall not be denied or abridged by the United States or by any State on account of sex.
> Congress shall have power to enforce this article by appropriate legislation.

It was a clear, straightforward and economically worded proposal. In a significant victory for Paul and Burns, the Senate sent it to the newly revived woman suffrage committee, which in June produced a favorable report. Immediately,

Paul organized another demonstration for late July 1913 to call for the amendment's passage. Five hundred supporters turned up in Hyattsville, Maryland, and sixty cars, decorated with bunting, headed from there into the capital, where they presented huge petitions before hearing in the Senate the first suffrage debate Congress had held since 1887.

Then, however, the surge abated and, despite the successful work of the two women during 1913, late that year the parent organization disagreed with them over policy. The NAWSA had focused on state campaigns to win suffrage for more than two decades. By 1912, women had equal suffrage in Wyoming, Colorado, Utah, Idaho, Washington, Arizona, Oregon, Kansas and California. The National led campaigns in many, but not all, of these states. Wyoming had come into the union with woman suffrage, while in 1911, California women had won the vote with a self-directed campaign. Nine equal suffrage states by 1912 was the result of 65 years of work[2] a number which signifies the doubtful effectiveness of the state strategy.

The weakness of the state amendment approach is clear in light of the expansion of the United States. At the time of Elizabeth Cady Stanton's call for suffrage in July of 1848, Wisconsin had just been admitted as the 30th state. A federal amendment then required twenty-three ratifications. By 1913 the union had forty-eight states, with thirty-six required for ratification. If state suffrage can be considered putative ratifications, 1912's nine ratifications in 1848 would have meant the job was more than one-third completed. However, in 1920, nine ratifications out of thirty-six was only one-quarter complete. In this light, the expansion of the union effectively pushed women backwards in the polity.

Yet NAWSA's focus just about excluded federal activity. Its congressional budget was $10 a year, sometimes never spent. President Anna Howard Shaw did not take federal campaigning seriously and when she put Paul and Burns in charge of the moribund Congressional Committee, she told them to raise their own funds. Partly with this fund-raising in mind, in mid–1913 Paul created the Congressional Union (CU), which, although separate from the NAWSA

Opposite: **The young suffragists' first office was in the basement of the smaller dark building at the top center of this photograph. The Treasury Building on 15th Street, only half a block from headquarters, was the only impediment to the two suffragists' view of the White House, where they immediately began to focus their campaign for the suffrage amendment. The crowd is witnessing the arrival of the Suffrage Pilgrims, who walked in the freezing cold from New Jersey to participate in the Great Suffrage March of March 3, 1913 (Library of Congress Prints and Photographs Division, Washington, D.C., Harris and Ewing Collection, Digital ID: http://www. loc.gov/pictures/item/hec2008001420/).**

In November 1915 the Congressional Union, much expanded since 1913, moved to Cameron House (the three-story building with bay windows, center) in Lafayette Square, which had an uninterrupted view of the White House. The Belasco Theatre is the tall building on the right. The NWP held many suffrage rallies here, including the one celebrating the November 1917 release of the suffragists from jail (Library of Congress Prints and Photographs Division, Washington, D.C., Harris & Ewing Collection, Digital ID: http://www.loc.gov/pictures/item/hec2009000285/).

Congressional Committee, had the same officers and the same offices. During the rest of the year, Paul attracted to her group some of the wealthy women who had previously supported NAWSA directly and donors leached from the National's fund-raising for general purposes. At this point, Shaw conveniently forgot she had told Paul and Burns to raise their own funds. NAWSA was, quite naturally, annoyed to see its general fund-raising diverted. To see it diverted to a perceived minor issue, especially by young women, was galling. Equally important, the NAWSA's leadership objected to new tactics that Paul

In early February 1918, after a sojourn in temporary and inadequate offices on Connecticut Avenue, the NWP moved its headquarters across Lafayette Square to 14 Jackson Place, and the party remained there until after ratification. Alice Paul displayed the Victory Flag over the balustrade of the balcony of the pillared entrance (Library of Congress Prints and Photographs Division, Washington, D.C., Harris & Ewing Collection, Digital ID: http://www.loc.gov/pictures/item/hec20090005 21/).

planned to use to force the amendment issue. The muddy situation over the fund-raising, therefore, provided the National with a good excuse at the National convention that year, to imply Paul's misuse of NAWSA funds and eject her from the Congressional Committee. Paul and Burns left NAWSA late in 1913. The two women and their supporters remained in the same offices, however, continuing their suffrage campaign as a separate entity. Paul explained the split and the money issue only in a published statement in the *Suffragist*, which the CU had begun to publish late in 1913, while the report of the CU's meeting that January also mentioned it.[3] Meanwhile, NAWSA criticized the CU's strategy and tactics openly, even as it early in 1914 copied it by opening its first offices ever in the nation's capital.

The CU was now poised for its next move, which the NAWSA abhorred: target the party in power. During 1913, Illinois had passed the Presidential and Municipal Voting Act—the first time women had won votes east of the Mississippi, increasing considerably the number of women voters nationally. Now, with ten states with various suffrage rights, Paul planned to use the British suffrage tactic of opposing in those states where women could vote all Democratic candidates or current representatives. Paul's tactic would hold Democrats responsible for the president's and Congress's failure to act on suffrage and would target both pro- and anti-suffrage Democrats. This was anathema to the NAWSA: leaders argued this meant supporting Republicans but it was a twisted logic indicating the partisanship of many of the NAWSA leadership. As the *Suffragist* repeatedly pointed out, while it meant currently opposing all Democrats as members of the party in power, the tactic could just as easily mean opposing Republicans if they controlled Congress or a legislature. In fact, in 1920, the CU opposed the Republicans for this very reason. Nevertheless, the party-in-power tactic signaled the ending of any potential cooperation between the National and the CU.

Something akin to an open attack on Paul's group broke out in March 1914, when the National's Congressional Committee maneuvered a Senate vote on the suffrage amendment, which resulted in defeat. NAWSA then attempted to undermine the work of the CU by having another, complicated suffrage amendment proposal introduced that would effectively leave the power to enfranchise women with the states. Known as the Shafroth-Palmer Amendment, if passed and ratified it would still have allowed a patchwork of state voting laws affecting women. Confusion reigned for the rest of the year over this proposal, while the defeat in the first vote on suffrage since 1887—a vote which the CU adamantly opposed—effectively killed any opportunity for the issue to come up again during the sixty-third Congress, even though it was reintroduced immediately in the Senate. Yet these events left two major legacies. The first was that Paul renamed the Bristow-Mondell Amendment the Susan B. Anthony Amendment to distinguish it clearly from NAWSA's proposal.[4] The second gave prominence and greater significance to a call for suffrage rallies across the nation that Paul had made that January. The purpose of the rallies was to shift the focus of woman suffrage from state to national level by demonstrating that suffrage was a concern of women all across the nation, not just in specific localities. This was necessary because politicians of both levels of government had given suffragists the runaround for decades, with both national and state elected representatives pointing to the other as responsible for deciding the issue.[5]

Rallies by women from across the nation would demonstrate that suffrage was a national problem. In fact, by the time of the failure of the Senate's vote, Paul and her emissaries had already been traveling in the states to raise local awareness of the plan. The rallies were to take place in cities everywhere on May 2, 1914, to be followed by a huge one the following week, made up of women from all over the country, in Washington, D.C. Carrie Chapman Catt of the NAWSA would later recognize how suffrage was a political football that politicians constantly kicked out of play, summarizing with great insight how they toyed with women over it for decades.[6] Perhaps such awareness even among leaders of the National led them, in spite of their objections to Paul's overall strategy, to agree to allow local affiliates to help organize these rallies. As a result, the May 2 demonstrations in countless cities across the country and the NAWSA's participation through its Congressional Committee in the succeeding procession to the Capitol on May 9, 1914, represented true cooperation between the two suffrage groups and a high point of the previous decade's campaign. From then, because of the huge gulf between them, initially over the party-in-power and, later, more assertive tactics, no further cooperation took place between the CU and NAWSA.[7]

Paul and the CU continued their delegations to the president, who in the face of the constant publicity for suffrage could no longer claim that he had known nothing of the subject. He now used two other ploys to avoid endorsing it, however. One was that voting rights were a state matter. The other was that woman suffrage was not a presidential but a party matter. When Paul tried delegations of women from industry and from women's clubs in addition to those from the CU, Wilson met with them only reluctantly and the women of the CU equally reluctantly had to accept that the president would not budge on the suffrage question.

In summer 1914 Paul sent Mabel Vernon—like Paul a graduate of Swarthmore, and one of her key lieutenants—to Nevada to support a state suffrage campaign, while that September, CU representatives left D.C. to spread out across the plains and the equal-suffrage states to raise money and support for the party-in-power strategy and to establish CU branches wherever they went. They carried out their groundbreaking campaign amid great controversy, some congressmen protesting them, others supporting them. The results in the midterm elections that year were mixed. Nevada voted for suffrage, as did Montana. Suffrage states then totaled eleven. The Dakotas, Nebraska, Missouri and Ohio, however, turned votes for women down. In addition, Democrats won three extra seats in nine states where the CU campaign took place.

The next year, 1915, was a year of momentous change. It began with a failure, when the House of Representatives for the first time voted the amendment down.[8] It ended in the dashing of the National's faith in state enfranchisement when the New York, Pennsylvania, New Jersey and Massachusetts campaigns all failed in spite of the higher visibility of suffrage in the nation's consciousness since the Great Suffrage March of 1913. Paul and the CU took no part in these campaigns, as they believed that state work diverted attention from the federal amendment.

In Washington, D.C., meanwhile, the CU had been forced into new tactics. A presidential meeting with a delegation of Democratic women that January had yielded results no better than before. Wilson's latest excuse was Europe: he was now too busy with war concerns to see *any* delegations. This, naturally, included the women. Now completely shut out, Paul and Burns determined to demonstrate the president's high-handedness to the world. They began almost immediately when Wilson started a campaign tour to prepare Americans for war. The women went in hot pursuit, 250 of them showing up at his hotel in New York the evening before he headed west, tackling him about promises he had made to talk to Congress about the amendment. He excused his failure by saying he was too busy. In Kansas, Mabel Vernon and 75 other women in that suffrage state went to see him at the governor's mansion, where he was staying, and stood on the sidewalk outside for an hour in the snow waiting patiently. When Wilson finally and reluctantly came out to see them, they handed him a petition for suffrage.

Back in D.C., in early May 1915, a group of Pennsylvania women were refused access to the president. Paul encouraged them to remain at the White House, where they conducted a sit-in for three days. This aroused outrage against the women but provided the opportunity for Paul and Burns, in an editorial on May 8 in the *Suffragist* to explain not only their nonviolent philosophy, but also Wilson's role in creating the situation. A sign of the magnitude of the women's struggle had occurred, however, the day before. On May 7, 1915, 128 Americans drowned in the torpedoing of the British liner *Lusitania* by a German submarine. War anxiety heightened. Such headlines were guaranteed not only to shunt women's so-called antics off any front pages, but also to push them to the back of the list of national concerns even as they were fighting for a space on the agenda. The CU nevertheless continued campaigning, that same month attempting to meet with Wilson at a formal naval luncheon at the New York Biltmore and then trying—but failing—to have a boat take them out to the U.S. yacht, *Mayflower*, when he was to review the Atlantic fleet. Again, when faced with public criticism of what they had done, the CU answered back, outlining the dynamics of presidential policy that were forcing them to these tactics in order to be heard.[9]

That year, Paul took to the road to raise money, leaving Lucy Burns in charge in Washington, D.C., where the latter oversaw publication of the *Suffragist*. She had much to report. Other members of the CU had again fanned out across the country, this time to tackle congressmen on their own ground about votes for women, to which some took offence. Another running story was a cross-country suffrage automobile trip. This would not be the first such trip; four women had already broken that ground in 1909 crossing the country by automobile from New York to San Francisco for the Maxwell-Briscoe Motor Company. Such a trip was rare, however, and Paul saw its publicity value: women driving across the country still challenged all conventions about what women could or could not, or should or should not, do. Making of it a political campaign to carry the message of votes for women to cities across the country additionally challenged convention, while both the feat and the signatures gathered for a petition to Congress would generate publicity for the cause. The trip also symbolized the idea of the already state-enfranchised women of the western United States carrying the liberating message of woman suffrage to the still-shackled women of the original colonies and other states further east. The CU had a booth throughout the Panama-Pacific Exposition in San Francisco that year and it held its three-day convention in the city that September. The women's groundbreaking political use of the latest mode of transport—itself inherently liberating—began at the end of the convention and attracted increasing publicity the further east the women travelled. The odyssey culminated in a ceremonial welcome in the Capitol in December 1915. During the period of this publicity for the federal amendment, NAWSA, disillusioned by the failures of its state campaigns, reorganized its hierarchy. Shaw declined to run again for president and Carrie Chapman Catt, who had already served immediately after Susan B. Anthony had resigned, took the reins once more. The CU, to close the year, moved from its first offices to a much larger venue. The move was significant. The new location, much more upscale than the one which they had vacated, expressed the higher public status of the CU and was now conveniently closer to the White House in order to carry on its work.

January of 1916, however, saw the CU trying to move the suffrage amendment favorably out of the House Judiciary Committee while facing the wrath of a Kansas Democrat who had been the target of CU party-in-power campaigning during the 1914 election. With such opposition, the committee voted the amendment down. Paul headed out to campaign, visiting several towns in Arkansas and Tennessee, where she set up affiliates of the CU. The visit to Little Rock demonstrates how the CU relied on networking to create its organization. In the capital city of Arkansas, a young society matron, Mrs. Adolphine Fletcher Terry, took the helm at the meeting, in the Marion Hotel, which promptly founded a CU branch. Terry knew Lucy Burns from their days at Vassar just before the turn of the century. Her sister Mary Fletcher was a student at the same time as Inez Milholland and likely attended the famous suffrage meeting that the latter had organized in a cemetery in defiance of the college president's ban.[10] Fletcher became the first president of the Political Equality League of Little Rock, founded in 1911, which later became the Arkansas Equal Suffrage Association and a NAWSA affiliate. When Paul visited in 1916, the NAWSA-affiliated women attended the meeting but kept their distance from the CU.

Meanwhile, Catt, the NAWSA's new president, began a national tour to sell a new strategy to affiliates across the country. What Catt called her "winning plan" was the older organization's attempt to catch up on the CU's work—thereby recognizing its importance to the cause. In sum, while effectively endorsing the federal amendment, the plan exhorted all members to continue their work at state level and, taking a leaf from the Illinois book, encouraged them to go for whatever kind of suffrage they could get. Constitutional amendment requirements for equal suffrage did not shackle unequal suffrage measures such as municipal and primary or presidential voting: they required only a bill from the state legislature and the governor's signature. Meanwhile, in April, Paul launched her "Suffrage Special"—a trainload of suffragists who for the next six weeks would tour the western states campaigning for the Susan B. Anthony Amendment. Paul organized the sendoff with her usual pageantry, which included a brass band.

Also during 1916, the CU continued its public attempts to meet with Wilson when he was away from the White House, which the CU had begun in 1915. On July 4, when the president was dedicating the cornerstone of the new building of the American Federation of Labor in D.C., Mabel Vernon, who was a platform dignitary representing labor, interrupted his speech extolling the virtues of liberty and justice for all by demanding to know why he contradicted himself by opposing the federal amendment for votes for women. The press promptly excoriated her. That October 20, a worse fate befell suffragists who picketed Wilson with banners when he was delivering a speech in Chicago: although peaceful, onlookers incensed by the challenge to the president's dismal suffrage record attacked them.

Meanwhile, early that July, Paul created the National Woman's Party (NWP), to be composed of members from the female suffrage states, which also controlled almost a quarter of the electoral college. The NWP had one goal: votes for women through federal amendment. The NWP's plan was to rerun the CU's 1914 party-in-power campaign, encouraging the four million women in the eleven female suffrage states to vote against both the Democratic Party and President Wilson, holding them responsible for the failure to pass suffrage. In September, Paul launched the western campaign and in October persuaded Inez Milholland—still remembered as the lady on the white horse at the head of the Great Suffrage March of 1913—to join it. Milholland, who was unwell, left to undertake fifty meetings in thirty days, with her tour ending in Chicago two days before the election on November 5, where Paul had arranged for her to speak to all twelve suffrage states simultaneously by phone to encourage women to get the vote for suffrage out.[11] This was Milholland's last campaign, for during a speech on October 23, she collapsed.

Wilson was reelected in spite of the party-in-power campaign, although the NWP found some satisfaction in the Democrats' loss of its overall majority in the House and the defeat of Representative Joseph Taggart of Kansas, the anti member of the powerful Judiciary Committee. NWP member Doris Stevens later reported that the women attributed this defeat to women's votes. She said that the NWP campaign had been pivotal and that Wilson's reelection was held in the balance for a week until the final tabulation of California's results.[12]

The suffragists' year had not yet ended: on November 25, Inez Milholland died. On December 5, 1916, during a presidential speech to Congress at the very moment when Wilson spoke in the House of extending the right to vote to males of the territory of Puerto Rico, Lucy Burns and Mabel Vernon unfurled a banner over the edge of the balcony: "Mr. President, what will you do for woman suffrage?" Front-page headlines the next day broadcast the story. To complete the year, that Christmas Day the NWP transformed the Statuary Hall of the Capitol with plants and the NWP's purple, white and gold pennants for a packed commemoration ceremony to celebrate Milholland's life and suffrage work. At this time, too, the National moved from its E Street NW offices to the more distant but distinctly more elegant former French embassy. The move signaled the huge differences in approach to suffrage between the CU and the NAWSA.

On January 9, 1917, a large NWP delegation to President Wilson took place. Requested in order to deliver to him resolutions passed during several memorial services held for Milholland, the women noted that yet another suffragist had died without seeing votes for women and again asked for the president's support for the cause. Wilson, however, refused again to endorse suffrage and left the delegation abruptly. The next morning, Paul and the CU upped the ante. From their headquarters, twelve women emerged and walked to the White House. They held aloft pennants with their suffrage colors and carried banners asking, "Mr. President, what will you do for woman suffrage?" and "How long must women wait for Liberty?" Flanking the White House gates, they were standing silently when the president returned from his daily golf game and pointedly ignored this new intrusion on his peace and quiet. Later, officials told the women that nothing would happen to them if no trouble arose. The story—as so often happened with Paul's tactics—made front-page news.

Paul and others of the CU, including Harriot Stanton Blatch, Elizabeth Cady Stanton's daughter, had been planning picketing as their next move should Wilson not budge on suffrage. Picketing was not new in the United States: it had often featured in industrial disputes. In 1914 the Clayton Antitrust Act had made it legal. The revolutionary twist on this traditional method of making a point very publicly was the key facts that women were doing it, that those women were largely professionals and that they were picketing the president on his very doorstep with a very pointed political demand. Again, Paul had seen the same kind of tactic used in Britain when she was campaigning there. In August 1909, Women's Freedom League members who had already been picketing the House of Commons for six weeks extended their protest to Number Ten Downing Street, the official home of the prime minister—the man in control of whether or not a bill could be introduced to enfranchise women. Those demonstrations had lasted fifteen weeks and Blatch had publicly defended the British women in the New York Times.[13]

The protest of January 10, 1917, was the start of three months of increasing creativity as Paul and her staff focused on keeping the pickets daily in front of the White House no matter the weather. The daily parade of women with their ever-changing banners provided entertainment for, and often won support from, passersby. It also attracted the inevitable criticism in the press, which found the idea of such women protesting on the president's doorstep far beneath the ladylike behavior women of their social standing were supposed to embrace. Catt of the National joined in this chorus of criticism: this behavior threatened, she believed, passage of the New York state amendment coming up before voters that November. Picketing of the president she declared to be wrong.[14]

The picketing continued despite these public objections and even from many voices within the CU and NWP. Paul's plan was to continue the tactic until after Wilson's second inauguration on March 4, which followed the CU's convention on March 1. In the meantime, however, Germany announced the resumption of submarine warfare on the high seas. When the United States severed relations with Germany, war now became likely and many people, including CU and NWP members, began to argue that national defense was a higher priority than votes for women and that—just as Paul's former organization, the WSPU, in Britain had done in August 1914—picketing and other protests should stop. Paul opposed this: she recalled the wholesale betrayal of women—Elizabeth Cady Stanton, Susan B. Anthony and other female abolitionists and woman's rights workers in particular—during the promotion and passage of the Reconstruction amendments after the Civil War. At that time, Wendell Phillips had declared that it was "the Negro's hour" and that votes for women should wait. Consequently, Paul wrote in the *Suffragist* early in February that each individual should make her own mind up. In contrast, the NAWSA, in spite of Catt's many years in the international peace movement, now set about redirecting its membership to war work.

The hysteria pushed the CU campaign out of the news and upended NWP plans for a repeat of the huge preinauguration parade of 1913. At the March 1 convention, the CU merged with the NWP with Paul at its helm, while the delegates now planned an inauguration day march around the White House grounds. Torrential rain transformed this lesser spectacle on March 4, 1917, into a poignant protest: the suffragists found all gates locked and guards resolutely against them when they tried to hand a petition in. Doris Stevens remembered how cold and wet was that day, made even colder and more dismal with President and Mrs. Wilson's icy stares when they left the White House in the comfort of their car. The memory of the Wilsons' hostility that day, said Stevens, kept the women going in the bone-chilling rain.[15]

In consolation, a small suffrage development did occur elsewhere. The next day, in Little Rock, Arkansas, Governor Brough signed a bill giving women the right to vote in primaries. This first southern state where women won some right to vote was a signal of some success for the NAWSA's plan to win suffrage by "knock[ing] at every door we see open," as Catt had described the tactic in the same city the previous year.[16] It was equally a measure of the distinctive problems women faced in the South. "The new Primary law was almost equal to the full suffrage, as where one party is so largely in the majority the primaries decide the elections," recorded the History of Woman Suffrage, outlining the operation of the then effective one-party rule.[17]

In Washington after the inauguration, the pickets backed off the White House—not, however, for long. Wilson called the War Session of Congress on April 2, 1917. Jeannette Rankin of Montana, the nation's first female congressional representative, spoke beforehand from the balcony of the new NAWSA headquarters and then suffrage women appeared in force both at the White House and at the Capitol. That day the House introduced the suffrage amendment. That day too, Wilson declared, "We shall fight for the things we have always carried nearest to our hearts—for democracy—for the right of those who submit to authority to have a voice in their own government." The Senate introduced suffrage on April 4, making suffrage's future look bright. The Democratic Party, however, still in control of both houses of Congress due to a House coalition, deemed that from this point it would consider only measures associated with the war effort unless the president deemed that a proposal was a "war measure." Promoting national suffrage as a war measure, therefore, wrote Doris Stevens, became the NWP's goal.

Now the NWP focused on the contradiction between the administration's crusade for democracy abroad even as it denied democracy at home.[18] A broadening acceptance of suffrage abroad heightened this inconsistency: Britain had announced support that March, while now Russia was openly considering enfranchising women. The NWP, therefore, began to quote the president on their banners. Starting with the late April visit to the White House of Arthur Balfour, foreign secretary of Britain, they displayed to the world Wilson's April 2 speech about fighting for democracy abroad.

As war preparations crowded votes for women out of the news, the NWP continued to picket faithfully; and while Maud Younger managed the work of an army of lobbyists tackling individual congressmen with the help of a revolutionary card data base on every single one,[19] Paul dispatched a campaign to the South, for their representatives in the new Congress constituted the major blockage against woman suffrage. In a move to stop the NWP, Catt sent an open letter to the press castigating the pickets for "hurting our cause in Congress," and, at least in Mississippi, a sprouting local NWP organization in Vicksburg died on the vine.[20] NWP members also conducted a campaign on the West Coast, to little effect.

With the NWP facing the need to do something striking to bring attention back to the cause, Lucy Burns and Dora Lewis upped the ante yet again. On June 20, 1917, anticipating the arrival of a Russian delegation, they unfurled a huge banner at the White House accusing Wilson of "deceiving" Russia about America's fight for democracy. They did so in spite of the new Espionage Act, which carried heavy penalties for statements or words that might interfere with the war effort. The truth was too much for some onlookers, who shouted their objections about the women helping Germany, while one enraged man knifed the banner and tore the shreds from the poles, leaving Burns and Lewis standing silently at the West Gate, their empty poles held aloft, speaking volumes silently. The next day young boys tore down another Russian banner, while that midday a banner at the East Gate declaring, "We demand democracy and self-government in our own land" attracted a huge crowd. A woman physically attacked one picketer, destroying her banner, and led the mob around to the West Gate to attack another picketer there. The picketers remained passive. The same afternoon, when Lucy Burns and Katherine Morey attempted to have a photograph taken with the Russian banner outside NWP headquarters and refused to return indoors, an officer tore it from the poles. Subsequently the two emerged with yet another banner quoting the president's April 2 war speech to start another session of peaceful picketing. Yet, in spite of the 1914 Clayton Act's legalization of such picketing, Burns and Morey were arrested, finally told that they had obstructed the traffic and then let go. This escalation in the NWP's tactics and its consequences for picketers led to further resignations from the organization, while Catt, objecting strongly to these stronger tactics and concerned about the eclipse of the NAWSA's approach, collaborated with Wilson's censorship office and the president himself not only to keep the NWP out of the news, but also to promote the NAWSA.

On June 23 and 24 the arrests continued. That weekend, on June 26, the first American soldiers arrived in France. Back home, the first trial of woman suffrage picketers—all six of them—took place on June 27. The women were charged with obstructing "the free use of [a] street," and the judge ruled that the women constituted "the proximate cause" of the disturbance and must "take the consequences." Sentenced to a $25 fine or three days in jail, they all chose jail. On arrival, Mabel Vernon, getting permission to play an organ she saw there, started a hymn service which other, mostly black, prisoners joined. Vernon finished with a suffrage speech that met with approval from their captive audience. The first NWP prisoners were released a day early. On July 4, Lucy Burns and Vida Milholland, the late Inez's sister, were only two of the thirteen picketers arrested after the latest attempt at peaceful demonstration by the picketers—a peaceful demonstration that a mob and the police disrupted.[21] The women again landed in jail, for three days.

Now the authorities responded in kind to NWP's more assertive tactics. The July 14 picket held banners quoting the French Revolution slogan, "Liberty, Equality, Fraternity." This raised virtually no disruption but still led to the arrest of sixteen socially prominent women, including later author Doris Stevens, who were sentenced to sixty days in the workhouse. Justice was showing itself to be decidedly unequal: not only did women live in the United States without equality under the law, but in the application of law for the same offences, a hugely different variety of penalties was also being levied.

The Occoquan Workhouse in Virginia[22] was a supposedly humane detention center concealing a dark secret: a creatively sadistic superintendent named Raymond Whittaker. The arrival of the arrested suffragists seemed to bring out the worst in him. He humiliated them first by having them strip naked. Then he insisted on their wearing heavy clothing even in the searing heat of July, while food and water—contaminated—were deliberately limited and correspondence with the families of the women was censored. Whittaker also used the race card in this southern state, where racial segregation still held sway, by imprisoning them with black women inmates, even though the prison routinely segregated prisoners by race at that time. This particular tactic—even though the Democratic president early in his first term had promoted racial segregation in federal government offices—shocked many when it was revealed. Long before Whittaker's crudeness was known, NWP supporters besieged the administration with protest telegrams, while Dudley Malone, Wilson's collector of the Port of New York, confronted the president face-to-face about the scandal. Wilson pardoned the prisoners, who were summarily released. Several weeks of peace and quiet descended on HQ. Yet the women were planning their next move.

On August 10, Lucy Burns strode out of NWP headquarters with a new banner, deliberately more provocative than anything previously. Calling the president "Kaiser Wilson," it said that twenty million Americans were not self-governed, yet he had sympathized with the Germans for having to live under a tyrannical régime. An incensed government clerk disposed of that banner, and two more produced the next day were destroyed. The word and the outrage spread and on August 14, when a picketer exited with the Kaiser Wilson banner, members of a large mob attacked her and destroyed it. Lucy Burns was assaulted and other banners were stolen. When Burns returned to HQ to drape a Kaiser Wilson banner out of the window, some of the mob tore it down. A bullet fired from among the crowd narrowly missed a suffragist inside the building. The watching police did nothing.

The next morning, August 15, 1917, Alice Paul, who had recently been ill from exhaustion, led the picket line to its planned position outside the White House. She and her colleagues were viciously attacked again, while bystanders also took some of the flack. On August 16, the police began to seize and destroy flags and banners, while the police chief informed Paul that further arrests would follow anymore picketing. Paul stuck to her guns, even producing that very afternoon a new banner declaring that the banners had been "destroyed because they tell the truth." Six picketers were arrested and sentenced to Occoquan, and the police chief announced there would be no more pardons. The women struggled with the same contaminated food and insanitary water, becoming increasingly weak, while they tackled Whittaker's latest contrivance to demean them in a racist society—the painting of the black women's dormitories and toilets. Later that month, however, he fired a matron. She headed immediately to the NWP. She reported what was happening, telling of the conditions inside Occoquan, including unsanitary sheets, failure to transfer infectious women to the hospital and regular abuse.

Dudley Malone, always till this point a staunch supporter of Wilson, resigned from his government post on September 7, incensed at the treatment of the picketers. Now acting for the NWP, he pressed the Board of Charities, which had oversight of the D.C. prisons, for a public enquiry, while gathering sworn statements from former guards and prisoners.[23] The Board of Charities supported Whittaker, however, blaming the suffragists for what was going on in Occoquan. But events had already overtaken the dilatory board. Twice more Paul had headed the picket line and was arrested. For October 6 she received a suspended sentence. For October 20, she received seven months, to be served in the Washington, D.C., jail.

Facing the intransigence of the administration, Paul now pressed into service yet another of the tactics from her WSPU days: a demand to be treated as a political prisoner. In Britain, suffragette Marion Wallace Dunlop, acting independently of any policy of the WSPU, introduced this tactic to the movement. She was imprisoned in June of 1909 for stenciling on the wall of St. Stephen's Hall in the British Houses of Parliament these words:

> *Women's Deputation June 29. Bill of Rights. It is the Right of the Subjects to Petition the King, and all Commitments and Prosecutions for Such Petitionings are Illegal.*

Held in Holloway Prison, she demanded in a letter to the home secretary to be treated as a political prisoner. Political prisoner status allowed prisoners privileges: the prisoners could wear their own clothes instead of prison uniforms; were exempt from prison work; were housed with their own group; could receive visitors, mail and food gifts; and have newspapers and books to read. Dunlop did more: she declared she would eat no food until that time. She fasted for 91 hours and then was freed.[24] Dunlop never won the status she demanded, but from then on the demand for political prisoner status and the hunger strike became regular WSPU tactics. Paul and Burns were arrested for the first time only a week after Dunlop's innovation and soon Paul would follow in the Scottish suffragette's footsteps. Now, eight years later, on November 5, 1917, protesting the food and conditions in the D.C. jail and having demanded political prisoner status and failed to win it, she went on hunger strike, as did Rose Winslow, the colleague jailed with her.[25] The next day, November 6, 1917, New York men voted to enfranchise women after a state campaign with a petition of well over a million signatures of women who wanted the vote.

The following Saturday in Washington, D.C., the suffragists set about crowding the jails. Forty-one were arrested and then freed on bail. Fifty more joined them on the Sunday at Paul's window at the district jail, where Paul told them of thrice-daily force-feeding and they shouted encouragement. Subsequently, authorities isolated her in the psychiatric ward and then boarded up her windows, while she had her sleep constantly disturbed. That same day, a huge meeting of newly enfranchised New Yorkers met as the nonpartisan Committee of One Thousand Women, excoriated President Wilson for his conduct of suffrage reform, holding him personally responsible for the treatment of the prisoners and "unspeakable conditions" in the jails in which they were held. One speaker threatened that if Wilson refused to endorse the amendment in the Congress that would convene that December, "the women voters of New York would not allow a single Democratic Congressman to be elected [in 1918]." The next morning a delegation left for D.C. to put pressure on the administration to change its conduct.[26]

That Monday, Judge Mullowney, unsure of how to deal with the suffragists, let them go. The women turned right around, picketed again and faced a mob that broke their protest up while the police ignored it until they arrested the women once again. This time, the judge doled out various sentences, including sixty days for some repeat offenders, and six months for Burns. They were all to serve their time in the district jail, where Paul was being held. But that night, the women found themselves at Occoquan, where Dora Lewis asked for political prisoner status. Instead, Whittaker treated the women to such brutality that November 14, 1917, was from then on known as the "Night of Terror," during which women were threatened, beaten up, left in solitary confinement, shoved into small cells with insufficient beds and browbeaten into silence. Warders also manacled Burns' hands above her head, refused the women food, ignored calls for medical help when one suffragist appeared to suffer a heart attack, and imprisoned women with the men.[27] Fifteen of the prisoners went on hunger strike in solidarity with Paul and Winslow. Whittaker and his staff did everything to entice them to eat, while further torturing them by moving them around regularly to confuse them further. Lucy Burns and Dora Lewis were forcibly fed.

While this torture of women campaigning for participation in the fundamental rights of American citizens—liberty and equality—by enfranchisement was going on in Washington, D.C., Maud Younger and Mabel Vernon were touring the heartland explaining the picket and hunger-strike tactics, which had split the country. In Little Rock, Arkansas, Vernon's advance guard, Jane Pincus, reserved city hall for a meeting on November 20; but when the local affiliate of the National heard of Vernon's plans, it protested, declaring she could expect "a Jack Frost welcome." Behind the scenes, the NWP's reservation for city hall was cancelled. The local history is silent, but the NWP history reveals that city worthies had closed ranks with the local women and cancelled the reservation. They did so, in fact, in four cities in total.[28] Pincus did hold a street meeting in the center of town on November 10, complete with D.C. picket banners, and Vernon did hold her rally in an alternate venue on November 20, with about fifty people attending. She also held a street meeting.[29]

The Arkansas NAWSA women were not only opposed to the NWP's methods, they also were in a snit, for they had been upstaged: at the same time Vernon was planning to visit to promote the NWP tactics for the federal amendment, the Arkansas NAWSA was welcoming home three of their own who had worked in the New York campaign.[30] The Arkansas NAWSA women were also enraged by what they deemed to be the insults to the president and the threats they believed the NWP tactics posed for the "Cause." Yet, on the very day the news broke of Alice Paul's hunger strike and the NWP campaign reached its most contentious stage, the nation's most populous state voted for suffrage. The NWP, obviously, had not harmed the New York suffrage vote; more likely, in fact, it had given it a considerable boost by keeping suffrage in the public eye and raising protests at the polls about the treatment of the women, or through establishing the National as a "reasonable" organization.[31] Despite NAWSA's various protests, with the potential doubling of the New York vote in future elections, the balance nationally had immediately shifted significantly towards a federal amendment. As the New York women had stated soon after the election, Democratic congressional seats—and consequently electoral votes—were now less safe than before. Even the simple *prospect* of the influence of this new electorate on the nation's politics was significant.[32]

With this important change in the national scenario, late in November 1917, as Paul and several other suffragists were forcibly fed, Mary Nolan was released after her six-day term. She sped to NWP headquarters to tell of the brutality at Occoquan. On November 23, the NWP attorney scheduled a court appearance in Alexandria, Virginia, petitioning for a writ of habeas corpus to have the women transferred from Occoquan to the D.C. jail, where the trial judge had originally decreed they should serve their sentences. Although as bad as Occoquan in many respects, a transfer to the District jail would represent a victory, which would make it easier for supporters to monitor how the women were doing and make them feel less isolated. The striking women, except Lucy Burns and Dora Lewis, who were too ill, were brought to court to testify, where their frail state was on display for all to see easily. On November 26 Judge Mullowney freed them all "because the jail was not equipped for their care."[33] Paul's tactic of crowding the jails had stretched facilities beyond their ability to cope: the interests of justice on that score at least demanded their release. Yet it was not completely back to the familiar place that the leaders repaired to recover and plan their next move: their headquarters had been bought out from under them and as the end of the year approached they had only temporary offices.

To some, the synchronicity of the suffrage win in New York State and the latest crescendo of the NWP campaign may have seemed either simple coincidence or something that occurred in spite of the NWP: what it was exactly is a matter of debate. What is not debatable is the fact that November 1917 was a pivotal point in the campaign. Even Catt's tone changed during the NAWSA convention in Washington, D.C., that December, when she now began to demand that the current Congress pass the federal amendment.[34] In the new year, with the prospect of a vote soon in the House, and undeterred by their eviction from their headquarters of the past two years, the NWP on January 2, 1918, challenged the president with the prospect of a Republican victory in November if he failed to bring the Democrats into line. "The situation at present is like this," said Abby Scott Baker, who represented the executive committee of the National Woman's Party. "The Federal Amendment is sure to pass if President Wilson will make it an Administration measure.... [I]t is strictly up to Wilson and the Democrats.... President Wilson is ... to all intents and purposes, the Democratic Party, so on his shoulders will fall the responsibility if Congress beats Suffrage next Thursday." The estimates Baker quoted for potential votes for suffrage supported her statement.[35]

Wilson and his party by this time were obviously concerned about the future the NWP promised. A week after Baker's challenge—on January 9, 1918, a year less one day to that when the first pickets had marched to the White House to broadcast to the world his hypocrisy about democracy—Wilson changed direction and came out in favor of votes for women. Going far beyond the observation of the niceties of protocol and gushing with epithets that treated Wilson as some kind of beneficent god, Carrie Chapman Catt said she was "thrilled" at the announcement, while former NAWSA president Anna Howard Shaw praised him as "the great leader of democracy." Susan B. Anthony's niece Lucy immediately placed Wilson on a pedestal in the pantheon of American greats beside Washington and Lincoln.

Yet, at this point, Wilson could hardly have done anything less. Not only did he have the new political reality at home to face, but opposition throughout Europe to suffrage had also been crumbling, with Russian, German and British women now having the vote—in the case of Britain, with restrictions— while Canada's intentions of suffrage brought the subject right to the back door of the United States. President Wilson—the leader in the war he himself declared was being fought for democracy—could hardly be seen as lagging behind the troops. More to the point, with many of them now in panic at the thought of abject defeat in the next election, House Democrats begged the president to guide them out of the thicket of the party platform of state's rights and war measures. This was the dirty political truth behind Wilson's about-face in encouraging a vote for suffrage. Many suffragists, however, took it as both magnanimous and stunning. In their response to Wilson's decision the NAWSA seems to acknowledge a gracious gift willingly granted. The NWP artfully and politely but pointedly and effectively commented, "About time too. And at such cost."[36] Now with the president's seal of approval for the Democrats, the amendment went to the vote, the first result duplicated in a recount—274 in favor to 136 opposed. The Susan B. Anthony Amendment had its two-thirds majority for a constitutional amendment for the first time in its history, but only just. The next challenge would be the Senate.

Concurrently, the NWP moved to new and permanent headquarters, a mansion centrally located within easy reach of the White House, allowing Paul to open a tearoom for supporters, congressmen and journalists. Paul's choice of the third headquarters of the NWP—excluding the temporary one used for the previous couple of months—demonstrated that Paul had no intention of easing the pressure until the amendment had been passed and ratified.

She wanted it done in time for the 1920 general election. In March, the U.S. Court of Appeals in D.C. ruled that the arrests of the picketers for obstructing traffic were unlawful: the women's right of assembly stood unless they used it for unlawful purposes.[37]

Lobbying of the Senate began immediately after the January House success. Eleven votes were needed. The NWP lobbyists had several successes, while new obstacles arose from a couple of senatorial deaths and the need to win over their replacements. By mid–June, still three senators short, the NWP workers in the field besieged senators with instructions to vote for the amendment. Meanwhile, Wilson had gone silent on suffrage, while an attempt in May by female munitions workers to prise support from him led to a two-week wait outside his door and no progress. "Nothing they could say could increase the President's interest in the matter.... [H]e ha[s] done everything he could with honor and propriety do in behalf of the passage of the amendment," Secretary Tumulty wrote.[38]

Under the United States Constitution, for promulgation of a constitutional amendment, two-thirds majorities of both the Senate and House were required, plus ratification by three-quarters of the states, 36 in all in 1918. As the 70-year history of woman suffrage had already demonstrated, these in themselves were huge obstacles for women to overcome and by mid–1918, they had overcome only one. In addition, the successes of state suffrage were a double-edged sword. While the mobilization of the woman's vote for party-in-power campaigns had been a groundbreaking technique, in 1918 there was no guarantee that suffrage states would help to ratify a national amendment for unequal suffrage states. Aware of these huge obstacles still ahead of them and with the goal of national woman suffrage in 1920, frustration in the NWP was building, even when the president that June urged woman suffrage at state level in Louisiana and expressed support for suffrage again to a delegation of the NAWSA. The NWP's frustration bubbled when Wilson—urging senators to vote for suffrage, during a delegation to the White House—based his support not on concern for American women, but on the international standing of the United States if it continued to exclude women from the vote.[39] The NWP's frustration boiled over when they read his Independence Day speech at Mount Vernon. Speaking from that lofty eminence over the Potomac, via a huge crowd, to the chained and huddled masses of the world and focusing on his postwar peace policy while proclaiming that the philosophy of the Founding Fathers applied to all mankind and it was the privilege of the United States in the continuing war to help ensure that all could share in and live by that philosophy, he proclaimed, "What we seek is the reign of law, based upon the consent of the governed...."[40] But nowhere did he mention any commitment to the female 50 percent of the United States population that was still working frantically for its own liberty at home. Infuriated, the NWP got into gear, even as Wilson wrote several senators opposed to the amendment asking them to change their minds on the grounds that passage was "an essential psychological element in the conduct of the war for democracy."[41] By this time, the NWP had had enough.

August 6 would have been Inez Milholland's birthday. That day about 100 women dressed in white left headquarters and walked to Lafayette's monument in Lafayette Square while holding aloft two banners and their familiar gold, white and purple pennants. One banner declared Milholland's by now well-known last words: "How Long Must Women Wait for Liberty?" The other protested "the Continued Disfranchisement of American Women for Which the President of the United States is Responsible." Veteran picketer, prisoner and hunger striker Dora Lewis had hardly begun to speak when police arrested her—and each succeeding speaker. In all, police arrested forty-eight people, including Paul. Authorities delayed trial while police tried to figure out what charges to bring against them. The *New York Times* opined that the women needed their heads examined: Wilson had already put up with enough very gracefully, done more than any president for suffrage and, in fact, might even have exceeded the chief executive's constitutional role.[42] This position is odd in light of the president's stated position on expansion of presidential powers. Nowadays it seems quaint, when presidential executive orders are run-of-the-mill.

The trial for the August 6 arrests was delayed until August 15. In the interlude the NWP conducted four more protests in Lafayette Square and many of the same women were arrested again. That day, twenty-four were sent to jail, this time to a deliberately resurrected condemned workhouse, where many of them fell ill. To counter their hunger strike, Louis Brownlow, chairman of the board of commissioners, had cooks fry ham to add torture to the inhumane conditions. The denial of freedom of speech and assembly to the women finally pricked Wilson's conscience and the women were freed on August 20 and given a permit to demonstrate in Lafayette Square.[43]

With the Senate vote stalled, the NWP went quiet, while Paul traveled to raise funds for the 1918 prisoner campaign in the suffrage states and called for a demonstration for mid–September in Lafayette Square. "The Senate suffrage situation is desperate," she said. "Nothing but a direct demand for action by the President will bring about the passage of the amendment.... Suffragists are confronted with ... centering attention on the injustice that the Democratic

Party is doing the women of the country, and on the inconsistency between the President's suffrage words and ... deeds so that the President will be compelled to take drastic measures to alter the lineup of forces in the Senate. We are determined that, unless it is passed before, the enfranchisement of women shall be a vital issue in the fall campaign."[44]

On the day of the NWP's announced demonstration, a delegation to the White House, arranged by NAWSA, of Democratic women from states with full or partial suffrage met the president. Mrs. Minnie Fisher Cunningham of Texas said that the president had promised "[to] do all that I can to urge the passage of the amendment by an early vote," a statement "not regarded by the [NWP] as holding out definite assurance of action by the Senate on the pending Federal Woman Suffragist amendment."[45] That same afternoon, from among a group assembling in Lafayette Square, Lucy Branham of Baltimore climbed on Lafayette's statue, held aloft the president's promise written on a piece of paper, and set his words alight, proclaiming, "The torch which I hold symbolizes the burning indignation of women who for a hundred years have been given words without action."[46]

In late September, the senatorial session approached its end. The matter was scheduled for discussion to start on September 26, with both pros and antis declaring they had the votes to pass the amendment, but as the debate progressed, the balance shifted clearly to the antis while supporters filibustered and the session was held over until Monday, September 30. That day, President Wilson finally and unexpectedly appeared before the Senate, urging, in his role of commander-in-chief, a "yes" vote for woman suffrage "as a vital war necessity."[47] But it was too little, too late: the next day, when the Senate voted on the amendment, it fell two votes short of a two-thirds majority.

Within a matter of days, the NWP announced a new, two-prong strategy: support the president, and for the midterm elections, target those senators up for reelection who had voted against the Susan B. Anthony Amendment. For NWP members it was time to return to picketing. On October 7, the women headed to the Capitol with a new banner drawing attention to the thirty-four senators who opposed suffrage, which "lined up the Senate with Prussia by denying self-government to the people." While some were simply hardheaded, Senator William Borah of Idaho objected to the amendment through the warped logic of not wanting to falsely raise the hopes of black women in the South with a guarantee of the opportunity to vote when it would likely not be fulfilled. Such concern had not prevented Congress giving black men suffrage during Reconstruction. The congressional picketing brought the women repeated imprisonment without charge by the Capitol police. When a judge ruled this illegal, the police stole the women's banners: they returned them only after yet another court challenge.

Even though the NWP conducted a strong1918 campaign in spite of the flu epidemic, several of these opponents of suffrage were reelected and, with the session ending on March 5, 1919, any potential vote on the amendment in the dying months of the sixty-fifth Congress looked no more likely to succeed than before. Wilson had said nothing about woman suffrage since his appearance in the Senate on October 1 before the failed vote. Now, on November 11, with the end of the Great War, war measures lost their importance and Wilson, with the Democrats still securely in power for a few more months, had shifted his sights even more decisively to foreign affairs and his policy of winning the peace.

But Paul had plans: her focus remained fixed on winning a Senate two-thirds majority in the current Congress, for many of the states were currently in session and could deal with ratification immediately. If the vote had to wait until the new Congress, the whole process would have to start over again, with both a House and a Senate vote. By then, state assemblies would have adjourned, in many cases for two years, and in an off-year, women would have to persuade governors, who had many competing interests to reconcile, to call for special sessions to ratify. In addition, after the sixty-fifth session ended, Congress was not scheduled to meet until December 1919. It was imperative that suffrage be won now. To this end, Paul turned once more to persuading the president to give his attention to his unfinished business at home. On December 16, while dark was descending, a long line of women with pennants, flags and banners held high emerged from HQ and assembled around the Lafayette statue once more and proceeded to burn "all the words [Wilson] has ever uttered or written on the subject of democracy." In the nighttime, with the light against the dark, the spectacle was striking, much more so than the burning of his words the first time during the day the previous September. On New Year's Day, NWP members appeared with a banner accusing the president of hypocrisy and set alight a fire that they intended to keep constantly burning opposite the White House, a reminder of his failed promise of democracy at home. This latest innovation in tactics, as usual, attracted an angry mob. Police arrested five women, including Paul. Such disturbances in the absence of war and without the excuse that the president was too busy with war revealed clearly the underlying prejudices against women's status and suffrage that held sway throughout the nation. It was clear that, in spite of all the social and educational progress of the nineteenth century and the progress of women during the war, women's position had not changed much since the mob assaulted Frances Wright when, as the first women in the United States to do so, she spoke about reform in public on the courthouse steps in Cincinnati back in 1828.

Nevertheless, and despite freezing weather, in Washington, D.C., in 1919 the women kept their fires burning night after night. On January 6, Paul and others were incarcerated yet again. Further demonstrations, arrests, prison sentences and hunger strikes ensued, while during the trials the women, refusing to recognize the court, were also sentenced for contempt. "Our Liberty bonfires are a symbol of our contempt for words unsupported by deeds. We will not sit in silence while the President presents himself to the people of Europe as the representative of a free people, when the American people are not free, and [Wilson] is chiefly responsible for it," a statement from the NWP Advisory Council said in the thick of this latest controversy.[48] On January 19, in defeated Germany where universal suffrage had been established, all men and women went to the polls to elect a new democratic government. NWP lobbyists, meanwhile, worked hard at the Senate trying to win the needed votes. On January 31, women in Indiana won a vote on partial suffrage. On February 3 in Congress, the amendment was set for vote for February 10, but the tally looked one short, even though Wilson was, in fact, attempting to persuade the Senator from Florida to fall into line.

This was not good enough for the NWP. On February 9, yet another colorful procession emerged from headquarters and building on the Watchfires attempted yet again to ignite Wilson's interest enough to make him put presidential influence behind the amendment. Marching to the White House, the NWP burnt him in effigy. While D.C. and military police and Boy Scouts rounded up the protesters, Sue White of Nashville, Tennessee, a recent recruit to the NWP from the NAWSA, declared, "We burn not the effigy of the President of a free people, but the leader of an autocratic party organization whose tyrannical power holds millions of women in political slavery," About forty of the arrested women were imprisoned. The protest was to no avail. On February 10, the amendment lost by one vote. Later that month, authorities clamped down on the women, arresting and detaining twenty-two NWP members in Boston even before they had had a chance to burn the president's speeches on his return from the Versailles Peace Conference in Europe. A week later, another attempt to introduce the amendment, this one modified, before the session ended, was unsuccessful. On March 4, 1919, the sixty-fifth Congress came to an end for the then usual months-long break after a Republican filibuster and a refusal to vote extra money for federal government spending. There was no sign of a special session of Congress in sight. The future of the

Susan B. Anthony Amendment—and votes for women in 1920—looked distinctly shaky.[49]

The week before, at the time the Senate scheduled the vote, Paul said, "Women recognize that it is entirely in the hands of the Democratic Party to pass the suffrage measure and will hold them responsible if it is not passed."[50] Five days after the vote, therefore, the previously postponed "Democracy Limited" Prison Special train of jailbird suffragettes outfitted in prison dress, led by prime jailbird and hunger-striker Lucy Burns, headed out from Union Station across the land, where huge crowds turned out to hear them speak. On March 4, Paul and a large group of picketers, staying close on the president's heels, attempted to burn Wilson's words again, this time outside the Metropolitan Opera House in New York, where the president was speaking about the progress of the Versailles Peace Conference. Before they could actually do anything, police and a mob destroyed the women's equipment, while Paul and five more were detained and later freed. On March 10, at a huge rally in Carnegie Hall to conclude the Prison Special tour, speaker Mrs. Henry O. Havemeyer said, "The Woman's Party is demanding, as all suffragists, will demand, that the President call an extra session of Congress. It is intolerable that the will of two-thirds of the people's representatives should be thwarted by the refusal of the President to summon Congress."

Two months later, on May 7, with pressure from Treasury Secretary Carter Glass to settle the funding of the federal government, the president called an extraordinary session of Congress for May 19. The unscheduled session would also bring up the Versailles Peace Treaty and the League of Nations.[51] As the sixty-sixth Congress approached, some quick calculations by Paul and the NWP following its lobbying in the interim indicated there could be enough votes in the Senate for the required majority, while the House remained secure in what would now be a Republican-controlled Congress. That May 19, 1919, when the session opened, for the first time ever—the seventh year since suffragists had been asking the president to do so—Wilson finally exhorted members to vote for the suffrage amendment. The reference to voting for the amendment in the cable from the president, still at the peace conference in France, went off like a damp squib: the women had already done all the work. On May 21, the reintroduced amendment passed the House again handily with 42 votes more than it needed. As attention turned towards the Senate, several new senatorial declarations of support indicated that the amendment should pass, but due to political maneuverings, the month went by with no news of new senators deciding to vote in favor of woman suffrage. Meanwhile, the Democratic National Committee, looking towards the 1920 election, now began to compare Wilson to Lincoln in his achievements and encourage states to ratify the amendment as soon as Congress passed it. Finally, on June 4, 1919, the Senate voted again on the Susan B. Anthony Amendment. It passed, 56 votes to 25.[52]

In anticipation of this successful congressional vote and still with the intention of having women voting across the nation in the 1920 presidential election, the NWP had already been getting into gear for the ratification campaign, opening offices in Chicago and San Francisco that May.[53] Opinion was in the balance, however, about whether the NWP's goal was realistic, given that thirteen states currently seemed against ratification and thirty-six out of forty-eight states were needed to ratify. Such a constitutional amendment process was the most difficult of any in the modern world, especially when it came not from the people in power but from the grass roots and when the supplicants were excluded from power. When Catt of the National received the gold pen used to sign the amendment after its passage in Congress, the *New York Times* noted that Paul of the "bolder, more original, more implacable" NWP should at least have received a brass inkstand for switching the slow suffrage campaign into "exceeding swiftness in the last few years." Reviewing the possibilities of ratification by 1920, it concluded success was doubtful.[54]

Ratifications started quickly, with Illinois, Wisconsin and Michigan ratifying within a week of passage. Kansas and Ohio followed swiftly and by mid–June New York had also ratified. Florida, whose assembly would not meet again before the 1920 election, however, refused to call a special session, while the New Jersey governor also refused because his state had a regular session early in 1920. North Dakota also refused, the governor declaring its legislature "would undoubtedly approve the amendment 'at the first reasonable opportunity.'" Meanwhile, Texas and Arkansas were competing to be the first southern state to ratify, with Arkansas' women offering to pay the expenses of the legislators when recalled. Texas won, ratifying on July 5, with Arkansas ratifying on July 28, marking one-third of the way to promulgation. Meanwhile, however, Alabama rejected the amendment. Even though the president urged Georgia to ratify, it looked unlikely that it would do so.[55]

Clearly anticipating a speedy ratification, on June 30, 1919, the NAWSA had closed its D.C. headquarters and taken steps to disband and reconstitute itself as the League of Woman Voters. In fact, Catt, speaking to the New Jersey Suffrage Ratification Committee that July, had early asserted that "the action of special and regular sessions of Legislatures [would] make it certain that from thirty to thirty-five states [will] have ratified before January first

[1920]...."[56] But the uneven nature of these early results spoke of a different possibility. By the end of the year, only 22 of the required 36 states had ratified, and the National's perennial over-optimism and limited political realism had become clear. By the end of March 1920, however, the 35th state, Washington, ratified and the pressure was on for just one more state.

Here the momentum stalled, dragging on, with the Republican governors in Delaware and Connecticut holding out in spite of their legislatures. Meanwhile, a solid bloc of the Democratic South had either rejected or not yet considered ratifying. The Republicans so far had provided the majority of ratifications across the country, outnumbering Democratic ratifications by more than six to one. By the end of March, of the 35 states that had then ratified, twenty-nine were Republican and only six were Democrats. That April, North Carolina voted no. Applying the party-in-power tactic yet again, on June 8 the NWP pickets were out in force outside the Republican National Convention in Chicago, this time protesting state Republican recalcitrance with a banner proclaiming, "Vote Against the Republican Party as Long as it Blocks Suffrage."[57] On June 28 the NWP attended the Democratic National Convention in San Francisco and won Democrats' support for ratification and a suffrage plank in its platform.

Meanwhile, the Supreme Court had ruled unconstitutional a referendum requirement to Ohio's ratification, leaving its ratification intact. Tennessee had a similar requirement, so this decision brought a previously unlikely state into play: if it ratified, it would be the historically important 36th state. The state senate ratified on August 13, but the Tennessee house vote was up for grabs. As the antis and pros readied for the battle, the NWP and all available prominent suffragists converged on Nashville, where, on August 18, the youngest representative, Harry Burn, changed his vote to a "yea" on the exhortation of his mother.

The news from Tennessee flashed across the country. In Washington, on August 20, a small group of women emerged from the double glass doors of their headquarters. Once outside, they gathered around the main entrance of the building, looking upwards as a small figure emerged onto the balcony above the door carrying a roll of fabric. The woman stepped forward and let the cloth tumble down over the balustrade to reveal a huge flag of gold, white and purple stripes. Sewn onto it were multiple stars. The group of women below cheered, raising their hands in victory.

The women on the street below the balcony were members of the National Woman's Party. The small figure who had unfurled the flag was Alice Paul, the famous leader of the campaign of the past eight years. The stars represented the 36 states that had ratified the Susan B. Anthony Amendment since June of 1919, making it the Nineteenth Amendment to the Constitution. Finally, after 72 years of campaigning, the women of the United States had won the vote and Paul and the NWP marked the event as they always did: with striking color, apt symbolism and a public demonstration, capturing this astounding achievement in a way that words alone could never do and marking it with a photograph that resonates down the years.

It is easy, in some ways, to imagine what was going through the minds of those women that day. They must have been exultant. And they had much to smile about, for they had overcome the opposition of more than 50 percent of the population in order to win for women the right to vote, a right which, from the founding of the nation, had been given automatically more and more to men. They would also be celebrating the ending of the relentless toil of the past almost eight years: petitioning, lobbying, tours, pageants and processions, organizing and fund-raising across the nation, all in addition to picketing the president, serving prison terms, and enduring brutality at the hands of their fellow citizens, the police, the judicial system, the administration and prison guards. For some of them it signaled the real end to enduring the torture of the force-feeding they had begun when they took the ultimate step of hunger strikes in order to win their goal. And, except for the violence of mobs and the authorities against them, they had achieved woman suffrage without fighting back. They had won, through a grass-roots movement and with hard-won support from members of Congress what had seemed a near impossibility, an amendment to the Constitution of the United States. In the process, they achieved woman suffrage with the first successful nonviolent civil rights campaign in the nation's history.

Yet, not being there, not being inside their heads, it is also difficult to know what was really going through the minds of the women that day in Washington, D.C. In particular, it is hard to know what was going through Paul's mind as she stood on that balcony, for she was well known for saying nothing, for moving on to the next obstacle or the next challenge without engaging in postmortems or recriminations. In the field of woman suffrage leadership, she stands out for not writing about the campaign or her experiences in prison.

Paul remains somewhat of an enigma. Inez Hayes Irwin, an early historian of Paul and the NWP, wrote that this Quaker from a wealthy family from Moorestown, New Jersey—only 26 when she launched the final campaign for woman suffrage in Washington, D.C., on March 3, 1913—was known for her extreme reserve, if not for seeming cold. She did not talk about herself.[58] Irwin listed Paul's considerable education and work experience before she became involved in suffrage: a Swarthmore BA in 1905, an MA and a PhD from the University of Pennsylvania in 1907 and 1912, respectively. She had also graduated from the New York School of Philanthropy in 1906, studied social work in England at Birmingham University in 1907 and 1908 and sociology and economics at London's School of Economics in 1908 and 1909. She had done a considerable amount of social work in New York, Birmingham and London and had been in charge of the woman's department of adult schools in Hoxton, England, in the summer of 1908. There was, ostensibly, nothing in this background to indicate that, by 1920, this apparently unassuming but studious and serious young woman would have masterminded the campaign that in only eight years converted Congress and 36 states from lack of interest in, or outright opposition to, suffrage towards actual ratification and rattled President Wilson enough to get him, if reluctantly, to put his influence behind suffrage. Although, like so many women of her time, Paul was breaking the bounds that throughout the nineteenth century had limited women's role to the domestic sphere or low-paying, meaningless and subservient jobs, her background was yet almost conventional, until in 1912 her search for a productive life led her to Washington, D.C., and a political campaign.

Jubilation, triumph and joy must have been coursing through Paul as she stood on that balcony above the victory flag; yet there is little to indicate what she was thinking at that specific moment, poised between victory over the past and what would come in the future. But it is not hard to *imagine* that running through the mind of this woman whose PhD dissertation had been about woman and the vote was a replay of the multitude of events, concerns and issues that had brought her to this place at the pinnacle of woman's history in the United States: the stories of not only her colleagues but also of the women who had gone before, who had started the work and left a legacy for a younger generation to pick up and complete, and of the arguments and problems they had to face and surmount in order to sway public and lawmakers' opinions and bring them round to the women's side. It is not hard to imagine, therefore, that accompanying Paul on that balcony, although in the ether, crowded those very women in whose footsteps she had followed. For the fact is that Paul and the NWP campaign was the flower at the end of the vine. It was both the goal and the result of a movement for woman's equality in the polity that had its seeds—so minuscule as to be almost invisible and easy to ignore—in the political thought before the Revolution in the colonies.

That tiny plant began to show its first shoots when women started to question the limited reach of the ideas of the American Revolution and the structures that the Founding Fathers created. The shoots developed in response both to deliberate exclusion of women from the polity early in the history of the new republic that was based on equality and on the practical experiences of women of comfortable circumstances helping poor women through the vicissitudes of a society evolving away from agriculture into an urban and industrial base. Soon, a few women spoke out for rights like those of men, while some women gained knowledge and practical experience from their work for others and against slavery in particular. The two distinct strands were later sundered through the pressures and betrayals of events, specifically Reconstruction. One branch supported the Reconstruction actions and betrayals and began to focus on organization, education and state suffrage reform. The other, incensed by the political equality extended to all the male sex by the Fourteenth and Fifteenth amendments, refused to endorse this reinforced inequality of women and set its sights on woman suffrage through an amendment similar to what the men had been given. For a time, that branch challenged the inequality through public activism and innovative use of the legal system. Later it returned to campaigning for federal constitutional change.

Still later, the two now almost completely separate strands of suffrage came together again; yet it was an unequal arrangement, with piecemeal voting reform overwhelming the pressure for a fundamental change. Proceeding in this way for years, progress stalled. Then, suffragism, reinvigorated by foreign influence, volunteered onto the American movement and forged ahead, aiming again for the stalled amendment to the nation's originating documents, which had ignored women's existence. At this point, with this new graft determinedly setting the pace, both branches of suffrage began to strengthen. Throughout this whole history, the separate and often competing versions of the woman's movement operated in the midst of a thicket of countless other reform movements—akin to theirs, some more prominent than others, each creating a challenge to the significance and importance of that of women per se, threatening independent survival. Viewed often as an illegitimate weed, suffrage resisted all attempts at killing it or rooting it out. Finally, in spite of its uneven growth and development and despite its surroundings, the movement blossomed in victory.

This victory, through Alice Paul's leadership and the campaign she directed via the NWP and its forebears, was the most revolutionary and successful civil rights movement ever conducted in the United States. Through her campaign, Paul jump-started the moribund federal amendment, which led directly to the passage and ratification of the Susan B. Anthony Amendment in 1920, an amendment that Anthony had first introduced in Congress in 1878. Paul bypassed the trundling and cumbersome state-by-state campaign, even as she attracted nonstop public prominence and publicity to all suffrage campaigns. Ultimately, she sucked into her orbit the reluctant two-million-strong and well-established National American Woman Suffrage Association, which finally recognized the rare opportunity Paul had created and belatedly followed her lead, even as its leadership claimed all the credit.[59] Paul's singular, revolutionary, achievement—and that of the NWP—in United States history inhered in the fact that women had won and also in what they won. It inhered in the consequences that flowed from that achievement. It existed in the issues that her campaign raised and dealt with or secured, and it was intrinsic in the character of the movement that Paul spearheaded for this victory.

CHAPTER 2

What the Suffragists' Victory Meant

To discuss the result of the suffrage victory—the vote for women—may seem redundant, yet it is seldom examined in very basic terms: the timing of the victory and what it meant in numbers of potential votes. These two issues, however, are important because they shed light on the significance of what the women achieved.

When the Vote Was Won

In August 1920, American women finally won the vote.

"TENNESSEE COMPLETES SUFFRAGE VICTORY," blared the front-page lead of the *New York Times* on August 19, 1920. In D.C. the same day, the *Washington Post* led with "TENNESSEE VOTES SUFFRAGE," declaring "Suffragists Jubilant" in a subheading. In this news, "suffrage" required no qualifier. The controversy over votes for women had been around forever and, due to Alice Paul's campaign, had been front-page news consistently since 1913. Suffrage, by definition, meant women. What may not have been clear was how amazing it was that women had won suffrage at that point instead of having to wait even longer.

The newspapers with those trumpeting headlines reported, however, the tentative nature of the victory in 1920. Harry Burn, the youngest member of the Tennessee house, prompted by a letter from his mother to do the right thing, had changed his mind and helped the measure over the final hurdle. The ratification, it seemed, was secured, when Banks Turner, a Democrat hedging his bets and waiting to see which way the dice would fall, asked for a change in his vote from "pass" to "yea." The final vote was 49 to 47—although until that last-minute maneuver by Banks, the amendment by whose ratification nearly 50 percent of the population would be enfranchised had passed by just one vote. Now, however, Tennessee antis plotted constitutional challenges, while in Washington, D.C., Paul called for the United States secretary of state, Bainbridge Colby, to promulgate the amendment as soon as he received Tennessee's certificate of ratification. While the required thirty-sixth ratification of the Susan B. Anthony Amendment actually occurred on Wednesday, August 18, 1920, it did not become part of the fundamental law of the land until more than a week later, on Thursday, August 26. By then its promulgation had become almost a cloak-and-dagger affair. A county judge issued an order forbidding Governor Albert Roberts from certifying Tennessee's ratification; the governor ignored the court order; Secretary Colby received it in the middle of the night on August 26, sent it for review to the department's attorney and finally signed it in private in his home. Astoundingly, for such a momentous event there were no witnesses. Colby said he signed the Nineteenth Amendment privately to avoid controversy, for, he claimed, there was disagreement between the NAWSA and the NWP about a how to conduct any ceremony. Yet, given the nature of the event, this decision was officious and seriously lacking in judgment. In the new age of movies, the NWP had wanted the amendment signed with cameras present: without that recording, without even stills available, nothing exists to show the actual moment in U.S. history when women finally became part of the national polity after 144 years. This act was, in fact, reprehensible and Colby was prejudiced to boot. Afterwards he was photographed in his office with Catt and a delegation from the NAWSA while he left Paul and the NWP's delegation kicking their heels even as he allowed a delegation from Spain to upstage them.[1] Paul never commented on this treatment, but veteran Oregon NWP activist Emma Wold expressed bitterness at the indignity meted out to Paul.[2] Wold's reaction was understandable: if it had not been for Paul and the militant campaign she orchestrated beginning in 1913, the NAWSA would likely in 1920 still have been struggling to make any headway in suffrage, for it was Paul's campaign that brought the subject to the front and center of the national agenda and tipped the balance at that moment in time.

One nameless southern congressman recognized, at least, what the NWP had achieved. "Your being so annoying and persistent and troublesome and being just like that sand that gets into your eyes when the wind blows, is what has put the suffrage amendment on the map. It is like a cinder in your eyes, you have to get rid of it. What your organization has done means this amendment is going through ten years sooner than it ever would have done without you," he said to Dora Lewis in 1919.[3] In other words, only Paul and the NWP had made passage and ratification of the amendment happen when it did. For something that had been in the works for 72 years, this in itself was a monumental achievement.

An estimate of passage ten years earlier than it might have, however, is probably an understatement, for while the NWP's goal was always the same, the political game was always shifting. The women constantly had to deal with the ever-changing makeup of Congress and the repeatedly renewing battle to reeducate returning and new representatives on the issue at each election or vote. A significant modification to the United States Constitution in 1913 — the introduction of popularly elected instead of state appointed senators — may or may not have helped suffrage, but an increase in the number of popular elections from 1914 may have added to the work that women had to do to educate and win candidates in favor. Regardless of the makeup of any Congress or administration, the women had always to counter the inveterate tendency of those in power to dismiss their concerns: they had little leverage and it was in the nature of the male Congress always to find something of a much higher priority to busy itself with. It would, in fact, have been surprising if woman suffrage in the United States had occurred even within another decade without the NWP campaign. Given the nation's insistence on going its own way, failure was possible even if other countries' opposition to women suffrage was falling like nine pins. Catt of the National expressed frustration that June about attending the Congress of the International Woman Suffrage Alliance in Geneva, Switzerland, with "the humiliation of representing the women of an unenfranchised nation."[4] The day after ratification in Tennessee, the *New York Times* reported that women had won the vote in twenty-two nations up to 1920, seventeen of them since the start of the Great War.[5]

Catt herself was aware of what an achievement suffrage represented when it finally came that August. Her calculation of what women did to win the vote was a total of 910 campaigns over the fifty-two years after the ratification of the Fourteenth Amendment, when the all-male Congress wrote the word "male" into the Constitution for the first time. This total is a measure of the monumentality of the 1920 victory. But the NAWSA's campaign was still involved in a long-drawn-out uphill operation at state level when Paul came on the scene. There were only nine full suffrage states in 1912 after a struggle of well over half a century, since Elizabeth Cady Stanton's cousin had woman suffrage entered as a plank in the Liberty Party platform in June 1848. In 1912, progress was uneven. Both new states added to the union that year—New

Mexico and Arizona—entered without woman suffrage. Each new state changed the number required for ratification. Later that year, however, Arizona women campaigned and won suffrage. New Mexico women won suffrage only through ratification of the Nineteenth Amendment. This scenario was like an echo of the Missouri Compromise of 1820 over slavery, with one state balancing another out. Also in 1912, Oregon and Kansas won equal suffrage, raising hopes of a surge in state suffrage wins. Paul, however, realized the many limitations of this strategy. Coming to the fore, she picked up the other strand of the history of woman suffrage, which had died with Susan B. Anthony in 1906: focus on winning a federal-level revolution in the vote.

The New Voters

The suffrage victory also had major national political implications, for just as Catt could measure the achievement by counting campaigns Paul and the NWP could measure the magnitude of their victory by the numbers. The new eligible nationally enfranchised electorate amounted to 26,500,000 women, according to the latest federal government statistics, a figure based on that year's census. The number of potential male voters stood in 1920 at 31,500,000.[6] Historians have more or less ignored this figure of the new female electorate. Of course, it could be argued that this is an unrealistic figure, for it was highly unlikely that 26,500,000 women would register to vote. In addition, there were the limitations on the reach of the new fundamental law and the barriers that states put up to registration. Besides, women themselves might not want to register, might not be interested in doing so or might not even know about their new eligibility. There was also no guarantee, either, that registered women would actually vote if registered. Such arguments can also apply to male voters, while nothing in them can take away from the stunning achievement of Paul and the NWP. Through the new amendment—a change in the fundamental law of the entire nation at the federal level—they almost doubled the potential size of the electorate. This achievement was phenomenal and it remains unsurpassed.

Invaluable evidence of the magnitude of the Nineteenth Amendment victory lies in a comparison of these 26,500,000 potential new voters with the numbers that other major federal measures enfranchised. The enfranchisement of women dwarfs all the others. Former freedmen became eligible for the vote by 1870 due to the Fourteenth and Fifteenth amendments; yet, based on the 1860 census, a total of only 875,877 former male slaves 21 and over became eligible to vote at that time.[7] The Voting Rights Act, which Congress passed in 1965 to prevent and stop discrimination against blacks in elections pursuant to those Reconstruction amendments and the Nineteenth Amendment, allowed for federal enforcement of enfranchisement of 10,906,235 nonwhites nationwide.[8] Discrimination and disfranchisement based on race, however, was endemic to the South, not the whole of the United States, so ten million plus disfranchised blacks is actually an overestimate of beneficiaries of the 1965 act. The total number of nonwhites in the South was 11,496,477 in 1960.[9] The total number of nonwhites[10] aged 20 and over amounted to 5,975,968, which again is an overestimation because 20-year-olds could not vote in 1965.[11] Neither the Reconstruction amendments nor the extremely belated legislation of the 1965 Voting Rights Act to enforce those amendments came close to the numbers of women who became eligible to vote under the Nineteenth Amendment.[12] Nonwhites aged 21 and older nationwide in 1965 constituted 41.16 percent of the new female 1920 federal electorate, while the percentage in only the South was 22.5—an overestimation that includes 20-year-olds. The Twenty-Sixth Amendment, ratified in record time in 1971, enfranchised eleven million young people, approximately the same number as the nationwide total of nonwhites[13] and constituting 41.50 percent of the number of new federal female electorate of 1920. Neither the Voting Rights Act nor the Twenty-Sixth Amendment remotely approached the vast numbers of newly eligible potential voters in 1920. By the straightforward numbers, therefore, the enfranchisement of women through the Nineteenth Amendment marks the most significant watershed in American electoral history.

Total Enfranchisement Due to the Nineteenth Amendment, the Voting Rights Act of 1965, and the Twenty-Sixth Amendment

Female 1920	Nonwhites, Nationwide 1965	Nonwhites, South 1965†	Youths Aged 18–21 1971
26,500,000	10,906,235	5,975,968*	11,000,000
Percentages			
100	41.16	22.55*	41.50

*Data based on the 1960 census. †An overestimation which includes 20-year-olds.

CHAPTER 3

How the Vote Was Won

The work of the National Woman's Party for suffrage was revolutionary in United States history. The party won its goal by bringing a president to his knees and a determinedly reluctant Congress round to its point of view. The work was also revolutionary because it brought about the largest enfranchisement of United States citizens at one time. Moreover, Alice Paul's work was revolutionary because of her methods.

Parades

The most visible mark of Paul's cutting-edge political campaign lay initially in parades. She was by no means the first to organize parades in the United States: they had been part of the fabric of the nation's life from its very beginning, organized to commemorate July 4 and other great national occasions. Days after the signing of the Declaration of Independence, for example, Williamsburg, Virginia, celebrated the historic event with a public reading of the document, a military parade, and the firing of volleys. Philadelphia was the first to organize a July 4 celebration including a parade on the actual anniversary of the Declaration in 1777.[1] United States cities often saw parades for other reasons. A Labor Day parade was held on Union Street in New York, for example, in September 1887, demonstrating union solidarity.[2]

Paul was not even the first person to organize a parade in support of woman suffrage. It is not absolutely certain who should receive that accolade, but it usually goes to Harriot Stanton Blatch, daughter of Elizabeth Cady Stanton. Blatch had spent twenty years in Britain, returning to the United States in 1902, and was aware of the long history of labor union protests in Britain such as the Labor Day event on May 1, 1894, in Edinburgh, which involved seventeen marching bands, "thirty-seven organizations, 10,000 marchers and an estimated 120,000 spectators."[3] Having lived there for so long, Blatch was finely attuned to events across the Atlantic that in 1903 would give birth to Emmeline Pankhurst's Women's Social and Political Union. With close ties to the British labor movement, and following its example, the WSPU initially heckled meetings, latched onto the publicity benefits of imprisonment and sent delegations to the prime minister at Number Ten Downing Street. In the spring of 1906, having secured with these tactics from prime minister Sir Henry Campbell-Bannerman an appointment with him for the woman suffrage cause,

> [t]he W.S.P.U. determined to make the occasion as public as possible, and began preparations for a procession and a demonstration. When the day came we assembled at the foot of the beautiful monument to the warrior-queen, Boadicea, that guards the entrance to Westminster Bridge, and from there we marched to the Foreign Office. At the meeting eight women spoke in behalf of an immediate suffrage measure, and Mr. Keir Hardie presented the argument for the suffrage members of Parliament. I spoke for the W.S.P.U., and I tried to make the Prime Minister see that no business could be more pressing than ours. I told him that the group of women organized in our Union felt so strongly the necessity for women enfranchisement that they were prepared to sacrifice for it everything they possessed, their means of livelihood, their very lives, if necessary. I begged him to make such a sacrifice needless by doing us justice now.[4]

This first parade of suffragettes in Britain set the scene for more marches and parades, starting with what became known as the "Mud March" on February 9, 1907, when 3,000 women walked from Hyde Park through London to bring attention to the cause.[5] A year later, following in these footsteps, the new American Suffragettes, later known as the Progressive Woman Suffrage Union, in New York were denied a permit for a suffrage parade in the city, although an unofficial march, comprising just over twenty suffragists, did walk together along Broadway on February 16, 1908.[6] Then the West took over. About 300 Californians organized a parade in Oakland that August to persuade the state Republican convention to take up woman suffrage.[7] Iowa followed in October the day after several suffragists, who attempted to meet with the New York City mayor to raise the question of woman suffrage, were escorted away by the police.[8] On the 29th of that month, about 150 women in the town of Boone, Iowa, headed from a church to downtown, marching or riding in cars and displaying suffrage banners. The British influence was clear here, for the march ended not only with a speech from NAWSA's president, Dr. Anna Howard Shaw, but also from two English suffragettes.[9] However, Little Rock, Arkansas, perhaps could actually claim to be the first place in the United States to hold a suffrage parade. In 1919, one recorder of the movement wrote the following: "About 1890 Mrs. Lida Merriweather of Tennessee was advertized to give 12 lectures under the auspices of the National Suffrage Society of Arkansas. Just before the lecture in Little Rock, the league, then consisting of some half dozen members, marched down Markham and Main streets carrying a banner announcing the time and place of the lecture. So there was a real suffrage parade in Little Rock about 30 years ago."[10] The likely influence here was temperance, for the membership of suffrage and temperance groups in Little Rock was largely interchangeable, with temperance being the larger movement. Women had marched outside saloons around U.S. towns since the early 1870s promoting temperance.[11]

It was on May 21, 1910, that large suffrage parades finally returned to the eastern United States. On that day Blatch and the Equality League of Self-Supporting Women and more than 400 supporters marched down Fifth Avenue to a mass meeting in Union Square, displaying British-style banners protesting the recalcitrance of New York assemblymen and their refusal to consider suffrage. Such parades became annual events in the Empire State.[12] Direct British influence, and that of Paul, can be discerned behind this event: Paul had spoken at Blatch's invitation in New York's Cooper Union that February 17, three months earlier.[13]

If Paul was not the first to organize a parade in the nation, she was equally not the first to organize a parade in the nation's capital. Ever since the start of Jefferson's second term, parades, although initially largely spontaneous, had been an integral part of inauguration ceremonies when sailors and bands accompanied the president riding back from the Capitol to the White House. The inauguration ceremony of 1837 saw the first horse-drawn floats, 1847 the first official organizing committee and 1885 the introduction of the presidential review, of both troops and civilian participants.[14] More memorable, in a sense because less usual, was President Andrew Johnson's Grand Review of the Armies after their parade along Pennsylvania Avenue on May 23 and 24, 1865, at the end of the Civil War.

Nevertheless, the first Great Suffrage March that Paul organized for March 3, 1913, places it at the head of the list in significance of parades in United States history, for it was revolutionary on several fronts. On that day, Paul introduced from her British experience—which included helping to organize the Great Suffrage March of October 1909 in Scotland's capital of Edinburgh—an event the type of which had never before been seen in the nation's capital. The details—the beauty, the discipline, the use of allegory, the carefully chosen colors and more—that Paul put on show with the Great

Suffrage March in Washington, D.C., are significant in themselves and are so many it is difficult to pin them all down. Other authors have examined them in depth.[15] What was more important, however, the March inaugurated a campaign that would continue this innovative approach nonstop until victory. Underpinning everything Paul engineered was her clearly thought out plan, based on in-depth study, widespread knowledge and hard-earned practical experience that produced the first successful such campaign in the United States. It also put to its own use a movement, one of whose protagonists was Woodrow Wilson, to give the federal government, as opposed to the states, the central role of governance in the United States. This was in part the advance of democracy, but Wilson promoted one aspect of it through his writings and speeches. In particular, he aimed to elevate the presidency from an equal position with Congress and the judiciary to the center of the federal constitution.

If Wilson spelled out his philosophy clearly, if he articulated it explicitly, if he wrote of his vision of a more powerful presidency long before he ever won the opportunity to try his vision out, Paul was equally explicit in her vision, less directly but with a range of expression far in advance of what the president thought of or had available. The president relied on verbal discourse and the exercise of the power in his office. Paul had determination, creativity, passion, art, femininity and the unique perspective of the politically dispossessed on her side, especially when the president talked so much about democracy. The Great Suffrage March of March 3, 1913, illustrated the kind of opponent that the new president was going to face. The parade was a huge statement, different from anything that had gone before. That March was not only the first move in a revolutionary campaign, but it was also revolutionary in itself, comprised as it was not of men but mainly of women and women's groups. It was revolutionary because its objective was to bring attention to a political goal for the benefit not of men but of women. It was revolutionary in the history of the nation up to then because all other marches along Pennsylvania Avenue had been celebratory and commemorative, not political, whereas the Great Suffrage March was about the fundamental civil right of citizenship, the right to vote. It broke new ground because women marched where only the men had marched before. It was cutting edge in the history of the nation's mass political movements because it was American women who were the first to stake the citizenry's claim to the U.S. capital's key ceremonial thoroughfare as a place for political protest, thereby laying the groundwork for every other political march in the nation's capital which has followed since. It was revolutionary because it wrested from the men their exclusive hold on one of the nation's most public spaces and asserted women's right to their own share in it as equals while at the same time demanding the ultimate share— political participation in the polity through the vote. Paul's triumph of winning Pennsylvania Avenue for the march was inspired, because it captured symbolically for women what had heretofore been a male space.

It is little wonder that Richard Sylvester tried to fob Paul off with the more spacious 16th Avenue or a date change to March 5. As he was chief of police in D.C., the crowds at the inauguration were a natural concern to him. Also, with the first Democratic president elected since 1897—a southerner to boot—the crowds of men in town for the event would perhaps be too jubilant for anyone to control. They might even roll out drunk from the nearby saloons. But perhaps Sylvester simply did not want ladies walking in public in the center of town. More important, protecting this male space may have been officials' unspoken objection. Remaining adamant about Pennsylvania Avenue, and with several society ladies backing her up, Paul went over Sylvester's head to the D.C. commissioners. She then went public. The *Washington Times* opined in the women's favor "since men's processions have already marched there."[16] The rest, as they say, is history.

It is not odd that the male onlookers, drunk or not, attacked the women. The United States has a long, ignominious and largely ignored history of mainly male audiences and onlookers attacking women in public, starting with the attack on Fanny Wright in Cincinnati in 1828 when, as a groundbreaking woman political orator in the United States, she faced down the rotten fruit, sexual slurs, and unruly mobs in order to speak against the injustices of poverty, exploitation, slavery and women's status in the nation. The degeneration of the Great Suffrage March into a free-for-all of male citizens, bringing out into the open their most deeply held prejudices about women, belongs to this long history. Despite much progress for some women, the men's prejudices were normally hidden under the veneer of the still-important and genteel philosophy of the "public" and "private" spheres. The male onlookers' response in 1913, however, was a clear sign that nothing much had changed since Frances Wright had first taken her place on the podium nearly ninety years before.

The mayhem was an eye-opener for some women of genteel background, teaching them for the first time what women of lower stations had to put up with every day. Dr. Nellie V. Mark, marshall of the fifty-strong women's professional division from Maryland who submitted written testimony to the ensuing Senate investigation on behalf of the Just Government League of Maryland, wrote, among many other disturbing details, of physical abuse of women and girls: "I saw some State militia throwing lighted cigarettes and matches onto our State flag and spitting upon it, and the police looked on and did nothing. I have never heard such vulgar, obscene, scurrilous, abusive language as was hurled at us that day by men—the voters of this country—and it amused the police. I did not know men could be such fiends."[17] Journalist Nellie Bly, a parade herald who saw the fracas from the inside, concluded in her ensuing article that suffragists were men's superiors.

The mayhem was also a clear sign that the men, drunk or not, understood clearly, even if only at a subconscious level, what the women's march meant. As one historian characterized it, with reference to suffragists having the temerity to drive automobiles into D.C., "it was a dangerous and usurping event in itself" at a time when women were still supposed to remain in their places.[18] Here they were taking over the center of the public stage, where women were not supposed to be.[19] Worse, with men imbued because of the history of parades on the avenue with the belief the meaning of parades was primarily commemorative and celebratory, a march on the eve of a key national celebration, and one that heralded a revolutionary political change, seemed inflammatory. Perhaps most important, the march of the women, no matter how beautifully arrayed, peaceful and entertaining they were, subliminally or otherwise represented on this avenue of celebrations and commemorations a capitulation of the male sex to the women. Meanwhile, the police largely stood idly by. The Great Suffrage March was by no means militant, but Paul had hit the jugular of male sensitivity in the United States, so powerful was her message. Whereas Wilson had words and the power of position for the struggle that Paul now so clearly had spelled out, in this march Paul demonstrated that she had at her command many more tools much more powerful than anything in the president's arsenal—and she had not even begun to bring them all to bear.

Every other aspect of the Great Suffrage March of 1913, unique and revolutionary in itself, supported Paul's message. The essentially unified design of the dress of the marchers, its unique floats and the hand-sewn banners all emphasized aspects of the feminine, from history to everyday life. Combined with its military formation, the march showed that women were as disciplined as men, yet more colorful compared with normal male parades. If not colorless, those generally relied on flags and military regalia for embellishment. One held at the United Veterans of the Confederacy Convention in Jacksonville, Florida, in 1914 shows men on horseback, men in uniform, men in automobiles and marching bands, and some women in cars with banners hanging over the doors.[20] Nothing in it compares to the Great Suffrage March of the previous year in Washington, D.C., all of which was designed for maximum visual impact, including the woman dressed in white riding a white horse at the head of the marchers. Even when both events are reduced to grainy old black-and-white silent film, the women's march looks much more interesting.

Paul's march leads in national history for even more features. The scope of female participation from all parts nationwide was hugely significant, for women were supposed to be at home. It stands out in the nation's history also because of its superb timing on the eve of the inauguration of President Wilson. Not only did the women have a ready-made audience who would not otherwise have attended, but the bunting on the avenue also enhanced the appearance of the whole. Latching onto the inauguration's timing, the march also benefited from the festive atmosphere, and the timing may, for some, have created the impression that woman suffrage was the policy of the new administration. And, even if suffrage was not actually a part of that policy, the march, its location and timing signaled clearly the intention for it to become so, whether the new president and his administration wanted it to be or not. Finally, the march won huge publicity for what had been a moribund subject—votes for women through a federal amendment—and Paul capitalized to the maximum on the even greater publicity that came her way because of the assaults by the male onlookers.

The Target

Peculiar as it may seem in an era when Washington, D.C., is the center of the American universe, many people a century ago thought it was extremely odd for Alice Paul to set up shop in the nation's capital. The Congressional Union raised eyebrows at the move:

> When the Congressional Union established its present headquarters in Washington many members, of the older suffrage organizations expressed astonishment that the Union had selected the national Capital as a permanent residence. Washington, they said, was a tomb except when Congress was in session. There was no public to address during the intervals of the sessions. New York was the proper place for permanent headquarters, and for the editorial rooms of "The Suffragist." A branch headquarters in the Capital, during the sessions of Congress was all that was necessary.

"Why Washington?" had come up so often that the *Suffragist* answered the question in its 1914 article, one which added more factors to consider in favor of D.C. besides its being the place where Congress met: "The truth is that Washington is the best center for suffrage work.... [It] is a city with a constantly changing population." The article pointed not just to honeymooners and holidaymakers, but also to people coming to "the greatest convention city in the country. Almost every week in the year sees some kind of assemblage or convention at the Capital ... [and] ... [t]he Congressional Union has taken advantage of all these conventions and assemblages to increase its membership and to obtain support for the [amendment]."[21]

The article listed several such recent conventions where the CU sold copies of the *Suffragist* and where members spoke, sometimes prompting suffrage resolutions among the delegates and even one to send a committee to Congress in support of suffrage. In these, and in a variety of other ways, the CU brought the federal amendment to the attention not only of the people who could change the law but also of countless voters and members of the public who, had they not been in D.C., might not otherwise have heard about the suffrage campaign through the normal channels. Such people might carry the news of the amendment back home. Some might sit up and take notice

From Wilson's inauguration on, suffragists sent countless deputations to the president in the White House asking for his support for the suffrage amendment. The deputations publicized their suffrage program with the banners they carried to the White House, as they did in this photograph from 1914 (Library of Congress Prints and Photographs Division, Washington, D.C., Harris & Ewing Collection, Digital ID: http://www.loc.gov/pictures/item/hec2008002612/).

and start to volunteer. Although the results of such actions were impossible to quantify, Paul obviously considered them an extremely effective form of publicity. In addition, suffrage had fewer diversions to compete with in D.C. than in New York and certainly not a state suffrage campaign. Paul's focus on Washington latched onto its then developing role for citizens as a business and vacation destination. It was, after all, the national capital, with—from the opening of Union Station for passenger traffic in 1907—a magnificent entryway. In fact, once the picketing began, the NWP's activities themselves became an attraction. One young married woman, for example, joined the pickets and was arrested, "and the groom spent his belated honeymoon indignantly lobbying the Congressmen of his own district."[22]

In January 1914, Alice Paul called for women across the country to rally for suffrage on May 2 and to converge in Washington the following week to present to Congress the signatures gathered that day. Between the call for the rallies and the two events, the NAWSA introduced an alternative amendment and maneuvered a vote on the issue. With its defeat, the May 2 and 9 rallies achieved heightened significance. Here members of the CU paste up billboards announcing the May 9 march to the Capitol with the suffrage petitions from across the nation (Library of Congress Prints and Photographs Division, Washington, D.C., Harris & Ewing Collection, Digital ID: http://www.loc.gov/pictures/item/hec2008002609/).

There was more about Washington in the CU's sights than its role in the nation. At the dedication of the Barry monument, the *Suffragist* admitted its prime target: "[Wilson made] the principal address [which] drew great crowds not only from Washington but from neighboring cities." The CU was there not only because of the crowds but also because of the president. Paul opened an office in Washington, D.C., and soon launched her campaign with a full-scale march right in the center of power to make certain that not just Congress but the president would sit up, take notice and act. To do so, she had latched onto a key part of the political philosophy of progressivism, at the point of progressivism's triumph and the modern start of the assumption by the president of the central role in the nation. This philosophy at that time swirled palpably in the air and echoed explicitly in the halls of power. Woodrow Wilson symbolized it.

In 1912, the United States did not have an overpowering central government as it has today, in which the focus is on the man in the White House and his leadership of one or other party in Congress. In the first decade of the twentieth century, the Constitution was not exactly operating in the minimalist manner in which the Founders intended, with a weak central government handling only those affairs that affected the nation as a whole and with essential political power residing close to the people of the nation within the several states. It was, however, much closer to that vision than it is today, hence a *New York Times* editorial several years later arguing that the suffragists were demanding action from the president when what they wanted was not in his bailiwick to deliver.[23] But the Constitution was evolving.

Originally, the states had their own representatives in Congress: under Article I, Section 3, Clauses 1 and 2, senators were elected by state legislatures and each state had two, signifying the essential equality of all the states in the nation. By 1900, however, that power distribution had moved far from the original intent by force of circumstances, by personality and by design, the change having started gradually from the beginning of the nation's history and increasing during the Civil War. During the rise of the Progressive era, arguments were increasingly put forward to modify this balance of power deliberately and drastically, to remove power largely from the states and to have it reside instead in the central government in Washington through direct election by the people—the expansion, in other words, of democracy and the eclipse of the republic. The key long-running signifier of this movement was gaining ground at the turn of the new century and reached its goal in 1912 with the passage of the amendment to provide for elections of senators by the voters instead of the states. It was ratified and promulgated as the Seventeenth

Amendment in 1913, coming into full operation for the first time in the 1914 elections. Still, the 1912 power distribution was less removed from the original intention than the modern one.

Meanwhile, however, the goal of revolutionizing the presidency was in the sights of Woodrow Wilson. In 1902, Wilson had become president of Princeton University, in Alice Paul's home state of New Jersey. He reformed it radically during his tenure, creating an academic bureaucracy to operate the larger academe, a mini-version of what would become his vision of a national government with a strong bureaucracy for carrying out delegated authority. Although more or less out of the public eye at the time, Wilson won widespread recognition for shaking up the elitist university and its student organizations. Becoming more prominent and now with a solid record of governance in his background, in 1910 he ran for governor of New Jersey. At that time, the Democratic Party had been out of the U.S. presidency since McKinley took over from Cleveland in 1897. The Democrats' ultimate goal was to regain the White House. New Jersey would be a stepping-stone to that grail: with his experience as New Jersey governor, Wilson could run for president in 1912.

Wilson was an effective leader of the Progressives, that wide-ranging movement for social change and reform that extended to political philosophy, if only because of the belief of many Progressives, that the forms of the United States government then in existence were inadequate for solving the modern national and world problems. Wilson was one of the key contributors to the new thinking on the United States Constitution. He deemed it to be a Newtonian machine no longer adequate to the demands of the late nineteenth and early twentieth centuries. The Constitution had to be Darwinian and able to evolve with the needs of each succeeding era of history. In particular, he argued, the role of the president had to be reconsidered for a modern, complex age. Originally, the president had been "the legal executive, the presiding and guiding authority in the application of law and the execution of policy. His veto upon legislation was only his 'check' on Congress,—was a power of restraint, not of guidance. He was empowered to prevent bad laws, but he was not to be given an opportunity to make good ones."

By 1910, when Wilson ran for governor of New Jersey, he had already articulated his own perception of the presidency of the twentieth-century nation: he was "becoming more and more a political and less and less an executive officer." While his "executive powers" would be increasingly delegated, his political powers were growing so that Americans would be "more and more inclined from generation to generation to look to the President as the unifying force ... the leader both of his party and of the nation."

"There is no national party choice except that of President," Wilson wrote, clearly articulating the cult of personality. "When he speaks in his true character, he speaks for no special interest. If he rightly interpret the national thought and boldly insist upon it, he is irresistible; and the country never feels the zest of action so much as when its President is of such insight and caliber. Its instinct is for unified action, and it craves a single leader. It is for this reason that it will often prefer to choose a man rather than a party."[24]

Such was the repeatedly stated political philosophy of the man who was elected governor of Paul's home state ten months after she returned from her suffragette sojourn in Britain. The significance of Wilson's views, published in 1908, could not have been lost on the learned and politically astute Alice Paul. Here was a political philosophy that may have been turning on its head the Founders' doctrine of small government with a limited executive, yet it fitted very well with what Paul had learned on the ground in Britain. There, to win the revolutionary reform that votes for women represented, women had to target and win over or wear down those men who were directly responsible for the acts of the government. Paul had not only seen this focus on a central power at work with the Pankhurst campaign in Britain, but she had also worked in such a campaign. When Paul and Burns became lieutenants for the WSPU, all laws for Great Britain—comprising Scotland, England and Wales plus the whole of Ireland at the time—were made and modified in the seat of government in the British Parliament based in London.

Unlike in the United States, where individual states exercised general police powers under the Constitution, no power over national legislation resided in the individual entities that constituted Great Britain and Ireland. The central focus for British suffragettes for their votes for women campaign, therefore, was automatically the king in Parliament in the main capital of London. Paul, therefore, became involved in a campaign that by definition focused on the center of political power. Such a campaign did not mean that the rest of the country was ignored. Other major cities, such as Edinburgh, Glasgow, Dundee, Manchester and Birmingham, were important to rally suffrage supporters at the grass roots; to focus on elections to fill an empty parliamentary seat during a parliament; to target ministers of the Crown when they spoke at constituency meetings or at major rallies in key cities; to try to engineer the defeat of current members of Parliament during general elections when they had opposed votes for women; and to create a majority with a pro-woman suffrage policy. The Pankhursts and the WSPU, the Women's Freedom League (WFL) and the National Union of Women's Suffrage Societies (NUWSS) each worked with a different emphasis in their campaign to change the law regarding suffrage in Britain, but every action of necessity ultimately focused on London, His Majesty's Government and even direct petitioning of the king. The aim was to change the mind of the government, not only to be in favor of, but also to promote, woman suffrage. If that did not occur, the aim was to prompt a change of heart and action through the majority party's fear of losing seats, and the government its power. This focus on the central government in London was the key to the British suffragettes' campaign for winning the vote. In the British context—as a process, although not in all its details— it was a logical and practical thing to do.

Back in the United States, Wilson had clearly outlined a position for the presidency in 1908 that merged with Paul's experiences in Britain. What he articulated was revolutionary in that it turned the Constitution on its head. Instead of "We, the People," he proposed if not "We, the President" then a position somewhere along a continuum from the founding to the monarchy that the founding had replaced. The president, Wilson unequivocally stated, "can dominate his party by being spokesman for the real sentiment and purpose of the country, by giving direction to opinion, by giving the country at once the information and the statements of policy.... [H]e is also the political leader of the nation ... the only national voice in affairs ... the representative ... of the whole people.... A President whom it trusts can not only lead [the country], but form it to his own views.... The President may also, if he will, stand within the party counsels and use the advantage of his power and personal force to control its actual programs."[25]

This whole philosophy, summarized in the latter statement in particular, Paul and Burns latched onto. If Wilson's own words were revolutionary in that they turned the Constitution on its head and approached the presidency as the leader instead of a representative of the nation, Paul's was equally revolutionary for taking the great man at his word. If the president was going to be the center of United States government, then Paul was going to make the president and his home the center of her work. Quite simply, for the suffrage campaign, if Wilson believed what he proclaimed, Alice Paul and her colleagues would make him act on his words.

CHAPTER 4

Where Paul Fits into Suffrage History

Paul's revolutionary and unwavering focus on the nation's capital and the man at the center of power derived from little in United States history. She did, however, have much to build on when she launched the final suffrage campaign in 1913. Soon her work influenced fellow suffragists and she combined with them to lead to victory.

Paul's campaign often petitioned Congress for action. This procedure was a long-established American tradition used to great effect in the past. Since the 1820s, women in particular conducted with determination great petition drives against slavery, which brought abolition to the fore as a serious matter for public and political debate. During the Civil War Susan B. Anthony and Elizabeth Cady Stanton spearheaded a national petition drive for abolition after discovering the extremely limited nature of Lincoln's much-vaunted Emancipation Proclamation. These campaigns focused on Congress, where legislative and constitutional amendment powers resided. Paul's petitions continued this tradition.

Her concerted focus on Washington, however, as the center of suffrage activism was new for suffrage. Although Anthony almost annually spent time in Washington from the late 1870s onward to promote the amendment, she was mostly alone and focused mostly on Congress. The closest to Paul's focus on D.C. was the march of Coxey's Army in 1894 to protest the economic disruption that the panic of 1893 caused and to lobby for job creation through public works. Like the purpose of petitioning, that march aimed primarily to make Congress act. The fact that the D.C. authorities never allowed the men right into the heart of the nation's capital city does not detract from their innovation.[1] The NWP's approach, however, was significantly different from

Coxey's. Coxey led a march for government help with poverty caused by recent economic collapse. Paul consciously launched a campaign to end a long-standing political inequity that women had been campaigning for decades to reverse. The Great Suffrage March was just the first salvo in what would be an extended campaign. Further, while Paul, like Coxey, went to the nation's capital, in the women's case the CU moved right in when Paul and Burns opened their office in January 1913.

Besides trying to win the president's influence, Paul had several good reasons to zero in on Washington. Women no longer needed to be educated about suffrage; it was now time for practical politics. Practical politics meant winning suffrage in the most efficient way. The state strategy had been proved inefficient. The federal amendment would change sex discrimination in all state voting laws at once and end the creation of further inequalities through piecemeal and partial state suffrage reforms. The amendment campaign once launched, therefore, Paul sustained it until victory, with the president at its center and Congress a close second, if not a virtually equal, target. It was the most insistent, creative and versatile civil rights crusade in the United States and the final ingredient in a 72-year constantly evolving movement spanning several generations.

Yet another distinguishing feature was its foreign influence, which significantly turned the tables, for suffrage struggles began in the United States. Paul never worked for suffrage before her sojourn abroad. Her campaign emerged from her extensive experience in Britain's WSPU. This influence imported the sense of purpose, direction and strategy that were at that time largely unknown at home. Even so, Paul owed much to her suffrage precursors. The federal amendment had been around from the 1870s, even if by 1912 it was moribund. Paul revived Anthony's work. Also helpful to Paul was what the NAWSA had done for decades to educate the public. Its nationwide grassroots organization, which Carrie Chapman Catt launched in 1895 when she became the National's organizer-in-chief, also proved invaluable.[2] This network was used for most of the victorious state campaigns up to the end of 1912. For most of 1913, as chair of the Congressional Committee of the NAWSA, Paul could use this network to call women to action. Her initial operation, therefore, benefited from not having to start everything from scratch.

Paul's work with the Congressional Committee also proved very useful, for it launched her work and established the structure to continue with after the NAWSA pulled back. In 1913 Paul had created the Congressional Union to raise funds after NAWSA had insisted she provide the financing for the federal campaign. The CU took on direction of all the amendment organization when the relationship with NAWSA collapsed: for the second time within a year, Paul did not have to start completely from scratch. Even in a separate organization, Paul benefited from the NAWSA's work at state level, not least from the fact that by 1912 two million women had won suffrage through the states by the state strategy. This vote was to grow: by the 1916 election four million women could vote in national elections, while woman suffrage states accounted for one-third of the electoral college. In 1917 the victory of votes for women in New York again raised the potential number of female voters across the nation. In Paul's head, every female vote represented invaluable leverage for party-in-power politics.[3]

The NWP further benefited from the experience of state campaigns, which early had derived new energy and creativity from the British example. In 1907, for example, visiting English suffragettes Anne Cobden-Sanderson and Bettina Borrman Wells promoted the use of British-style activism,[4] while in October 1909 Emmeline Pankhurst found an enthusiastic welcome on a speaking tour that she began that month.[5] By 1912, in many of the states which had recently won equal suffrage, women had canvassed the entire potential voter base, utilizing such British techniques as street-corner speech making and soap box and automobile orations, some of which Paul herself introduced after 1910 to Philadelphia. Just as their British counterparts had done, the women also chalked sidewalks, pasted billboards, distributed handbills, and turned every mass communication innovation, including the press and movies, to their benefit. To carry themselves and their message across whichever terrain they faced, the women pressed into service not just trains, but also automobiles and planes, in addition to the traditional carts, traps, horses and foot slogging.

In many states, therefore, women already knew how to win suffrage and some of the veterans of these campaigns later chose to work for the NWP and the national amendment. Louise Bryant, Clara Wold and Alice and Betty Gram, for example, who campaigned for suffrage in Oregon, worked for Paul's campaign, becoming picketers and prisoners in 1917. Wold later went on hunger strike.[6] Harriot Stanton Blatch of New York in 1916 brought her organization, the Women's Political Union, into the NWP. The announcement of this move by the NWP praised Blatch and the WPU for the 1910 suffrage parade in New York adding that "the greatest contribution of this association to suffrage work in New York was the introduction of direct political action in dealing with the state legislature. Under the leadership of ... Blatch, suffragists, who had previously expended their energies in propaganda work, excellent in character, but with no definite political object, turned public attention on the state legislature, and put the responsibility for favorable action on suffrage squarely upon political leaders at Albany...."[7] The latter half of this quote nails the difference between the old (NAWSA) educational approach to winning the vote and the new (NWP) direct political action approach.

The Great Suffrage March also shifted into high gear a momentum which began at state level, for after a slow start, parades had featured in 1910 in New York, while California, Kansas, Arizona, and Oregon had used them to win suffrage. Increasingly, women at state level also celebrated with striking and innovative tactics, such as the New York City torchlight procession to celebrate that year's western victories. In fact, the November 10, 1912, New York City parade might have been a dress rehearsal for the substantial gear change from state to national campaigning that would emerge the next year, for this huge and stunningly picturesque parade featured several floats, suffrage banners and Anna Howard Shaw marching along to great cheers. It also featured at its head a woman—Inez Milholland—with a white horse. Milholland wore only a flimsy white Grecian-style gown in the cold night air and reined her horse from a chariot.[8] Paul arrived on the scene at the pivotal time to focus much of this disparate energy into one combined goal.

In addition to the advantage of having had so much suffrage groundwork to build on, Paul had suffrage precedent beyond Susan B. Anthony's yearly canvassing of Congress for the amendment after its introduction in 1878. A history of civil activism by women, for its time as revolutionary as Paul's would be, had triggered Anthony's missions to the nation's capital. This was the "New Departure" that came to public attention in St. Louis in 1869 and was an attempt to overturn the restrictions of the Reconstruction amendments and win for female citizens a favorable judicial interpretation of woman suffrage under the privileges and immunities clause of the Fourteenth Amendment.[9] This new tactic prompted incensed suffrage women from 1868 onward to attempt to vote. Anthony, for example, voted for President Grant in the 1872 election. Accused of breaking the law, at her trial the judge denied her a jury and sentenced her to prison when she refused to pay the fine. The only reason her case did not make it to the Supreme Court was because her lawyer, out of misplaced gallantry and against her wishes, forestalled imprisonment by paying up. It was one of the most famous trials of the nineteenth century, and Anthony then publicized the judicial system's unequal treatment of a woman in court by publishing a book.[10] Meanwhile, Virginia Minor's legal challenge, following the denial of her attempt to register to vote in St. Louis, Missouri, in 1872, did reach the Supreme Court. The dismissal of her case—whereby the justices ruled that, while women are citizens, citizenship does not confer the right to vote—immediately prompted Anthony and Stanton to begin to promote the federal amendment.[11]

These protests emerged from the radical strain of the NAWSA in the originally distinct National Woman Suffrage Association that Susan B. Anthony and Elizabeth Cady Stanton created in 1869 as a result of the Reconstruction amendments' betrayal of U.S. women. In her later campaign for the federal amendment and its conduct in Washington, Paul was effectively returning to these roots. Just as Anthony had upped the ante in 1873 by refusing to pay her fine, Paul upped the ante during her campaign when an obdurate Wilson and Democratic Party blocked her goal. The turning point came in 1917, when the NWP turned to overt civil disobedience, or, as one author calls it, "unruly citizenship."[12] In 1917, Paul and the NWP introduced their modern twist on the women's previous historic protests—the January 10 first-ever introduction of pickets at the gates of the White House, an innovation that over the next two years involved several hundred women, and countless other new tactics to fire up supporters and wear the president and Congress down.

Paul benefited considerably, therefore, from the work done by women in the decades before she came on the scene. Even so, her work in turn influenced the older suffragists who were still active. Primarily, if, while inside the NAWSA in 1913, Paul could not pull it along with her vision, she did so once she was on the outside by setting the pace and raising the stakes. The heightened interest in suffrage from the NWP campaign kept suffrage before the public eye. The campaign brought suffrage to women's attention in an exciting way hardly seen since Anthony's time. Paul's methods may have been controversial, but that was helpful to the NAWSA, for it helped establish the older and much more staid organization as reasonable and moderate and they quickly prophesied doom from the NWP's "antics."

The NWP, in effect, created a dynamic that the NAWSA could not ignore, even if the latter's prophecies proved wrong, at least in the New York campaign when the Empire State women won the vote even as Alice Paul was being forcibly fed in November 1917. Yet the National castigated the NWP. Opponents in the press swiftly labeled "militant" the tactics that Paul introduced in 1917. Catt, who late in 1915 had replaced Anna Howard Shaw as president of NAWSA, joined in this hue and cry. Militancy was a touchy subject because of what had happened in Britain when the suffragette movement had transitioned from political protest via militancy to a campaign of violence. Although largely against property, that campaign also targeted some government ministers. With the Pankhurst protégée at the helm, it was natural to assume that the NWP actions would copy the WSPU's. During a war it was equally natural for citizens to turn uncritically patriotic and follow the president with a narrow and intolerant vision of patriotism. Concern about suffragists being painted with that brush was, perhaps, logical. The National underestimated Paul's uniqueness of vision.

For the NAWSA, the adjective "militant" too easily served as a convenient slur on the NWP. Almost anything outside of the bounds of ladylike behavior the NWP women did could be described as militant, partly because so many of the CU's picketers were women of some social standing. Such women, even in 1917, were not supposed to behave as they did. Catt and the NAWSA used the militant slur to make themselves look reasonable. Yet, as the war progressed and Paul and the NWP not only refused to back down but upped the ante regularly, Catt still benefited from the negative publicity. As the treatment of the so-called militants by the Wilson régime raised public concern and ire to such great heights that the tide of public sentiment turned in favor of suffrage, Catt—an able politico—turned the new pro-suffrage reality to her own advantage. Catt, born in Wisconsin and raised from the age of seven in Iowa, obviously knew how the "true woman," as opposed to the "new woman," behaved. Alternatively, she had learned enough of the behavior of the "Southern Lady" to play that role to Wilson's "Southern Gentleman" persona. She flattered and soothed the ego of this famous ladies' man while wheedling, cajoling and entreating him to support woman suffrage. Once Paul and the NWP had changed the political landscape on votes for women, particularly with the Catt-castigated picketing-prison-and-hunger-strike campaign, they had thereby set the scene for Catt to sweep in, put her personal style and access to the president into overdrive and demand his support for suffrage as the way to get those young harridans off his back so he could concentrate on what really mattered. To him, and many of the NAWSA, a just peace and the creation of the League of Nations were what mattered.

Of dramatic political bearing at this point, which seals Paul's role in the suffrage victory, however, was Paul's unique vision of a just peace. She had earlier refused to stop campaigning when the United States went to war, due to lessons learned from a critical mistake women made in 1861 and from Susan B. Anthony, who was against women's suspension of their equal rights activities when the Civil War began. Without Paul's contentious decision it is highly unlikely that suffrage would even have featured on the political radar when war ended in 1918. Women then would have faced the very political oblivion and consequent exclusion from the peacemaking plans that they had faced exactly fifty years before. Paul's refusal to allow war to derail suffrage was revolutionary not simply because she did it: it was revolutionary because of her interpretation of the terms under which Americans went the war. If Wilson said the war was to fight for democracy abroad, she said the NWP fought for democracy at home. In effect, she supported the purpose of the United States in going to war by reframing the woman's struggle in the same terms as the men used, although emphasizing a different theater. She also supported war aims by continuing to fight for democracy on the home front after the war for democracy abroad ended: a just peace at home meant suffrage. Keeping Wilson's feet, almost literally, to the fire on the issue, she thereby ensured that one right of half of American humanity on this belated occasion did indeed become part of the peace.

In this sense is it correct to say that women won suffrage because of the war. It was, however, only in this one sense: suffrage became part of the peace due to Paul's astute, unexpected and radical interpretation of the war propaganda. It was also due to her use of the hothouse circumstances the war created and by forcing authorities' adherence to the terms under which Wilson fought it and then fought to win the peace. This made suffrage the major issue that it actually was even if the powers-that-were never accorded it that status in their agendas. Catt's role would have been almost nonexistent, while passage of the amendment and federal woman suffrage would have been doubtful without Paul's campaign.

Together, however, the NWP and the NAWSA contributed to the victory. They both worked during ratification, each organization lobbying in states across the nation until suffrage was secured against mounting opposition from antis, old-world Southern Gentlemen, and groups such as the liquor interests. They worked in more than the thirty-six states successful states, campaigning in several states that voted no and, after Tennessee's vote, in two more just to make sure.[13] It was an incredible, unforgettable, monumental achievement. Yet in American history, it has largely been forgotten. At least Paul and the NWP women were largely forgotten. While struggling to catch up on the NWP, Catt positioned herself and the National as the group that won suffrage for American women, conveniently forgetting how the CU/NWP had set the pace since 1913 and created the conditions that made it possible. Catt herself and the NAWSA's publications dismissed very ungraciously the pivotal and critical role of Paul and the NWP in a victory without which United States history would be very different, while Catt cooperated in Secretary Colby's dismissal of Paul when he signed the amendment.

Catt, however, had acknowledged early on in private that her adversaries within the cause had vaulted the issue of woman suffrage from merely a state to a national issue. "There is no doubt that the Congressional Union has pushed the federal Amendment to the front no matter what anybody says about it," she stated in a letter in January 1916 soon after she returned to the presidency of NAWSA.[14] This letter clearly demonstrates the gulf that existed between the two organizations, for Catt is unsure even in 1916 whether the federal goal is possible, whereas the actions of the CU and Paul at the time demonstrate certainty of victory. In fact, Doris Stevens had discovered that with Paul, like Susan B. Anthony, failure was not countenanced, even if victory took

During a congressional debate about the First World War in February 1917, the NWP focused on how long women had been waiting for the right to vote. It was now fifty years since they had been told to wait because it was "the Negro's hour," when freedmen were given the vote after the Civil War. The cavalier treatment during Reconstruction of women who had fought to free the slaves still rankled, especially when, with the massive immigration to the United States during the late nineteenth century, men born abroad and often unable to speak English were automatically given the right to vote on becoming U.S. citizens or even, in some states, simply by declaring the intention to do so. American-born women had long seen these multiple standards as a stunning injustice that demanded speedy rectification (Library of Congress Prints and Photographs Division, Washington, D.C., Harris & Ewing Collection, Digital ID: http://www.loc.gov/pictures/item/hec2008006816/).

When the NWP planned major demonstrations, such as the walk around the White House in the rain for Wilson's second inauguration, which took place just three months after the suffragists began to picket him in his residence, they advertised their plans by walking through the streets with placards (Library of Congress Prints and Photographs Division, Washington, D.C., Harris & Ewing Collection, 1917, Digital ID: http://www.loc.gov/pictures/item/hec2008005371/).

an interminably long time. Paul made this clear when she said in 1913, Stevens related, that passage and ratification could occur even during that Congress if enough women demanded it.[15] The passion to win fired the NWP and gave it a power that the NAWSA lacked. Only during ratification did NAWSA demonstrate that it had even the same goal. Even then the tactics differed, with the National leadership then more presumptive about early victory.

Such presumption may have emanated from the National's political sympathies. Catt, with a closer relationship to the Democrats and Wilson than Paul had, used that to her benefit when pressing the president to support suffrage in order to rid his agenda of troublesome women. But beyond such a relationship, Catt's letter to the National's state presidents points to NAWSA's distinct political leanings. Even though the National professed nonpartisanship, it was significantly pro–Democrat. The near identification of the NAWSA with the Democratic Party emerged in the League of Woman Voters,

Standing outside their Cameron House headquarters in Lafayette Square in 1917, suffragists display a range of banners used to provoke action from a recalcitrant Wilson (Library of Congress Prints and Photographs Division, Washington, D.C., Harris & Ewing Collection, Digital ID: http://www.loc.gov/pictures/item/hec2008005759/).

which succeeded the NAWSA in 1920 and immediately took on the character of a "progressive-liberal organization."[16] This Democratic bent had long been evident in the South. In Arkansas, for example, after its women won primary suffrage in 1917, suffragists reorganized into an Equal Suffrage State Central Committee along political lines, while leading suffrage women began to appear regularly in the roster of local Democratic Party officials.[17] In contrast, the NWP remained nonpartisan. In June 1920, in what was ultimately late in the ratification campaign but before Tennessee came unexpectedly into the running, the NWP blamed the Republican Party for blocking ratification because the Republican governors of Vermont and Connecticut blocked ratification in the two remaining states which did not have constitutional obstacles to delay ratification beyond the 1920 election. The women, therefore, picketed the Republicans at their convention in Chicago.[18]

If Democratic leanings did confer some benefits, therefore, the closeness of the National to the Democrats also signaled a weakness: it could not, like

KAISER WILSON

HAVE YOU FORGOTTEN
YOUR SYMPATHY WITH
THE POOR GERMANS
BECAUSE THEY WERE NOT
SELF-GOVERNED?

20,000,000
AMERICAN WOMEN ARE NOT
SELF-GOVERNED.

TAKE THE BEAM
OUT OF YOUR OWN EYE.

Paul and the NWP, go for the political jugular in pursuit of suffrage. In her letter to the National's presidents, Catt disapproves of the CU/NWP's policy of putting the blame on the party in power for stopping the amendment in Congress, for that tactic meant opposing Democrats. The NAWSA, in other words, not only did not have the passion but did not possess the kind of killer instinct that an intended victory required. The NWP took a no-holds-barred approach, which gave them the greater impact.

In summary, from the very beginning Paul built on what her suffrage precursors in the United States had done, using her forebears' educational and organizational groundwork. If Elizabeth Cady Stanton was the original philosopher and face of the movement and Susan B. Anthony the relentless campaigner and instigator of suffrage action and Carrie Chapman Catt the quintessential organizer, Alice Paul was the consummate strategist who pulled these strands together, making them work effectively and pushing tactics to the limits during very stressful times in order to win. Alice Paul could not have done this without the groundwork of her predecessors. But no demand for national woman suffrage could have reached a successful conclusion, no matter what Catt might have claimed, without the shock troop activity of Alice Paul and the NWP in the fervid atmosphere of a world war. Her campaign bypassed the old-fashioned and ineffective rut the movement had become stuck in. Paul introduced major innovations from Britain, thereby breaking new ground for United States suffrage activism. She grafted onto

Opposite: From the suffrage perspective, if there was any difference between a president who played politics with the women who campaigned for suffrage and the tyrannical Kaiser Wilhelm of Germany, with whom the United States went to war in April 1917, the difference was merely one of degree: only tyrants denied liberty to their subjects or treated citizens as subjects. The Kaiser Wilson banner demonstrated this uncomfortable truth so clearly that onlookers physically attacked the women who displayed them peacefully.

The banner points to another uncomfortable truth: the growth in the injustice to women since they were refused the vote during Reconstruction. It refers to "20,000,000 American women [who] are not self-governed" without the vote. When the Nineteenth Amendment finally banned sex discrimination in voting, in fact, 26,500,000 women were enfranchised. In contrast, 7.3 million women were excluded from the vote during the Reconstruction amendments, while the number of freedmen enfranchised then was less than one million. Congress's refusal to deal with the issue of woman suffrage fifty years before, therefore, had allowed the injustice to more than triple in size through the years and demonstrates the contrast in the manner of dealing with injustices to women and injustices to men (Library of Congress Prints and Photographs Division, Washington, D.C., Harris & Ewing Collection, Digital ID: http://www.loc.gov/pictures/item/hec2008006861/).

what had gone before a completely new approach and combined it with tactics that the NWP members devised as needs arose. It was this combination which finally broke the national dam of resistance against suffrage. Alice Paul, following directly in Anthony's footsteps, led suffrage to victory. Even within suffrage, therefore, her work was new and revolutionary, yet another reason for recognizing her importance and that of the NWP in American history.

CHAPTER 5

Imagination, Creativity and Nonviolence

In September 1918, with the amendment stalled and the president effectively ignoring it, the National Woman's Party upped the ante yet again, this time choosing to burn Wilson's empty words about democracy.[1] Later, the women raised the stakes higher still by lighting fires outside the White House, keeping them alight throughout the night or for as long as it took authorities to put them out. Initially, they burned the fires openly in an urn, but soon the police began to arrest them. Then the women smuggled the logs under their overcoats. They used logs soaked in oil, which water could not extinguish. The police were reduced to stamping them out, which scattered the embers and fascinated onlookers. The women often lit several fires, setting a new one alight when police were already dealing with an earlier one. Later they used asbestos coils, which were easier than logs to transport. In reading this part of the NWP's story, it is difficult not to cheer the suffragists on as they circumvent the law. The image of the fires illuminating the darkness of the night alone seems magical, but the flames themselves seem alive, fires appearing seemingly from nowhere, with spectators bedazzled by the suffragists' sleight-of-hand.[2] This cat-and-mouse game with the police must have appeared to bystanders like a live version of the Keystone Kops. The ensuing laughter and gasps of admiration must have garnered the NWP some outright support.

The Watchfires for Freedom comprised the latest tactic revealing the imagination and creativity of the NWP members. From the start, for recruitment and publicity, the NWP had employed pageants and parades beautifully designed, emphasizing the feminine and woman's contribution to the nation while pointing out the pains and penalties imposed on unequal female citizens. They marched in and on Washington, they drove cross-country to stir and

79

organize the grass roots, they collected signatures from all over for petitions, they used planes and balloons to broadcast suffrage messages, they worked hard for every inch of press coverage before and after organization, mobilization and celebrations.[3] The efficiency of their lobbying of congressional representatives came from a system that Maud Younger designed for the NWP, which created the blueprint for lobbying in Washington today.[4] Party-in-power targeting was another innovation.[5] Paul's campaign also harnessed its own uniqueness—the very fact that women *were* this campaign—to make the public stop and think. In fact, just about everything that, only because of convention, women were not supposed to do, the women of the CU/NWP women went ahead and did, with all their putative rule breaking heightening the publicity they sought in the goal of ultimate victory. And, while it also involved women of all social classes, it relied on the social position of its leaders to shock and stir.

The Watchfires for Freedom demonstrated clearly the knowledge these women possessed. It is not difficult to discern in them the brains of women well versed in chemistry, with knowledge of and access to the most appropriate tool for their purpose and the focus to carry out their plan. If Paul still needed to demonstrate the quality and independent spirit of the "new woman" of the twentieth century as opposed to the "true woman" of the nineteenth—and she was demonstrating clearly this difference from the Great Suffrage March onward—she did it brilliantly with the Watchfires, for what those Watchfires demonstrated without doubt was the educational attainments of the suffragists. The fires established clearly, for those still refusing to face the facts, that the women were President Wilson's intellectual equals.

They were his intellectual equals not only because of the knowledge, such as that they called on for the Watchfires, which they applied to details of the campaign, they were his intellectual equals because they had a solid philosophy on which they based their whole work, the one that required the imagination and creativity that they demonstrated so often: nonviolence. It may have been politically expedient for many reasons for people such as Catt, who saw her thunder being stolen by young upstarts, to characterize the NWP as extremists. Yet this was a distortion that ignored the nuances which that word encompassed. It also downplayed the competence of the women themselves to draw a line which divided militancy from violence and to act nonviolently. The simple fact is that the NWP was never militant in the sense the British suffragettes Paul had worked with were. Two windows apparently were broken, it is true. One, however, Paul broke to allow air into a prison. The other was to enable NWP members to release themselves from illegal imprisonment by Capitol police. Stories about American women chaining themselves up sometimes surface, but there appears to be no foundation for them. Such activity did occur in Britain, but so far it had not been shown in the United States.[6] The use of the word "militant," however, in the suffragist sense and with reference to the NWP specifically, is still incorrectly conflated with violence. Yet the NWP understood the difference, defining militancy as a strong assertion within the boundaries of the law of the right to the vote and the right to demand it.[7] To dismiss the NWP as extremist is to ignore what actually happened. Besides targeting the president in the capital as the national leader of policy, Paul espoused peaceful protest. In other words, her approach was wholly dedicated to nonviolence, "based on well established political and military strategy, and upon a deep knowledge of the history of all reform movements" and planned by "women of education, scholarly attainments and gentle culture," said picketer, prisoner and campaigner Doris Stevens in an article in the *Suffragist* in July of 1919.

Stevens wrote when the amendment was wending its way through ratification and described the two main prongs of the suffrage campaign as military and political. The military prong focused on the weakest point of the adversary, which the NWP identified as the president and Congress. They were markedly weak during the war. "[O]ur boasted crusade for world democracy [contrasted] with the glaring inconsistency of the denial of democracy at home. That was the untenable position of President Wilson and the Democratic Administration." The second prong was the political strategy of opposing the party in power, which "not only harassed the offending party, but ... forced down the opposition of the minority party." "[H]istory had taught us that no great reform could hope to succeed without a downright fight," she continued. But "[n]ot necessarily a fight with arms; perhaps merely with brains, wits, and devoted sacrifice, but a real fight." "Action," Stevens wrote, "was the 'acid test' of words.... We merely sought to dramatize this weakness with the only weapons at hand to which a powerless class which does not take up arms can resort."

Listing "every known scientific device ... which [men used] to annihilate the enemy," from bayonets to poison gas to tanks to firearms, Stevens wrote, "We could not and would not fight with such weapons.... How were we to make our fight seem more heroic and important by the side of men's world conflagration? How could we, with reasonable speed, rout the enemy without weapons, and we a class without power and recognition? Our simple, peaceful, almost quaint device was a BANNER!"

On the banners "were inscribed pertinent truths and burning questions, fiery challenges and sedate quotations from no less respectable sources than the Declaration of Independence, the Bible, President Wilson's learned volumes ... Abraham Lincoln ... and so on." In those early days, when movies were silent and reading was widespread, the women had hit on the original form of the sound bite, the now century-old precursor of "if you like your plan, you can keep it." In her article, Stevens lists several women in the NWP who worked on the details of this overall strategy with Paul and how they had thought of it in advance. "Ridiculed? Of course. But we had nothing to lose.... Woman is more or less used to that weapon of men anyway. But a president and a cabinet simply cannot stand being made ridiculous, especially by women. That is what hurts."

Consequently, through the "stupidity" of imprisoning the picketers and finding an endless "stream of women willing to submit to the indignities of prison," the all-powerful administration was finally forced to admit the failure of its own tactics. "The women had won ... [and] were not bitter. They could afford to forgive stupidity which had worked as a boomerang upon the government." Stevens concluded: "And so I repeat what has never been a secret. We set out to embarrass an administration unwilling to enfranchise women. We succeeded so well that we began to get results. The minute the government began to move we changed our strategy."[8]

Stevens was fudging the issue somewhat when she wrote, "How could we possibly know a banner would create such a panic among presidents and cabinet ministers, congressmen and the populace?" NWP members must have known what could happen and discussed what they would do because they had already encountered—from the public and some local authorities, if not from the federal government—the potential of the banners, which lay in the response of viewers. During the 1916 party-in-power campaign in the West, "the Democrats ... exhibited when encountering the Woman's Party, a degree of passion truly amazing," an item in the *Suffragist* had reported. In Denver, Colorado, a member of the NWP was arrested for distributing literature about the Democratic record on suffrage, while in Colorado Springs, the "Great Demand" banner was "arrested" and put in jail for the night, removing it from the sight of speaker William Jennings Bryan, who, at that point, was still campaigning against suffrage. In Chicago, a member of the NWP was attacked apparently because she wore the gold, white and purple of the party. Following this, a mob completely destroyed the NWP's banners challenging Wilson and the Democrats' position on suffrage when he arrived in the city.[9]

However, Stevens was correct in saying that the women had no *guarantee* of the response of authorities: they just had to wait and see. They were acting peacefully, within citizens' legal rights that the recent Clayton Act of 1914 outlined. Violence against *them,* and then *their* arrest and imprisonment were not a foregone conclusion even if they knew it was possible or even highly likely. The simple fact was that if Wilson and Congress had not been so hard-headed and dismissive of the women they could have passed the amendment much sooner than they did with much less controversy and pain all around. More to the point, if in the 1860s—fifty years before—Congress had omitted one little word, "male," from the Fourteenth Amendment and included one little word, "sex," in the Fifteenth, the campaign of Paul and the NWP would not have been necessary at all. These two little words, however, were the tip of a huge iceberg of prejudice, discrimination and even outright misogyny. Because of these restrictions, which the United States Supreme Court later reinforced, by the start of the picket campaign in 1917 the women's position in the federal polity had not changed even as those previous amendments had created further inequalities. While Wilson might have professed, as he did in a speech in 1890, that "the ear of the leader must ring with the voices of the people," it seemed, that the "voices of the people" mattered to him only when they said what he had said in the first place. In spite of being president beginning in 1913, he remained on the suffrage issue very much "the closeted recluse" with his "uncompromising thought," a "luxury" he obviously otherwise considered not very useful in practical politics.[10]

Historians Adams and Keene cite three influences on Paul's campaign of nonviolence. The first is her Quaker faith, her extended family antecedents in that faith, and the pacifist history of Quakers in United States history, including the foundation of Pennsylvania by William Penn, the refusal of Quakers to fight in the American Revolution and the divisiveness of the Civil War on their communities when some Quakers chose to fight as the lesser of two evils: war or the continuation of slavery. Associated with her Quakerism was the early example of such luminaries as the abolitionist Baptist William Lloyd Garrison, who, like some Quakers, began his crusade against slavery as a pacifist, only later to fall in on the side of war as the only solution to this great divide in the United States, even if President Lincoln fought not over slavery but about the illegality of secession. Adams and Keene also credit Paul's Quaker faith with her obviously burning and inviolable sense of mission with which she approached the campaign for suffrage, for Quakerism espoused the notion of an individual's unique mission in life. Action, in this approach to life, followed belief. Words, simply a profession of a belief, were not enough. This truth applied especially to the Hicksite group to which Paul and her family belonged. Each member sought her unique purpose for being on earth, the purpose being one which helped not merely to ameliorate conditions in society, but also to reform and restructure society for the greater good. This is why Paul rejected social work: only woman suffrage set the fire burning in her soul, for ennobling women through winning them a political life would involve not only the inclusion of women in the polity but also the end of a searing injustice in that polity. It would signal a revolution, an understated, peaceful revolution, but a revolution nonetheless. There is no simple coincidence that the WSPU fired her up, for its slogan was "Deeds, Not Words"—not just defiant but with great spiritual resonance for Paul.[11]

Adams and Keene also include in Paul's influences the philosophy of Henry David Thoreau. By the time Paul attended Swarthmore, his 1849 *Civil Disobedience* was recommended reading for its advocacy of nonviolent opposition to a federal government which, at the time of his writing, not only had not had the moral courage to end slavery across the nation, but also engaged in such wars as the one with Mexico that ended in 1848. When governments violated the "individual's sense of right and wrong" they had not just a right but a moral duty to protest that government, even if the civil disobedience they engaged in led to their own repression or worse. Thoreau, like Garrison and many Quakers of the time, ultimately fell in line with the Civil War.

A third influence was Leo Tolstoy's *The Kingdom of God Is Within You,* originally banned in Russia, published in Germany in 1894 and soon translated and reaching its twenty-second edition by 1905. Paul's own faith resonated with Tolstoy's philosophy, which was also based on Christ's example of several principles: turning the other cheek; accepting the very worst that the authorities can throw; forgiving them for doing so in the cause of loving one's neighbor as oneself; and bringing an end to the circle of violence, thereby improving life for all the world in which one lives. Paul was a voracious reader, even during the campaign refusing to read nothing but books on suffrage and women's rights because she wanted no distractions from her goal. Every snippet of information also added to the knowledge with which she could campaign more effectively. The influence of Tolstoy, therefore, likely came from her own reading, but there was also the word of close contacts, such as her brother Parry, who worked for the Friends in Russia, and from people such as Jane Addams, who immersed herself in Tolstoy's works and visited the writer at his home near Moscow in 1896.

Alice Paul's nonviolence and peaceful protest and the work she based on that foundation is the most understated, least understood, unknown or even dismissed aspect of her campaign for suffrage. Yet it was the crucial aspect of a sustained and victorious campaign, the one that should make it stand out as the beacon it was, pointing the way for every succeeding movement for justice in the history of the United States. The campaign of Paul and the NWP was the first successful nonviolent civil rights campaign in the history of the nation, and it was by infusing her colleagues with the fire of her own commitment that Paul led a relatively small group to sacrifice themselves in the cause of rights for all American women.

She has often been criticized for her apparently autocratic leadership style in pursuit of woman suffrage.[12] Viewed through the lens of the perceived necessity of democratic leadership for a movement for a democratic goal—one that aimed to expand potential involvement of the people in the polity by 100 percent— her leadership seems to represent a contradiction in terms. Yet it represents no such thing. The leadership was not simply in the hands of Alice Paul and directed by her ego: the real situation was that all the members and workers were of one mind and they acted in concert, while Paul was the conductor of an incredibly broad-ranging, exceedingly complex and intricately detailed symphony that was played out with precision, astuteness, knowledge and sensitivity to the constantly changing dynamics. It was also executed with superb timing. Viewed in the light of a spiritually inspired crusade, Paul's leadership was only one aspect of a tightly knit movement. Prisoner Doris Stevens wrote about this approach late in the campaign, describing militancy as "a state of mind" which informs political action, not the action itself. NWP members were well aware of the significance of their groundbreaking role in United States history, "the first organized militant political action in America," wrote Stevens.[13]

In spite of any other potential philosophical influences, the NWP acknowledged only one in its approach to suffrage, and that was of Susan B. Anthony, which also implicitly incorporated the influence of the Friends' teachings. By association it incorporates Thoreau as well, for he wrote his *Civil Disobedience* when Anthony was awakening to the rights of women. Anthony was also a friend of feminist Margaret Fuller, who was a friend of Thoreau. Yet, action being more important than words, it was Anthony's actions and example that spoke most loudly to Paul and the NWP members. In addition to the famous Anthony trial following her "voting without the lawful right to vote" when Anthony refused to be silenced by the court, the NWP cited her solitary stand in contrast to all the other equal-rights women who deferred to others during the Civil War, an action with the haunting and long-term consequence of the constitutional inequity Paul in the twentieth century was trying to bring to an end. For Paul, this was a lesson women did not need to submit to again.

Militancy for the wartime twentieth-century suffragists came from the fact that for Anthony "to think meant also to act, to translate the conclusions she had arrived at into deeds. Throughout her whole life she lived consistently up to the maxim she urged upon the women of her time [during her trial]: 'Resistance to tyranny is obedience to God.'" The NWP also cited Anthony's own short-lived newspaper, *Revolution*, which heralded the philosophy "principle not policy, justice not favors."[14] The NWP retold the story of Anthony's protest at the exclusion of women in Philadelphia from the centennial celebrations. At that event, she interrupted the proceedings to present the Declaration of the Rights of Woman to an astounded international gathering of male dignitaries. Then she commandeered an empty bandstand to read it aloud to the crowds and afterwards handed it out with great dignity.[15] "Miss Anthony had reminded the nation of the hollowness of its celebration of an independence that excluded women."[16] It is for such actions that Paul and the NWP came to call the suffrage amendment the Susan B. Anthony Amendment.

Anthony's cohorts in such civil disobedience were relatively few, but important advocates of the cause. In 1868, one woman in Lawrence, Massachusetts, and in Vineland, New Jersey, 172 women both white and black voted in that year's federal election. Several others did their part also before Anthony voted.[17] Virginia Minor's protest led to her celebrated defeat in the Supreme Court. Women used militancy elsewhere. In 1886, during the dedication of the Statue of Liberty, which is a woman representing Liberty, a group hired a boat and sailed to what was then named Bedloe's Island to register their protest at women's complete exclusion from the event.[18] In more recent events Paul had witnessed nonviolent militancy across the Atlantic, which action is often forgotten or lost in the emblazoning of the WSPU's deeds in the British headlines. This nonviolent militant action had come from the Women's Freedom League (WFL), a 1907 breakaway from the Pankhurst organization over what they saw as the Pankhursts' autocracy. Its constitution stated that it was nonpartisan; it would hold the party in power responsible for woman suffrage and oppose government parties for failure to act. It would conduct "[v]igorous agitation upon lines justified by the position of outlawry to which women are at present condemned"; and it would work to organize women all over Britain and educate them on women's rights. Besides votes for women, the additional object of the WFL was "to use the power thus obtained" to establish "equality of rights and opportunities between the sexes."[19]

Much less flamboyant and incendiary than the WSPU, the WFL still made its mark. In addition to caravan campaigns each summer throughout rural Britain, in 1909 it achieved prominence for its silent picket of the houses of Parliament:

Perhaps one of the most striking protests organised by our League has been the picketing of the House of Commons. This "epical siege," as the Daily News called it, has continued since July 5th. At eight o'clock on that night a deputation of delegates from public meetings went to the House of Commons with a petition which they desired to present to Mr. Asquith. They have been waiting there ever since making an aggregate of 14,000 hours, in all weathers, asking that a public servant shall give half an hour of public time to consider a matter of public importance. It is the most monumental example of patience and endurance on record.[20]

During that summer, the WFL picket was extended to Number Ten Downing Street, the official home of the prime minister. Police arrested ten women.[21]

The WFL conducted this "Great Watch" at the House of Commons when Alice Paul was first jailed in England and afterwards travelling through the United Kingdom with Emmeline Pankhurst. Paul could hardly have avoided knowing about it. The story was significant enough to reach the letters pages of the *New York Times,* with Alice Stone Blackwell, daughter of nineteenth-century suffragist Lucy Stone, anticipating that elected officials of the government would never mete out such treatment to women in the United States.[22] The WFL's militancy, although not espousing violence to people or private property, did extend to the use of chemicals on some public property during the election of November 1909 when they destroyed some executed ballot papers, which the WFL deemed appropriate when women could not vote. Nora Blatch DeForest, granddaughter of Elizabeth Cady Stanton, defended this action as understandable given both the continued refusal of the vote to women and the cavalier and insulting treatment of women, with Parliament and the prime minister ignoring them "while delegation after delegation of men from every walk of life [was] ushered through the sacred portals."[23] These two letters demonstrate the openness in 1909 to militancy among American suffragists who were frustrated by their endless work in response to the political games of elected officials.[24]

Eight years later, in the NWP's nonviolent campaign, the women of the United States—having gone through thorough grassroots organizing, continuous education, parlor meetings, publishing newspapers, street corner speech making, parades and political campaigns, deputations, petitions, lobbying and picketing, ridicule, arrest, imprisonment and brutality against them—were forced to adopt the most extreme measure against the continuing obduracy of the régime in order to stand their ground and press the suffrage demand to its conclusion during a war being fought for democracy. It was this further step, along with the nation's shock and outrage at that régime's continued brutality, which led to the latter's capitulation. Already on the front line (this is what the NWP called its picketing campaign in its own publication), the extreme measure the women finally adopted was the hunger strike. Like young American men fighting abroad, the women now put their lives right on the line in the famed fight for democracy, although they did so at home in a struggle against a domestic autocrat. World War I was called the "war to end all wars" and as it progressed the NWP pressed into service terminology from that overseas struggle to establish their own intentions clearly. Such words as "the last trench," used in the *Suffragist*, emphasized that as far as the NWP was concerned their own "war" for suffrage would be the final one: its only goal was victory. As the overseas war to end all wars ended, the NWP could point to many an example of old establishments and régimes finally capitulating to suffrage. Yet, after the armistice, in November 1918, in spite of everything, Wilson left for the Peace Conference in Paris as the representative of the only English-speaking nation in which women had not won the vote by December 1918.[25]

One precedent that Paul and the NWP women cited for the hunger strike was ancient Celtic law from Ireland and Brittany in which an individual who was owed a debt sat outside the house of the debtor and fasted to force payment. Other influences were fasting in Hindu law and hunger strikes by prisoners in Russia within the previous fifty years. Doris Stevens compared American women's lack of say in legislation to these other protests that a lack of legal remedy triggered.[26] The hunger strikes of suffragettes that began in Britain in 1909 drew their main inspiration from the Russian precedent.[27] Scottish artist Marian Wallace Dunlop introduced the tactic independently but it quickly became WSPU policy. It received publicity in the United States when Paul's hunger strike and force-feeding appeared in the papers. Upon her arrival home in the United States in January 1910, reporters besieged Paul to tell her story.

Besides having an immediate impact on the British suffragette movement and being publicized across the Atlantic, Dunlop's new tactic was influential further afield. After the initial frenzy, the influence was fitful, for the British suffragettes suspended their militant campaign in January 1910, resuming late in 1911. But then Ireland picked up the tactic, with the first hunger strike of Irish suffragettes taking place in August 1912, followed in 1913 by that of Irish nationalist James Connolly. Hunger strikes appeared in the United States in 1914. The first was that of International Workers of the World member Becky Edelson that April.[28] Upton Sinclair, imprisoned for protesting against John D. Rockefeller and the Standard Oil Company in a strike in Colorado, announced his own protest that May in emulation of the British suffragettes.

Two women sentenced with him also went on hunger strike.[29] Back in Europe, Irish nationalists resumed hunger strikes in 1916, while in January 1917 Ethel Byrne, the sister of Margaret Sanger imprisoned for distributing birth control information, went on hunger strike in the United States.[30] In October 1917, the NWP noted that Irish political prisoners had "won" their hunger strike in their "demand to be treated as political or interned prisoners" on the death of Thomas Ashe after a botched forced feeding.[31] This strike occurred within the context of the violent anti–British uprising which began at Easter 1916. It was not part of a nonviolent campaign.

As hunger strikes by 1917 had assumed an increasing role in protest internationally, the *Suffragist* drew parallels between what the Irish had won through their hunger strike and what the women in Occoquan at that time were demanding. Like so much of what Paul did, the introduction of such strikes as a suffrage campaign tactic in the United States, was not completely original. It was, however, based on personal experience. The NWP had little

The Great Demand Banner, here displayed before a 1914 procession, was a central feature of all the suffrage pageantry from March 1913 on (Library of Congress Prints and Photographs Division, Washington, D.C., Harris & Ewing Collection, Digital ID: http://www.loc.gov/pictures/item/hec2008002911/).

WE DEMAND
THAT THE
AMERICAN GOVERNMENT GIVE
ALICE PAUL
A POLITICAL OFFENDER.
THE PRIVILEGES RUSSIA GAVE MIYUNOFF

TO ASK FREEDOM
FOR WOMEN IS NOT
A CRIME
SUFFRAGE PRISONERS
SHOULD NOT BE TREATED
AS CRIMINALS

The picketers, from January 1917 on, were called Silent Sentinels. Their banners called both for the vote and for freedom or liberty for women—the vote being how women would be liberated or freed from laws passed and enforced against them without their consent. Freedom became more prominent once the picketers were imprisoned, and especially when Alice Paul was sent to jail in October 1917. These picketers are demanding not only freedom but also political prisoner status for Paul because her only "crime" was to protest her lack of political freedom in a nation which denied the vote on account of sex (Library of Congress Prints and Photographs Division, Washington, D.C., Harris & Ewing Collection, 1917, Digital ID: http://www.loc.gov/pictures/item/hec2008007152/).

need for a cue from anyone else to decide to start hunger strikes, for as suffragettes Paul and Burns had participated in the original WSPU campaign. Paul had described her hunger strike and force-feeding dockside on her return to the United States in 1910.[32] She also described it in the Cooper Union in New York for the Equality League of Self-Supporting Women at the invitation of Harriot Stanton Blatch in February 1910.[33] Before that, she had already addressed her fellow Quakers about it, calling it one of "the full array of rhetorical techniques" available to win suffrage, while placing the use of these devices of nonviolent protest for change within the historical context of the American Revolution.[34] Paul spoke out in this manner in 1910 even though before her departure from London she had said that "for the present, she did not intend to take a part in the suffragette movement" in the United States.[35] Directly from her experiences in Britain, therefore, Paul was aware of everything at her disposal that could be necessary to campaign for votes for women. Even if she did not immediately start activism in the United States, Paul had known for years the hunger strike was a possibility, and she knew from experience what it did to the body. Paul also knew what force-feeding was like. The hunger strike was a decision entered into with full awareness of its role in nonviolence.

Originally, however, Paul had not thought hunger strikes would likely be necessary for women in the United States to win the vote: "The women here will not have to pursue militant methods to gain equal franchise with men. Their position is far in advance of that of the English women, and if they really want the vote they can get it ... unless the trusts and big corporations and the political bosses oppose them. Of course, they might take the place of the cabinet ministers and the House of Lords, but I don't believe they could be so ignorant and stubborn."[36] Even with others' individual hunger strikes in the United States, therefore, this departure of the NWP suffragists in Washington, D.C., was revolutionary, for the women employed it not only fully aware of what they were going into, but also took it up as the most extreme measure of a long-running and ongoing nonviolent campaign for political reform. When Alice Paul and Rose Winslow began their hunger strike, fifteen others in Occoquan at the same time also stopped eating.[37] But Paul and her colleagues took something previously done and raised it to a higher level. Not only did the suffragists of the NWP became the first protesters in the United States to utilize the tactic successfully in a civil rights campaign, they also did so while employing the hunger strike and enduring force-feeding in the same nonviolent spirit that the women had endured ridicule, imprisonment, brutality and everything else that the authorities and the American public could throw at them, without allowing, in other words, their own behavior to be part of, or to degenerate into, the violence they faced or to denigrate their opponents as they were denigrated. In a Christian framework, this would be the spirit of turning the other cheek and "Father, forgive them for they know not what they do."[38]

The first to conduct a wholly nonviolent civil rights campaign in the United States, these NWP women were also the first to use the hunger strike successfully in nonviolent political protest in an international context. That international trend ranged far and wide. Historian Kevin Grant notes that when Wallace Dunlop introduced the hunger strike to the suffrage movement in Britain, she brought the tactic into the British Empire. This innovation was not lost on Ireland and India, from whom others around the world later took their cue.[39] The NWP action, a direct spin-off from Marion Wallace Dunlop's, occurred within this international context. It was during the ultimately victorious NWP suffrage campaign—in the months after Wilson caved and released the women strikers—that in India in 1918 such strikes became a tactic of the independence movement in that country. Those hunger strikes continued until 1947. Gandhi, famous for his peaceful protest and hunger strikes for Indian independence and having observed early on the suffragettes in action in London, set his philosophy and actions up in contrast to the adoption of violence by the WSPU.[40] Yet his final successful employment of the range of tactics of nonviolent protest, including the hunger strike, occurred long after American women had successfully employed those same methods and the victory of Paul and the National Woman's Party in the last decade of the 72-year campaign for votes for women in the United States. Alice Paul, Lucy Burns and the National Woman's Party today deserve to be recognized as the first, successful pioneers in modern nonviolent protest for political reform anywhere.

CHAPTER 6

When the Right to Vote
Is Not the Right to Vote

In Dallas, Texas, on October 8, 1920, an attorney sought dismissal of a petition against his client, a husband whose wife had taken him to court. The attorney contended "that with women enjoying equal suffrage privileges, they should be no more entitled to protection against desertion or cruel treatment than men. For the same reason he would abolish alimony," a news story reported.[1] In Kansas City that September, a woman had asked a policeman for directions. W.H. Scott, recently appointed to his job, helped her on her way. "'Thanks,' said the woman, and reaching into a pocket of her coat she took out a plug of tobacco and bit off a chew. Scott arrested her on a charge of disturbing the peace. In Municipal Court this morning, Judge John M. Kennedy dismissed the case. 'If women may vote, why shouldn't they chew?' inquired the judge."[2]

These two news items appeared outside the states where the events occurred, for although small they were news, unusual and extremely topical incidents. Light as they were, they served as fillers for what might have been some empty column inches. To history they are invaluable. The headline of the first ran "New Hope in Woman Suffrage," while that of the second went "Seems Ladies Now Have All Men's Rights." They are two important vignettes about perceptions far from Washington, D.C., regarding the impact the Nineteenth Amendment had soon after it was promulgated on the relations of ordinary people in American society. The attorney argued the amendment had changed everything between men and women. The policeman, however, made no link between what a woman did on the street with the new fundamental law of the land. The judge obviously knew that women and men were now in a different relationship. One headline writer—presumably and most likely male—obviously believed and even hoped that the new fundamental law presaged further changes, while the other concluded that the two sexes were now completely equal under the law and the whole of society would treat them as such. The men's perceptions are fairly clear. The situation with the women is less so. The Kansas woman, asking directions, obviously did not know Kansas City and likely was just visiting the big city from rural parts. She may have been a tobacco chewer almost all her life and when she chose to do so then and there she may have acted just as she had always done and in a way that was acceptable to her own community. On the other hand, she may have done what she did in order to test the reach of the new reality for women across America. Either way, she encountered immediately one man's boundaries of acceptable behavior for women in the big city, at least as opposed to rural areas and regardless of the new law, and found there was more than one inter-pretation of that new reality. The Dallas woman was silent, though presumably her attorney would have much to say on her behalf. All parties involved in these two stories raised questions about the impact of the Nineteenth Amend-ment: was it a lot, or did it amount to not very much at all?

Every single aspect of these events possessed a grain of the truth that the Nineteenth Amendment was significant, yet so many historians down the years have missed this essential point,[3] usually sliding past the complex history, impact and potential of woman suffrage with the comment that women were "given" the vote in 1920 in favor of events considered more significant that year, such as the presidential election or the League of Nations controversy. Even the women who had worked for suffrage made this specific mistake of terminology. A front-page cartoon published a year before ratification in the NAWSA's *Woman Citizen,* stated, "The United States Grants Universal Suf-frage to All," when it celebrated the continuing ratification process after pas-sage of the amendment in Congress. It even portrayed the male image of Uncle Sam standing beside a billboard where the words proclaimed, "And I'm Mighty Proud of the Job Too!"[4] The irony of the cartoon seems to have escaped the editors who chose to publish it, for what it contained was far from the truth. The fact is that it was mostly women who *won* the vote in 1920 and it was a victory they fought hard for. As Catt described it later, women conducted a total of 910 campaigns for the vote over the fifty-two years after ratification of the Fourteenth Amendment.[5] This does not include the work done in the twenty years beginning in 1848 in which women worked to secure equal rights for themselves, including the vote. Further, as Catt tended to write about NAWSA alone, this total may not count the NWP's nationwide campaigns.

Catt's figures represented a large part of the truth, however, and referred only to Suffrage, for she knew not to confuse the vote with anything more. The fact was that the Nineteenth Amendment was not the comprehensive reform that many parties in 1920 tended to assume. In fact, the statement that women won the vote is not even quite correct, which the amendment itself reveals clearly. What women won in 1920 was not the right to vote, but the removal of the sex discrimination in qualifying for the vote. The wording, which Susan B. Anthony and Elizabeth Cady Stanton had chosen, reflected that of the Fifteenth Amendment, basically adding "on account of sex" to that amendment—more than fifty years after the first failed campaign to have the phrase added and all women consequently included in the polity. The Nineteenth Amendment, therefore, established only the right not to be discriminated against in voting laws simply because women were women. It applied to both sexes, although only to women in effect, for all male citizens of the United States had been eligible to vote under the Constitution since Reconstruction. The removal of sex discrimination in this area of the law was a hugely important distinction from the belief that it conferred a right to vote, for it made the issue of woman suffrage less clear-cut than might be initially apparent. Specifically, even though they were now eligible to vote, women were still not, in 1920, men's political equals in the matter of elections, for the amendment's reach did not encompass every aspect of voting law. This problem arose from the fundamental structure of the United States. The amendment impinged clearly upon state jurisdiction, which was one major reason that the South fought so strongly against it. Because of each state's police powers, questions were raised even before ratification as to whether the amendment was enough to enfranchise women in states without equal suffrage. The concern erupted nationally after a pronouncement by the attorney general of Massachusetts, which had become the eighth state to ratify the amendment, on June 25, 1919, that "in addition to the ratification of the amendment it is necessary that suffrage be conferred upon [women] by either state action or congressional legislation."[6] Such an interpretation of the new legalities produced a flurry of state legislation after promulgation to allow women to register and vote. Democrats in Maryland, which had not ratified, called for a special session to extend the time for women to register, with Connecticut and Maine right behind.[7] They were part of what was a general trend: in a survey of thirty-three states immediately after promulgation, to which twenty-seven replied quickly, the NWP found that only Mississippi had so far definitively decided that women could not vote in spite of the new amendment, because of the tardiness of the promulgation in a general election year. Immediately after the election, because of the exclusion of women in Georgia and Mississippi and other shortcomings that had swiftly appeared during the election, the NWP called for "an enforcement act" from Congress, pursuant to clause two of the amendment to protect women from restrictive state legislation.[8]

Other limitations for women in the exercise of the vote in 1920 had already appeared. The NAWSA cartoon had trumpeted "universal suffrage" for all women, but even that claim was incorrect, for restrictive legislation still applied to women even after the promulgation of the new amendment. At the federal level, according to the Census Bureau, an estimated 1,500,000 women in the United States would still be ineligible to vote. These included the logical exclusion of "at least 1,000,000 of 5,250,000 foreign-born women ... not yet ... naturalized." Also excluded from the vote, however, were 60,000 American-born Indian women, "most of whom were living in reservations." These women did not get the right to vote until 1924. Even then, removal of state laws restricting Indian votes required several legal cases before they were struck down. Further, 8,607 Chinese and Japanese women were excluded too. At the time, Asians by definition were denied citizenship and, by extension, the franchise. Chinese Americans were first allowed to become citizens and eligible to vote in 1943. For Asian Indians, it was 1946. Japanese Americans and other Asian Americans were not accepted equally until 1952. Some of these restrictions already applied to men, but now women doubled the numbers of each of those excluded categories. A further doubling of exclusions occurred when the insane and felons were enumerated. For decades, law-abiding women had been incensed by being clumped with what they considered undesirables in exclusion from the vote. On the one hand, therefore, the amendment finally brought that to an end. On the other hand, even if women now had the right to vote, if they were a felon or insane they could not vote, just like men. Even more anomalies arose from the application of federal law to women only. "American women married to aliens are not eligible to vote, the Department of Justice has held, but foreign-born women married to American citizens or whose fathers have become American citizens are entitled to the ballot without naturalization proceedings," the Census Bureau reported.[9]

Restrictions on the woman vote rendering it less than "universal" occurred also at the state level. According to the Census Bureau and reported in the same news item that dealt with the potential female vote, there was "a larger number [of women than previously specified] deprived of the ballot under state statutes in harmony with constitutional provisions." This is the point at which the constitutional structure of the nation could render an apparently clear constitutional amendment muddy and uneven in its reach. Article I, Section 2, of the Constitution awarded to the states the power to determine who should vote. Individual states had been exercising this power ever since the Constitution came into force in 1789. Supreme Court decisions made the situation muddy, however. Even with the promulgation of the Fourteenth and Fifteenth amendments, which purported to limit the scope of this state power, the court in several decisions in the late nineteenth century had declared constitutional some legislation whose effect was to restrict voting rights.[10] Legislation and Supreme Court decisions are famous for contributing to the Jim Crow laws of the South and notorious for restricting and therefore controlling the vote, often specifically to keep black men away from the polls. These laws and decisions, however, conveniently for political bosses cast their net much wider than the black voter. State qualifications beyond citizenship also excluded white men in many states throughout the nation from the polls. Women now came face to face with these same restrictive state laws, in spite of the new amendment.

Probably the most notorious of the "state statutes in harmony with constitutional provisions" was the poll tax, which along with literacy tests is traditionally considered the key measure designed to keep black voters from the polls. An indication of how oppressive the tax could be is that of Arkansas, where, in 1929 the tax was $1 annually when the annual average per capita income in the state was $310.[11] This poll tax cut many poor whites out of the franchise along with blacks. When women won the vote, the tax hit them disproportionately because their wages were traditionally lower than those of men. A further complication might arise with poor married couples. In spite of a low income, a household might yet manage to scrape together the dollar for one member of the family to vote. When both husband and wife could vote, however, the poll tax automatically doubled. When faced with this punitive doubling of the tax and the consequent inability to pay to exercise the second vote, the question in a poor household would become which member of the household should vote. Given the traditional preeminence of males at home, the likelihood of a husband deferring to his wife in this matter, or of a wife not deferring to her husband, was low. Further, if the poll tax raised a financial problem and the wife wanted to exercise the franchise, the anti-suffrage argument that woman suffrage could produce marital discord might suddenly appear well grounded.

The problems that the poll tax raised did not end with these considerations, however, for it could trip up a voter's prospects whether or not it was affordable. This became clear even before the amendment. Women in Arkansas won the primary vote through legislation in 1917—the first female suffrage in the South and a significant victory for the state under Catt's "Winning Plan" introduced in 1916. Yet the women faced no smooth sailing that year: a local suffragist warned that the poll tax receipts being issued to women appeared not to fulfill the very specific legal requirements for such receipts and were probably invalid.[12] This was a potential problem linked with women's unfamiliarity with voting procedures and their inability, therefore, to watch with eagle eyes to ensure that everything had been done correctly to qualify them. Failure to issue receipts fulfilling all the legal requirements might also be a cunning and deliberate attempt to invalidate female votes. There were, however, in this case, no follow-up reports of actual invalidations occurring. If the poll tax didn't work, other means to cut women out of the vote could be tried. One candidate defeated in the 1917 primaries in Fort Smith, Arkansas, filed suit to contest the election on the grounds that woman primary suffrage was invalid under the state constitution and state law and because of their sex.[13]

The poll tax debate arose in several places in 1920 after promulgation of the Nineteenth Amendment. In Alabama, which failed to ratify, officials decided that women in their state required no poll tax receipt to vote that November, while in Texas, a judge in Harris County ordered that women could also vote that year without a poll tax receipt. But poll tax provisions were applied unevenly across the states. In Arkansas in 1920 officials initially gave conflicting advice on whether poll tax payment was required for women to vote, but two days before the general election, the state's attorney general confirmed that such payment was required of women to vote.[14] The Arkansas decision was perhaps understandable, because women had been eligible for primary suffrage since 1917. In a state dominated by the Democrats, primary suffrage was the virtual, although indirect, equivalent of voting for president, and to vote in primaries women were required to have paid their poll tax. It was a legitimate position to take that they should have paid the tax six months before the election if they wanted to participate; but in a one-party state, it is hard to avoid intimating that the poll-tax decision was a plan to restrict the women's vote. The apparently sound argument regarding being ready to vote when a voter didn't know whether she would be allowed to was not watertight and the uncertainty likely depressed the female vote at the very least. The general election was about much more than the president, and Republican women might have been deterred from paying a tax to vote in the primaries purely because of the futility of the exercise in a one-party state. Waiting to pay the tax until it was clear that the women could vote in the actual general election might have seemed a good tactic in a state with the lowest average annual wages regionally and a high poll tax relative to that, especially in the case of poor women, for

In January 1918, the House of Representatives voted for woman suffrage after President Wilson grudgingly encouraged House Democrats to do so. The battle to win the Senate now began, but by summer once again the amendment was stuck. Wilson, during a July 4, 1918, speech, had extolled the virtues of "the reign of law based upon the consent of the governed" even as he again studiously ignored the women. In response, NWP members began demonstrations at the Lafayette Monument. Another series of arrests ensued and on August 20, in an attempt to ignite enthusiasm in Wilson for democracy at home through a quick Senate vote before the end of the current Congress, the women began to burn the president's empty words. The president's support, again grudging, failed to win the Senate (Library of Congress Prints and Photographs Division, Washington, D.C., Harris & Ewing Collection, Digital ID: http://www.loc.gov/pictures/collection/hec/item/hec2008 008110/).

whom it was punitive. If all such women in Arkansas did choose to wait and see, however, it cost them their vote in 1920.

The situation for new women voters was problematic for other reasons. They were also subject to the residence, property and tax qualifications, literacy tests and awkward registration requirements that men also had to fulfill in order to vote.[15] Citizens who wanted to register in Mississippi, for example, had only one day to do so in their precinct during registration, which finished four months before the election.[16] Mississippi refused to ratify the Nineteenth Amendment and also refused to let women vote in 1920 because promulgation occurred too late to allow women to register within the legal time frame. Georgia came up with a similar excuse. Such strictures, however, did not prevent all women in Georgia from casting the newly won vote. In November 1919, it was reported, one woman had actually cast her ballot. The newsworthiness of the story lay in the fact that not only was she apparently the only one to succeed in voting in her area, and even the state, but that she somehow had contrived to fulfill the legal requirements even though female suffrage was not the law at the time she did so. "Mrs. Mary Jarett White of Stephens county ... paid her taxes and registered at Toccoa, six months before the election, thus complying with the state law. Other women were barred by the six months registration law, but there was no explanation of how Mrs. White managed to get her name registered before the Nineteenth Amendment was adopted."[17]

Another clear way in which women did not achieve equal political status

The influence of the suffragists' methods, which included the innovation of women marching in political parades in Washington, D.C., appeared in American life very quickly, as this group of women, dressed in white and in strict formation as the suffragists had first done. They are participating in a war preparedness parade in 1916 (Library of Congress Prints and Photographs Division, Washington, D.C., Harris & Ewing Collection, Digital ID: http://www.loc.gov/pictures/item/hec2008004 484/).

with men with the promulgation of the Nineteenth Amendment was in the matter of running and serving in public office. While it would seem natural to assume that a corollary of female suffrage would be that women could run for and serve in elective office, this was not automatically the case. It was true at the federal level, with the first female representative to the United States Congress sworn in three years before equal suffrage became law. Jeannette Rankin of Montana had campaigned for woman suffrage in New York and Washington, but her greatest suffrage victory was her campaign in her home state in 1914. Now able to vote, and also run, in the election of 1916, she stumped the whole state she knew so well from her suffrage work and won. She was sworn in on March 3, 1917. An irony of the promulgation of the Nineteenth Amendment, however, was that the nation's second elected representative to the Congress was an anti-suffragist, Alice Robertson, elected in 1920 from Kansas' second district. Running against the advice of friends, Robertson defeated "veteran Democrat incumbent, Will Hastings."[18] Rebecca Latimer Felton, an advocate of suffrage, equal pay and several progressive programs such as prison and educational reform and also a white supremacist, was the first female U.S. Senator. Sworn in on November 21, 1922, to fill a vacancy due to a death, the 87-year-old activist served only twenty-four hours before the newly elected replacement took over.[19] Hattie Caraway of Arkansas was the first woman to win election to the Senate, in 1932.

While women could run at the federal level, women were not automatically eligible to run for office at the state level. Arkansas suffrage veteran Dr. Ida Joe Brooks discovered this immediately after ratification in 1920. Brooks had worked for votes for women in Little Rock, Arkansas, in the late 1880s and upon moving to Boston to study medicine was involved with the Boston NAWSA in the early 1890s, occasionally writing for the *Woman's Journal*. With that pedigree, she was a natural for public office. The very week of Tennessee's ratification of the amendment, she announced her intention to run for the state office of superintendent of public instruction. Early that following October, however, the state's attorney general declared that under current Arkansas law, women were ineligible for office, a decision which kept another female candidate, Julia Ward Pennington, off the ballot also.[20] A constitutional amendment to remove this ban on women officeholders was attempted that November, but the results remained unclear. Arkansas passed legislation in 1921 to allow women to put themselves forward for election to public office. Such exclusion of women from state officeholding was not confined to the South: that December, Governor Coolidge of Massachusetts had to recommend that lawmakers change the law to make women eligible during the upcoming municipal elections, which would be "a forerunner of legislation to make women eligible for any office in the State."[21]

Besides these obvious limitations to the Nineteenth Amendment, another less obvious one that did not by design establish or maintain political inequalities was the fact that the amendment did not compel women to register for the vote. Neither did it reach practices that were designed to create political inequalities, such as stringent literacy tests for some races, or stop activities such as vote buying by a candidate by paying the poll tax of voters willing to trade the vote for cash. Nor did the amendment prevent intimidation that stopped voters considering voting or getting to the polls on election day. In this case, women were actually in a slightly better position than men: they were less likely to face the overt threats and actual harm that black men in particular faced when they might have thought of voting. One of the reasons many Southerners fought so long and hard against the amendment was that the prospect of black women voting forced them to face the hypocrisies of their own white racism, their attitudes to women and the question of how far they would go, even against black women, to prevent the latter voting. Further, the amendment did not even prevent any cumbersome rule or location to make voting difficult if not impossible for the poor. It did not bring an end to partisan manipulation of the vote either, by both parties. In Georgia, for example, which excluded women from voting in 1920 in spite of the amendment, "some 75 negro women were permitted by the Republican election manager to cast ballots in the Sixth ward in Atlanta over the protest of the Democratic manager, but it was announced later that the ballots, which were specially marked, were thrown out when the count started."[22]

In short, the Nineteenth Amendment did not do what many observers assumed, wished or hoped it would do and it left untouched in 1920 some significant residues of the old order. In fact, the political inequalities that remained after promulgation demonstrates that the amendment represented the end of a 72-year-long nationwide campaign to bring women into the polity, a campaign which had started out with the aim of making women fully equal in the nation and a campaign which, in the process, had concluded that winning the vote was the necessary first step to all the rest of the goals laid out in the Declaration of Sentiments at the Seneca Falls Convention in 1848.

Yet the amendment was a monumental achievement, the mark of a revolution in American life and politics: one, if measured by the size of the results and how long the victory had required to win, which was as significant as the abolition of slavery in the nineteenth century. For it is important not to forget that women had actually done the almost impossible: amended the United

States Constitution, the most difficult of any constitution to amend, requiring unusual, if not unlikely, majorities in the House of Representatives and the Senate, plus ratification by three-quarters of the states of the union, the number of which had grown throughout the time women were campaigning to win the vote. Unlike so many other amendments, this one came from the grass roots, emanating from the wishes of members of the populace right to the very end, which required convincing succeeding generations of politicians, ever changing down the never-ending decades, to vote in its favor. Unlike every other amendment, except temperance, women achieved what they had set out to do when the odds were stacked against them right to the very end, for they won what they wanted in both instances without even having the tool usually needed for any political victory, the vote. They achieved it largely without the support, if not the outright opposition, not only of large numbers of women but also, for most of the movement's history, of the people in power: the male half of the population—through numberless campaigns. Finally, and perhaps most significantly, they won the vote peacefully, without causing a single injury and without a single shot being fired. It was the first, successful nonviolent civil rights campaign in United States history.

CHAPTER 7

Equal Suffrage
and Equal Rights

The limitations of the Nineteenth Amendment extended much further than exercising of the vote and eligibility for office. Suffragists had never seen it as a catchall for equal rights. They had considered it only the means to win equality. In August 1920, Alice Paul summarized the situation. It was "a great victory ... [with] many victories over sex discrimination yet to be won. But with the vote as a tool, women can accomplish anything."[1]

The discrepancies between the understanding and expectations of some and the continuing reality of women emerged in a group photograph that appeared in newspapers on November 4, 1920, two days after American women had voted under the amendment. It captured an all-woman jury, this rare animal sighted in Bayonne, New Jersey.[2] This was not actually the very first. That September, the first known all-female jury in Missouri was empanelled in Joplin,[3] while in February 1920, the NAWSA's newspaper, the *Woman Citizen,* carried a photograph of the all-female jury empanelled in 1916 in San Diego, California. That "first-ever," as the writer calls it—she does not state clearly whether it was the first ever in the county, the state or nation, although it is likely the last—was revealing. She reported the cynicism, sexism and outright stupidity of some men encountering the idea. They predicted doom while dismissing the women's aptitude for such civic responsibilities.[4]

These news stories capture important snatches of that watershed time a century ago when women finally broke into the national polity, particularly the prejudice that women still faced from a traditional and widespread paradigm which saw women's further encroachments into previously reserved areas of the public sphere as inherently objectionable and disastrous. Equally interesting is the newsworthiness of an all-woman jury, for it demonstrates clearly how novel it was. An even more startling circumstance across the country was the fact that women were still not considered for jury duty in most states at that time.

Jury pools were usually drawn from lists of registered voters, but in 1920, as women were winning the vote through the Nineteenth Amendment, a new sticking point in women's role in the polity was shaping up. In Raleigh, North Carolina, the attorney general announced that women did not become liable for jury duty with promulgation because "[the] right to vote plays no part in the qualification of a juror." For women to serve on juries, he said, an act of the legislature was required.[5] Arkansas, although the twelfth state and the second in the South to ratify the Nineteenth Amendment in July 1919, had done nothing since then to admit women to juries and they were still barred under the state's constitution. It was only in October 1920 that both political parties endorsed the submission of an amendment to voters in the November election to sanction female jury service.[6] In Alabama the same month, officials deemed that winning the vote did not mean that women would be required to serve on juries.[7] Already, in 1919, as only six states allowed and only one required jury duty of women, the attorney general of Oklahoma ruled that women there could not serve because the state's constitution called for juries of twelve *men.*[8]

The history of female jury service was mixed across the nation. In Wyoming, where women voted beginning in 1869, the year it became a territory, women were called to jury duty even before they voted there, although female jury duty was later discontinued.[9] Later, when women won the vote in California, Idaho, Illinois, Kansas, Michigan, Nevada, Oregon, Utah, and Washington, "local magistrates assumed that all voters ... were to be drawn from [voters lists]," but soon the attorneys general in California, Illinois, Oregon, and Washington declared female jurors illegal without special legislation. Still later, the six other suffrage states—Arizona, Colorado, Montana, New York, Oklahoma and South Dakota—deemed female jurors illegal. By 1920, Washington and California had legalized female jury service. By May that year, Oregon and New York were in the process of legalizing female jurors. In Illinois in 1913, women had won restricted suffrage. Only with ratification, in August of 1920, was the potential jury responsibility of women as full voters being touted.

With such a variety of possibilities in jury service, it is clear the vote could be, and very often was, seen separately from other civic activities: they were not necessarily dependent upon each other. This suited some, as it laid to rest the anti-suffrage objections of women who, for reasons of delicacy, did not want be a juror and of many men who felt women should not have to hear about murder, rape, prostitution and wife-beating along with all the unsavory details. Such exclusions also short-circuited out-and-out antis who had used the prospect of jury service to frighten voters off suffrage. Yet it appalled others. Many women considered that the sex of jury members was a key aspect, although almost completely ignored since the country's founding, of the constitutional provisions of trial by jury. Article III, Section 2, specified that all criminal trials be heard by a jury and that they be heard in the state where the crime was committed, while the Sixth Amendment deemed that juries had to be "impartial." Sex, in the view of many women, was an essential part of "impartiality." Without females at least eligible for juries, women never had been and never would be tried by an impartial jury.

Depending upon the individual's perspective, jury service could be viewed as a right, a duty or an unwelcome obligation. In criminal trials, a female accused might or might not welcome women on the jury, especially in a legal world where women were still a tiny minority group. Perhaps women of the jury could radically affect the outcome of such trials, but only after some history and statistics had been accrued and studied would it be possible to assess the impact exactly.[10] In civil matters the outcome might equally be affected. The exclusion of women from jury service was, therefore, of great significance to those at the center of trials. As for female jury membership, attorneys general could excuse women from this potential civil role. Alternatively, they could deprive and deny women of what some considered a right. It all depended on the individual's perspective. Such exceptions were easy for attorneys general to make, for the old English common law, then still exerting great influence, excluded women *proper defectum sexus*: on account of the defect of sex.[11] The process of extending jury duty, however, was in train by 1920, but the small number of female jury states demonstrated clearly another limit of the Nineteenth Amendment. By 1927, only nineteen states called women to jury duty, leaving twenty-nine still with laws and practices barring female citizens from a key civic role. Yet the Supreme Court of the United States had deemed unconstitutional the barring of black men "because the debarment would brand them as an inferior class of citizens, and deprive them of the equal protection of the law which is guaranteed by the National Constitution."[12]

The situation with juries demonstrated clearly that not all laws, even apart from voting laws, stopped discriminating against women with the passage of the Nineteenth Amendment. In the wide-ranging legal field, it was not only jury duty that excluded women. In Arkansas, the appointive office of notary was still closed to women pending new legislation,[13] while the NWP was now bringing up the question of the numbers of "women on the bench," yet another issue with an effect on women's employment and also an impact, potentially great, on the outcome of trials of female defendants. The service of state judges, like juries, depended on a plethora of differing state laws and regulations. These issues permeating the legal field demonstrated clearly how many aspects of women's lives and how their freedom to make their way in the world differed from men's even among the individual states.

In April of 1920, the now monthly NWP newspaper, *Suffragist,* published the first of several articles listing bills before Congress to change laws that discriminated against women or filled inequitable gaps. One such bill was to establish ranks for army nurses. Another provided that, after ratification of the amendment, an American woman who married a foreigner would not lose her citizenship, while foreign women marrying Americans would no longer automatically acquire U.S. citizenship. Another bill provided for the creation of a woman-led Department of Labor woman's bureau that would oversee regulations to set standards for the conditions of working women. A fourth bill, known as the Sheppard-Towner Bill, proposed appropriations for the federal government to work with the states in promoting maternity and infant care. A fifth proposed the amendment of civil service law to exclude sex from lists of eligible candidates and at least two women on a five-member civil service commission.[14] This list of proposed laws dealt with only some of the many areas identified as still discriminating against women even when women had the vote. Such laws referred to federal jurisdiction only. As with the Nineteenth Amendment, such laws, if passed, would regularly encounter state constitutions, laws and regulations that could restrict or limit their impact.

After the Nineteenth Amendment was promulgated, Alice Paul affirmed this constricted nature of the amendment's effect both in both federal and state law. Examples of discriminatory state laws that treated men and women differently pepper both major women's newspapers of the time—the *Suffragist* and the *Woman Citizen.* One such area of law, which particularly offended women, was the double standard in prostitution cases, in which women were prosecuted but men were not. Further double standards applied in laws such as that reported in Iowa where a judge ruled "that a man cannot be addressed by the health authorities on suspicion of having a venereal disease, and compelled to submit to examination. These high-handed measures are still being taken in regard to women, however, in many of our states."[15]

Former suffragists also identified a need for laws to prevent discrimination against women where the problem emanated not necessarily or exclusively from state action but from the action of third parties. The most important example of such a wished-for enactment was equal pay. Proposals were already proceeding through the New York state legislature in 1919 to deal with a well-known inequity which in some cases had worsened during the war. The disparities along sex lines appeared clearly in a report that compared male and female earnings in boot and shoe manufacturing in the Northeast. In one analysis of workers in a selected number of companies, an average full-time weekly male wage in all occupations of $15.43 in 1914 had almost doubled to $30.08 in 1920. By contrast, an average full-time weekly wage for females in 1914 of $11.05 had become by 1920 only $17.89. This represented an increase of only 62 percent. The disparity between males and females had actually increased and the female wage in these industries was now only 59 percent of men's.[16] The same trend towards increased disparity between male and female wages appeared in an analysis of all the establishments surveyed, although it was less obvious when averaged over several industries.[17] In spite of the work that the Great War had opened up to women and the increasing wages, therefore, it could be said that some women had effectively fallen behind men in earnings over that time.

Also relating to work was the question of equal opportunity. This was not the normal exclusion of women from certain jobs and professions or the greater difficulties they faced in entering into traditionally male jobs, but exclusion with an additional twist, for with the end of the war a controversy had erupted over the enforced removal of women from war jobs. "This is ... man's now-you-see-it-and-now-you-don't philosophy as to women's work," wrote the anonymous journalist in the *Woman Citizen* with an asperity that even today reveals her exasperation at the constantly shifting standards women faced in the constantly shifting job market, where women were seen as useful or expendable depending on the changing circumstances.

> "Come hither," said mere man to mere woman when the jobs were yawning empty. "Back to your kennels," snaps the master's whip when the need is over.
> "The country will care for your children" cry the sociologists when the mother is needed at the factory. But they sneer at her lack of maternal feeling when "with children who might reasonably be expected to need her care," she still sticks on her job to which they called her only yesterday.[18]

Still requiring reform, in the minds of women, was a huge array of laws with no common standard over a vast range of areas. One report published in 1919 detailed only those laws across the country relating to the process of getting married, which differed in each state. The low marriageable age for females of 12 years and for males of 14 years was in Virginia, with almost equally low marriageable ages in ten other states. The high was in Wyoming and ten other states where the marriage age was 18 for males and 16 for females.[19] Not only was the contrast in marriage ages clear across geographical lines, but it was also clear across suffrage and nonsuffrage lines. "[W]omen are trying at the polls ... to stabilize the home and lift it out of bad social ruts," wrote one reviewer of the report.[20] This variety in the laws relating to the process of getting wed was just the tip of the iceberg of all the laws affecting women's lives, often to their detriment compared with men. This report did not even begin to list or assess those relating to men and women under marriage, inheritance or divorce or in relation to children. Many of the inequalities for women were still based on the ancient legal fiction of coverture whereby on marriage a woman as a legal entity was merged into the person of her husband. But none of this nationwide listing of the process to get married even began to touch on the limitations which severely curtailed the opportunities for women single or without children. Nor did they begin to address the range of conventions, regulations or practices which severely restricted women's choices in the still-powerful "public," as opposed to the private, sphere. The inescapable conclusion is that federal and state laws and regulations, even after women won the vote, continued to limit the possibilities of, and deny opportunities in, women's lives. In many cases, too, whether intentional or not, they resulted in the penalization of women who were not married, purely because they were women.

This concern about inequality after ratification is not surprising: in 1848, the Declaration of Sentiments had recorded a comprehensive list of areas in which women faced injustices under many laws and conventions. In the ensuing seven decades-plus, many changes had taken place in such areas as marriage, divorce and inheritance laws; education opportunities had improved at all levels; some professions such as medicine and law had opened up; and women of all classes had surged into the paid workforce most recently under the specific impetus of war. Yet they still faced major inequities compared with men. In addition, during the second half of the nineteenth century, more women stayed single, and at that time, by definition, remained child-free, secretly or otherwise.[21] These women, still defined by the notion that women were wives and mothers even if they were not, also continued to experience great restrictions on their lives, both by law and by convention. In fact, by 1920, the only victory approaching what could be called a comprehensive reform that women had achieved which had featured in the Declaration of Sentiments of Seneca Falls was the originally contentious one of woman suffrage, achieved through the long-fought-for Nineteenth Amendment to the United States Constitution.

Alice Paul, on the eve of the 1921 NWP convention to decide the future course of the party, linked directly the position of American women in 1920 with that far-off time of 1848: "Almost seventy-three years from the date of that first convention, the women of the United States again meet to consider where they stand. During these seventy-three years, women have won the right without which all others are insecure, the right of a full and equal voice in the government under which they live...."[22] The previous year, at the time of the Nineteenth Amendment's promulgation, however, Paul had spelled out precisely the real picture facing American women: "With their power to vote achieved, women still have before them the task of supplementing political equality with equality in all other fields. In State and national legislation, as well as in other fields, women are not yet on an equal basis with men."[23]

The vote, just as for many previous suffragists, was still only the means to an end. It had never been considered by suffragists as the panacea that observers saw it as during the long decades of the struggle. Now, in 1921 surveying the new reality, Paul also wrote:

> At that first convention in 1848, one of the resolutions unanimously adopted read:
> "RESOLVED, That the women of this country ought to be enlightened in regard to the laws under which they live, that they may no longer publish their degradation by declaring themselves satisfied with their present position, not their ignorance by asserting that they have all the rights they want."
> This resolution still applies to the women of today. They have gained much since 1848, but they have made their gains piecemeal; rights which they possess in one state, they do not possess in another.[24]

Paul added that, because of the number of states and the fact that laws were not coded in many of them, it was almost impossible to assess all details relating to where American women stood in 1921, but she concluded that "enough facts have been collected to prove that the 'present position' is not 'satisfactory.'"

Paul clearly knew and emphasized again and again, therefore, from the time of the promulgation of the Nineteenth Amendment, that the suffrage victory represented a monumental milestone in American history. It was, however, a monumental milestone in a journey that still continued. She emphasized that the dramatic significance of the victory brought problems in its wake, for there existed the "danger that because of a great victory women will believe their whole struggle for independence [has] ended," whereas "[t]hey have still far to go."[25] In other words, now that women had the means to effect change they needed to reassess where they stood and start to use the vote to win true equality for themselves. The Nineteenth Amendment represented, therefore, a monumental victory in American history not just for removing the sex disqualification from voting across the nation, but also for being the gateway to more reforms in the law for women.

Several different approaches to winning more reforms were already evident in 1921, almost mirroring the beginnings of the campaign for the rights of women. One approach was to concentrate on changing discriminatory laws at individual state level. A second was to eradicate discrimination by specific reforms at the federal level, where they were clearly identifiable. A third was to promote legal reforms aimed at improving specific aspects of women's lives because women were women, at either state or federal level. Each of these approaches had advantages and supporters. Changing laws at state level represented an application of the founding philosophy, which intended that the relationship of the individual to government, above the municipal level, should primarily be through the individual's state. It was within this specifically defined geographical, political and historical area that the wishes of that specific population were best expressed. In some states, for example, such as Utah, a specific religion held prominence, while the northern part of the eastern seaboard states reflected the Puritan heritage. Western pioneering states in the nineteenth and early twentieth centuries broke more ground than the earlier pioneers of former colonies, not just geographically but also in their outlook. This manifested in differing laws, such as the earlier introduction and victories in the votes for women campaign. Southern states' outstanding characteristic was race. Agricultural states were very different from highly industrialized states. In every case, the underlying outlook and philosophy of the people in each state was reflected in its laws and customs. Individuals in each state were also much closer to their specific problems. As the report on the marriage process demonstrated, researching and collating the information on all laws relating to women, although not necessarily easy, was easier in one state than for the forty-eight that existed in 1920. Nationally the project became unmanageable, if not beyond comprehension.

The state was also the traditional level at which reforms for women had been tackled. Arkansas Territory in 1835, for example, passed a bill to protect the property of married women. When it became the twenty-fifth state in 1836, that law became the first such law in the nation, even if it proved inadequate and over time judicial decisions gutted both it and succeeding measures. Mississippi enacted its own Married Woman's Property Law in 1839, in its turn providing an example for a still later act in Arkansas.[26] Back East, New

York women launched their first attempts at married woman's property reforms in the legislature in 1836 and 1837, with women petitioning for the first time ever on the subject. The Married Woman's Property Act was finally passed in April 1848.[27] A later act in 1860 protected married women's earnings and their right to custody of their children, although it was gutted when women gave up their campaign for women's rights at the start of the Civil War. Votes for women had also been won partly through state reforms.

With suffrage now secured in the Constitution, which affected all states, many women therefore returned to the specific problems of women at the local and state levels. As already outlined, jury service was a key issue tackled at state level. One unique local movement for reform occurred with the formation of a new organization in the District of Columbia to fight for the right of D.C. residents to vote there in those days when the residents had no rights at all in their own governance. Two other key issues that arose were woman notaries and the poll tax. Arkansas, for example, which had categorically denied women in 1920 the right of appointment as notary, by 1928 had the position open to women.[28] Women also repeatedly attempted to eradicate the state poll taxes, which expressed separate state policy specified under Article I, Section 2, of the United States Constitution, but which still curtailed their right to vote under the Nineteenth Amendment. Between 1920 and 1950, North Carolina, Louisiana, Georgia, Florida, Arkansas and Tennessee repealed the tax.[29] In the meantime, in the landmark case of *Breedlove v. Suttle* of 1937[30] the United States Supreme Court found the tax constitutional and—in an echo of the strategy that women had to adopt—the tax was ultimately repealed in national elections only through federal amendment in 1964.[31] It was only in 1966 that poll taxes in state elections were judged unconstitutional by the United States Supreme Court under the Fourteenth Amendment's Equal Protection Clause of the Constitution.[32]

Recommendations approved in February 1920 at the Chicago meeting of the NAWSA, which at that point handed the torch of civic reform campaigns over to the newly formed national League of Woman Voters (LWV), revealed the wide-ranging nature of this relaunched campaign for equal rights for women and became the map for civic work for numerous women for many years to come. The recommendations emerged from the report of the National's Committee on Uniform Laws Concerning Women, which was made up of members from thirty-seven states and the District of Columbia.[33] The stated reason for the existence of this committee was the historic fact that "before the women of the United States wanted the suffrage, they wanted their rights," most particularly equal rights within marriage and the opening of education and the professions to women. In these 1920 recommendations, besides changes in marriage laws and the better treatment of juveniles by the courts, the National called, among other things, for the replacement of the postelection political spoils with equal access for women in civil service exams and appointments.[34]

Campaigns for this huge variety of reforms continued in the decades after the suffrage amendment, with various victories. One victory in the 1920 recommendations about reform of civil service appointments at all levels also contributed to the second approach to further reforms for women after ratification—the campaigns for reforms which had to be dealt with at the federal level—for one major success of LWV women ultimately was the 1938 and 1939 federal legislation which transformed many political spoils jobs into civil service jobs with appointment based on merit. Reform of married women's citizenship, the creation of ranks for army nurses and the amendment of civil service law to exclude sex from eligible candidates' lists and the appointment of at least two women on a five-member Civil Service Commission, which the NWP also outlined as goals in April 1920, are further examples of such legal reforms many former suffragists worked for.[35] Campaigns dealing with changes in discriminatory laws either at state or at federal level were specific and easily identifiable and called for focused campaigns, usually removal of a very clear discrimination based on sex. The work the women did in this period—such as that for legislation based on the 1920 LWV's recommendations and also the prodigious amount of legislation that the NWP drafted for both federal and state reforms during this time[36]—gives the lie to the clear picture arising from the continued marginalization of women in the histories, that work for women's rights died after women won the vote.

The third approach by women to reforms for women, pursued at both the state and federal level, promoted legal reforms aimed at improving specific aspects of women's lives because women were women. This approach, today called "social feminism," aimed at reforms in such areas as working hours, child employment and maternity and child care. At the federal level, newly enfranchised and politically active women, through a combination of eight women's groups that came together in 1920 as the Women's Joint Congressional Committee, set yet a third agenda in 1921 for federal legislation to cover prohibition, education both physical and mental, protection of infants, protection of women in industry and arms reduction for international peace.[37] All these different groups of women were interlinked, and at the federal level their major achievement after the war was the passage in 1921 of the Sheppard-Towner Act, the nation's first major law to promote "the welfare and hygiene of maternity and infancy." Reform of prisons for women was also a significant victory in 1924, and an amendment banning child labor passed Congress and was sent to the states for ratification, although it was never ratified.

Women's progress received assistance also at the federal government level. In 1913, the Wilson administration had established the United States Department of Labor, which during the Great War spawned the War Labor Administration (WLA) to manage most federal government war work manning plans. The WLA itself spawned the Woman in Industry Service to promote women's employment while overseeing their health and welfare. After the war, Congress established a permanent Women's Bureau in the Department of Labor, which operates to this day.[38] This bureau carried out studies about women's work at the request of 31 different states and helped to create policies and standards for women in work which influenced women's working conditions and hours for decades.

Long before the federal amendment, reform-minded women had worked for legal changes to benefit the lives of women and children. In Arkansas, for example, Little Rock society matron Adolphine Fletcher Terry was instrumental in the creation of the juvenile justice system and chaired its board for two decades. Elsewhere, state suffrage victories for women led directly to women-focused reforms in some areas, partly because of unequal pay and partly because many women were also working mothers. Oregon women won the vote in 1912 through a hard-fought state referendum. The next year, suffragist Carolyn Gleeson produced a historic report on the working conditions of women there.[39] This led directly to that state's first minimum wage law, which set an example that other states later followed. It still later provided a model for the first federal minimum wage law. Oregon's reformed constitution, now complete with women voters, created pensions for single mothers. The women also spearheaded legislation such as workman's compensation, safety boards, and the abolition of the death penalty.[40] These trends continued on a broader level after women won the vote.

During the same era that suffragists won the vote, women as individuals became more able to break out of some old conventions that restricted them, while developments of the First World War had helped them along. Whereas dress reform through the Bloomer movement in the early 1850s had been ridiculed out of existence—like most women's attempts at reform, including the call for the vote at that time—by the 1920s women's clothes had freed up, imparting the psychological freedom that looser styles allowed. Some of these style changes had come about because of war shortages: lack of steel hastened the demise of corsets, for example, while fabric shortages led to simpler styles altogether. But these changes also came about partly because of the war work in industry that women went into in great numbers, work which demanded simpler clothing. Military uniforms also influenced fashion. The influences behind such momentous changes in fashion as occurred between 1910 and 1920 are many and some trends were already in train before the war, but the net result was clothes that women could move and breathe in. The Flapper era of the 1920s—itself a complex phenomenon—was both triggered in part by, and was a manifestation of, this new freedom that some women, particularly the young, displayed during that decade.

Yet many women were unwilling or unable to change their own traditional self-image. They were supported and reinforced in doing so and even forced to follow this path, not only by the prevailing mind-set of the populace, not only because of economic and legal constraints on the opportunities for expressing women's possibilities if they wanted to, but also because under-girding all of American life remained two conflicting philosophies that had existed since the time of the founding. One philosophy was the individual's right to self-determination, based on John Locke's natural rights theory. The other relied on Scottish enlightenment theories which conflated rights and duties. The former applied to men and the latter applied to women. The two philosophies devolved into the public and private spheres and the conventions and expectations about women's role and duties primarily as wives and mothers, no matter what the reality of women's lives of whatever class or the effect on women of severe restrictions on the quality of their health and freedom. This second philosophy has dogged American women ever since. It was through the framers' and drafters' uses of these two philosophies as it suited them, employing terminology which was both all-encompassing and exclusive at the same time, that women's lives were securely limited. The new United States of America was founded on the rights of man, purportedly referring in the Declaration of Independence to all members of humanity through the assertion that "all men are created equal." In its verbal flourishes, therefore, the new nation subscribed to the notion of the equality of all of its members. From the start, however, reality—in the shape of attitudes, laws and conventions—restricted women's freedom. This duality was perhaps not immediately recognized in federal fundamental documents, but after the end of the Civil War that more restrictive philosophy, which conflated rights with duties, emerged openly in the drafting of the Fourteenth Amendment, when rights for the first time in the United States Constitution were restricted to man as the male sex. The introduction of the word "male" in regard to voting practices drew a much clearer line between men and women in the republic and raised the stakes in the struggle for equal rights for women, including the vote, to a much higher level.[41]

With these conflicting philosophies still undergirding American society in the 1920s, no matter how many changes women had amassed through their own hard work both nationally and in the states through the years, it was easy for anti-woman positions to take the starring role whenever they popped up. Hence, after the First World War women had to give up the jobs they had done during the emergency and return to the home in order to allow discharged servicemen to fit back in. This long-standing philosophy, bred unconsciously into the American psyche, appeared and showed its power and potential during the expansion of federal power in Roosevelt's New Deal when even the *right* of married women to work was questioned. Women also were the overt target of discrimination in New Deal federal job creation that focused on men under Section 213 of the Economy Act of 1932.[42] The same expanding and then contracting opportunities for, and demands and constrictions on, women occurred again during the Second World War and the years afterwards.

Ratification of the Nineteenth Amendment left other things unchanged, such as the mind of Alice Robertson of Oklahoma, the woman elected to Congress in 1920. The amendment did not eradicate either the feelings of women who did not really care about the vote or the ones who were apprehensive about voting or even going to the polls, which up to now had been a very masculine arena, much like a saloon. It did not change by the stroke of a pen any inhibitions and prejudices about proper sex roles by which many still thought both men and women should live.

Progress beyond suffrage, therefore, did occur, but it had its limitations. To give just one example, while twenty-five states had opened the office of notary to women by 1928, at that time twenty-three still banned women from the position.[43] This kind of progress was like suffrage all over again—uneven and interminable. This was the central characteristic of reform through the individual states and, while specific federal reforms applied nationally, reforms of individual laws left much to be desired, for it involved huge amounts of work for only very specific results. The remaining inequalities that still pertained at the national level emerged clearly during the Second World War, and one job in the services provided a particularly pertinent example. Because of the crisis, in order to free male pilots up for combat duties and service abroad, ultimately a total of 1074 women were recruited for the Women's Airforce Service Pilot (WASP) program to take on flying jobs at home. The WASPs were women who already knew how to fly and they often carried out work so dangerous that men avoided doing it. The women ended up after the war, unlike male members of the military, with no pension or benefits for their service. In December 1944, their work unceremoniously came to an end.

"When different [women] showed up [from a mission], what they might have said was, 'Your orders have come. You're through.' That was it. No Discharge. Nothing," said a former WASP, then 90-year-old Sara Payne Hayden, in 2010 when the remaining WASPs and relatives of dead WASPs went to D.C. to receive the Congressional Gold Medal. Unlike enlisted airmen, the military didn't even pay the WASPs' way home. "[Hayden] was told she could take a ride on a military airplane—if there was a flight out of Randolph Army Air Base before midnight. She caught a flight to Fort Bragg and from there returned to Charlotte, where she went back to secretarial work."[44]

WASPs finally won the right of discharge and military benefits but only in 1977.

CHAPTER 8

The Unfinished Business
of the Civil War

In contrast to these ongoing piecemeal approaches to equality for women beginning in 1920, with their unequal results, Alice Paul adopted her own unique idea to tackle the complicated state of women's inequality after suffrage. In 1923, she and the NWP launched the Equal Rights Amendment (ERA) in an attempt to establish nationally the principle of equality for women under the law. Discrimination on account of sex banned in the fundamental law would require the complete overhaul of laws, both federal and state, that discriminated against women. It would also have influence during the creation of new laws and begin to permeate the legal rulings from all courts, from the United States Supreme Court all the way down. Establishing a national standard, it could even have an effect on conventions that led to a wholesale prohibition of women from certain activities, such as jobs that required physical strength, whether or not individual women might succeed in any tests required. It could even affect attitudes prejudicial to women but based on no solid ground, such as those the WASPs had encountered in the military.

The precedent for such a global amendment as Paul proposed had existed in the United States Constitution since 1870. The Fifteenth Amendment banned discrimination on account of "race, color or previous condition of servitude" and at the time of that amendment's passage, leading woman's rights advocates had campaigned to have the word "sex" included. They were pointedly and deliberately ignored. The ERA would try again to win what women failed to do even with a desperate campaign for women's rights during the progress of what became the Fourteenth and Fifteenth amendments. They also later failed to win a Sixteenth Amendment to cover women specifically.

Paul and the NWP would, in other words, be working to finish the unfinished business of the Civil War.

Paul and the NWP launched the ERA at Seneca Falls on the 75th anniversary of the Seneca Falls Convention and the Declaration of Sentiments. Adhering to the nation's founding philosophy that "all men are created equal," it ensured that the ringing phrase from the Declaration of Independence applied unequivocally to both sexes. The ERA, which was later reworded, stated, "Men and women shall have equal rights throughout the United States and every place subject to its jurisdiction. Congress shall have power to enforce this article by appropriate legislation."

Republicans introduced the amendment in Congress for the first time in December 1923 and every Congress introduced it from then until 1970. The only vote occurred in the Senate, in 1946, which the NWP lobbied for. Members of the Women's Joint Congressional Committee, a combination of all groups which endorsed the ERA and formed under the NWP's urging, supported this effort to capitalize on the heightened regard for women that women in industry and the services had evoked during the war. The move foundered when discharged servicemen began to return home and the traditional social structure with women at home began to resurface. A strong coalition of antis emanating from the federal Women's Bureau, which created the National Coalition to Defeat the Unequal Rights Amendment, successfully worked against it. This combination of twenty-seven groups comprised progressive or left-wing organizations including the ACLU and boasted prominent supporters like Eleanor Roosevelt.[1] These antis also produced a winning strategy to defeat the ERA when it passed votes in Congress in 1950 and 1953, even with additional wording which undermined its whole premise. Even President Eisenhower's plea to a joint session of Congress in 1958 to pass the ERA achieved nothing, while again the unacceptable addition was included.

This short history of the initial voting record encapsulates the basic problem that Paul's ERA encountered from the very beginning, which was the fact that social feminists and others of the same ilk, from the 1920s on, opposed the ERA because the guarantee of equality to both men and women threatened programs of protective legislation for women across the nation, as well as the protective legislation of labor unions. The unacceptable addition to the ERA, known as the Hayden rider, stated, "The provisions of this article shall not be construed to impair any rights, benefits, or exemptions now or hereafter conferred by law upon persons of the female sex." Intended to preserve protective legislation for women, its inclusion imported an unacceptable contradiction in terms to equal rights on account of sex.

Paul's ERA was a deceptively simple idea, aimed at avoiding a considerable amount of repetitive work both at state and national level. Yet it would also incorporate in United States fundamental law a comprehensive principle that would ultimately have practical results and, in theory, affect the American psyche: equality on account of sex. This object has been a can of worms. The major obstacle which the ERA immediately ran into could easily have been anticipated, not only because individual women after the suffrage win espoused different and even competing approaches to further reforms for women, but also because of the continuing existence of the two competing philosophies from the founding period, which have permeated the United States from the start, inhibiting the progress of women. Paul's ERA encapsulated the philosophy of the natural rights of man (as humankind) and ensured that the founding principle that "all men are created equal" actually—and finally without question—would include and apply to women. The problem with the ERA for social feminists was that if men and women were to be equal under the law, legislation devised to protect women would not fit. Logically, social feminists could not support the ERA and neither could labor unions, because they were creating preferential treatment for some groups. The ERA, therefore, while deceptively simple, was also both challenging and disturbing to the very fundamentals of American life.

The fundamental conflict between the ERA and social feminists lay in that old Scottish Enlightenment philosophy of equal rights, which fed right back into traditional sex roles, particularly those of the female sex. Men and women were equal in the sight of God; the rights that emanated from God implied duties; with men and women the duties were different. Women produced offspring and their duties arose because they became wives and mothers. It was by extension, therefore, though not necessarily logical, that woman's role was to become a wife and mother. Because of that role—which now became her duty—by extension it was woman's right to receive special considerations or privileges to support that role. This was the philosophical foundation, whether spelled out or not, whether understood or not, for creating the ideology of the public and private spheres and putting women on a pedestal in the nineteenth century. In the late nineteenth century and well into the twentieth century, this allowed the development of protective legislation for women.

The confusing philosophy of duties, rights and privileges depended on a biological interpretation of women—which, apparently naturally, did not apply to men. It defined and constricted the possibilities of women's lives by their ability to bear children, by assuming that all women would become mothers, and by ignoring the fact that many women, for whatever reason, would not. This philosophy was like a snake eating its own tail, but it had such deep roots in the American psyche that it was virtually invisible. It carried with it major implications for American women and had a deep and abiding impact on them. In particular, the protective legislation that was intended to protect women often ended up protecting male jobs because it provided employers with excuses to avoid hiring women when restrictions on women's hours and what they could do physically within a particular job made them less valuable workers. When women were employed, it also provided a rationale—if any were needed—for the long-standing tradition of paying women less than men. In addition to the piecemeal nature of individual reforms at both the federal and state level, therefore, it was for hampering, and not helping, women that Paul and the NWP opposed protective legislation and preferred an ERA to help attack the philosophical basis of women's legal, social and economic inequality.

The support of the ERA by the political parties tended to mirror these two competing philosophies, with the Republican Party at first ignoring but ultimately including the ERA in its platform from 1940 on. The Democrat Party did so in 1944. Within that party, a combination of interest groups both northern and southern, for whom protective legislation remained the holy grail, continued to oppose it for decades—such as Labor unions, New Dealers and Eleanor Roosevelt. Meanwhile, women made some inroads in American politics itself, with each administration after 1920, due to campaigning by women themselves, appointing women to federal and policy-making positions. Women's clout to lobby for inclusion of women arose because, soon after women won the vote, both Republicans and Democrats brought women into party positions, the Democrats in 1920 doubling the size of its national committee to include a woman from each state, and the Republicans finally allowing women into the National Committee in 1924.[2]

The significance of developments such as these was relative, however, and by the late 1960s one researcher could conclude with justification that women had not achieved political equality or much visibility, in spite of the variety of ways in which they had progressed in the political arena. Even the very idea of women in politics was still a debatable proposition and women's qualifications for such roles were still automatically dismissed.[3] The overriding impression from the histories of this time is that suffrage had been a damp squib, that it changed nothing of women's contribution to the polity, even though one of the arguments for winning the vote was to facilitate it. However, while at national level the conclusion that the women's inroads could be interpreted as largely tokenism—in spite of the abilities of the women who broke through—at state and local level the truth was very different. In 1963, as an effort to have a recalcitrant President Kennedy recognize women's contribution to party politics by appointing capable women to appropriate positions, Clayton Fritchey, who had served on the Democratic National Committee, stated bluntly not only that women were voting in increasing numbers, but that women were also "virtually running local politics" and that such women noticed their exclusion from the highest levels.[4] Women's involvement in politics in the South demonstrates clearly this involvement of women in politics at local levels.[5] Political involvement did not, however, necessarily mean belonging to a party. It could also mean participation in clubs identifying with one or other political party, as with members of women's Republican clubs.[6]

In December 1961, President Kennedy announced his Commission on the Status of Women as a sop to party women because of his less than stellar record on women in his administration.[7] Even long-term ERA anti Eleanor Roosevelt agreed to chair the commission. The justice of a continuing demand for equal rights for women was underlined by the commission's report, which appeared in October 1963. Yet, even the women's inequalities which the report outlined were not enough to raise support for the ERA. In fact, the report promoted a backward-looking move—pursuing equal rights through the Equal Protection Clause of the Fourteenth Amendment.[8] Commission member Pauli Murray had resurrected the very idea Susan B. Anthony had abandoned in the case of suffrage in the mid–1870s after the Supreme Court had held that women were not persons for the purposes of voting.[9] Murray proposed the Fourteenth Amendment approach for several reasons: to attempt to bring social feminists and pro–ERA women together; to try to hitch women's rights to what had been for several years the successful tactics of black civil rights; and to promote the cause of black women within any push for women's rights. A rapprochement between pro–ERA women and those who supported this latest move emerged.

Meanwhile, the piecemeal equality for women reforms continued with some success. In 1963, the Equal Pay Act banned discrimination in pay on account of sex in some circumstances. The measure represented somewhat of an advance for women, bringing the federal government for the first time into the field of sex discrimination enforcement.[10] Then, in 1964, the Civil Rights Act included sex as a category in its Title VII—Equal Employment—section. The inclusion of sex has often been characterized as an antiblack move by the NWP and other women who were attempting to upend the whole bill in connivance with a racist southern congressman, Democratic representative

Howard Smith of Virginia, chairman of the House Rules Committee. This telling holds that the move was Smith's idea alone and that some women, sensing opportunity, quickly acted in support of the inclusion of sex and won. Smith's maneuver thus failed.[11]

Such a characterization is at best inadequate. At worst, it is prejudiced. If the introduction of sex was such a cynical move, it was the replay of a political game as old as the hills, the counterpart to that whereby congressmen of any stripe would introduce the race card to truncate or kill suffrage. In this case, it was using the sex card: either way, sex and race were political footballs. If, as Smith declared, it was an honest attempt to include a ban on discrimination that affected the largest discriminated-against group in the nation, which was women, then it was about time that some attention was paid to sex discrimination instead of only to race and other inequalities. Supporting this view is the fact that Smith had sponsored the Equal Rights Amendment for many years. Some women, it is true, did consider that a move to include a prohibition of sex discrimination in work opportunities at a time of the promotion of black rights was frivolous because, in their view, civil rights for blacks represented a higher priority than civil rights for women. Then, and still in the 1960s, this view represented a powerful position to adopt. Yet it may be as cynical as the notion that the women were trying to destroy the whole bill. To espouse equality for one section of the population at the expense of another once again asserted the fundamental contradiction in terms that the Founders refused to face: it prioritized equalities, creating inequalities, which was particularly ironic in a nation founded on the principle of equality. If the Civil Rights Act had excluded sex as a category in Title VII, it would have been a straightforward replay of Reconstruction history—events which further institutionalized inequality throughout the nation. There were, therefore, many good reasons to include it.

The negative characterization of the inclusion of sex as a category in Title VII is also wrong because it came about, in fact, as a result of intensive lobbying by Alice Paul and the NWP and other women who, from the time of the introduction of the Civil Rights Bill late in 1963, were determined to win some civil rights for women. One object was to ensure that if protection in work was to be extended to black workers the bill's definition of such workers would include women. Including the word "sex" was to prevent the situation where, as Representative Martha Griffiths, stated, "The bill as written *would leave white women with no protection at all,* since black women would have a cause of action against employers who hired only white men but white women would not...."[12]

The immediate response of Congress to the proposed addition to the Civil Rights Bill indicated how very little progress women had made in American society. While civil rights for blacks were taken seriously, even narrow equal rights for women elicited hoots of laughter from members of Congress—much like a proposal to give women the vote had been treated in 1868 in Arkansas. Representative Griffiths made sure to point the double standards out in her reply to this behavior and because of women's astute political maneuvering during the debate—itself likely grounds for criticism of their motives—sex became a category in the Civil Rights Act in 1964, which resulted in the federal government's yet again getting involved in tackling sex discrimination.

Yet, that involvement was ultimately limited: the 1963 Equal Pay Act defined discrimination in pay on account of sex in an extremely narrow manner, while the Equal Employment Opportunities Commission (EEOC) refused to consider sex discrimination cases. By late in the 1960s, women, enraged by this discriminatory treatment against women directly by the federal bureaucracy, had created the National Organization of Women (NOW) to fight for women's equality, while the litigation approach was gathering enough steam to lead in 1971 to a case from Idaho in which, for the first time, the Supreme Court used the Equal Protection Clause of the Fourteenth Amendment to make a decision favorable to women.[13] The case challenged a state law automatically giving men preference over women in appointment as the administrator of an estate and seemed to represent a major departure in law. The decision's unexpected legacy was that it underlined Paul's wisdom about the advisability and necessity of a blanket amendment for equal rights on account of sex, for the Supreme Court applied a standard of proof that was lower than—and was therefore not equal to—the strict scrutiny that applied to cases involving race discrimination. It was, in short, improved treatment but without equality, a continuing theme in women's history in the United States.

The Equal Rights Amendment, meanwhile—the much older second prong of the dual strategy that evolved in the 1960s—had actually been progressing during this same time. In spite of the labors of countless women, including Paul, during the fifty intervening years, there had been no broad-based movement of women demanding equal rights. Now there was. The increased anger of women triggered by the distinctly discriminatory treatment of women by the EEOC and consequent activism through NOW, combined with the eruption into prominence of women's rights passion as "Women's Liberation" by 1969. These together were the ingredients missing since 1920 for passage of an amendment—widespread demand by women for equal rights on account of sex.

Congress finally passed and sent the proposed amendment to the states in 1972. It contained a deadline for ratification of seven years, which Representative Martha Griffith had included, despite the lack of any such stipulation in Article V of the Constitution, for a deadline was considered the only politically feasible way to get the ERA through Congress. Seven years later, in 1979 it had only 35 of the 38 ratifications, the further expansion of the United States having yet again pushed back the cause of women's equality. In 1923, it would have required only 36 ratifications, like suffrage. Congress passed a three-year extension, but no further ratifications transpired, while some states, in a fit of regret, rescinded theirs. In 1982 the ERA was pronounced dead.[14] During that time, the hope the 1971 Supreme Court decision in *Reed v. Reed* raised also crumbled. The justices declined in their decisions to extend to sex discrimination the equal status with race discrimination, while further decisions tended to further refine the application of the Equal Protection Clause in sex discrimination cases. The Fourteenth Amendment strategy was revealing major inadequacies. The strategy, as an alternative, possibly successful, approach to equal rights also compromised the ERA. The latter seemed less necessary when the justices might do the work of Congress. The 1970s, therefore, in spite of the dual strategy, had ultimately left women both without equality under the Equal Protection Clause and without the Equal Rights Amendment.[15]

Like most of women's history in the United States, equal rights for women after the 1970s have inched forward. Today, many of the most glaring inequalities may or may not have been removed or have gone underground. Women, however, are still not equal under the law. Yet a poll conducted in 2001 found that 72 percent of the population believed that the ERA was ratified.[16] In the intervening years since the declared death of the ERA, there have been developments. In 1996, the Supreme Court created an intermediate test under the Equal Protection Clause heightening the standards for sex discrimination cases. The new standard was still not the strict scrutiny that applies to race cases, so even if women in some cases by that ruling had a better chance of success under the so-called equal protection clause, it is still not equality.[17] In fact, Supreme Court justice Antonin Scalia stated in an interview with *California Lawyer* in January 2011 that no equality according to sex applies under the U.S. Constitution: "'Certainly the Constitution does not require discrimination on the basis of sex,' said Justice Scalia with reference to the Fourteenth Amendment. 'The only issue is whether it prohibits it. It doesn't. Nobody ever thought that that's what it meant. Nobody ever voted for that.'"[18]

Laws and judicial review are still often touted as the way to deal with continuing women's legal inequalities in the U.S., but that approach has serious shortcomings. In 2007, the failure of Lilly Ledbetter to win equal pay in her suit against the Goodyear Tire and Rubber Company demonstrated the fragility of statutory equal rights for women when sex equality faces judicial review with a Constitution without equal rights on account of sex. When that decision all but gutted equal pay laws for women, it necessitated a new act of Congress to deal with it. The Lilly Ledbetter Fair Pay Act was signed into law in January 2009.[19]

Another shortcoming is the insecurity of statute as opposed to fundamental law: if sexual equality exists only in statute law, such laws can always be repealed with only a one-vote margin in Congress. They do not have the solid position in the Constitution that an amendment would have, while without an amendment, statutes and even judicial holdings do not have to conform to a strict interpretation of sex discrimination that the ERA has attempted to create, elevating sex to the same level as other groups.[20]

More than ninety years after its first introduction the ERA still lacks three state ratifications. More than thirty years after it was pronounced dead, it is, however, still holding on. In response to its declared expiration the ERA has been reintroduced in every Congress since the end of the extended deadline in 1982, in an approach called the start-over strategy. This requires 38 ratifications. More important, however, is the three-state strategy, which is based on opinions of constitutional scholars that states could still ratify the ERA and only three more ratifications would cause promulgation. This strategy relies on a position that any deadline on any amendment steps beyond constitutional requirements, for there is no stipulation of deadlines in Article V of the Constitution. Consequently, the argument goes, the deadline on the ERA never had any validity and even now does not apply. Even the three-year extension was unnecessary because the original seven-year time limit had no validity. This analysis emanated from a legal opinion arising from the ratification in 1992 of the Twenty-Seventh Amendment—one of two proposed amendments that didn't make it into the Bill of Rights in 1791. Prohibiting members of Congress from awarding themselves pay raises without going to the voters, the ratification of that amendment after more than 200 years raised the question of the continuing viability of old proposed amendments, especially those with deadlines, the ERA being the key one among them.[21] Besides leading to a major presidential legal memo on the issue,[22] the ratification of the Twenty-Seventh Amendment led to a new strategy, in which members of Congress repeatedly attempted to have resolutions passed affirming that the

ERA would become part of the Constitution when the number of ratifications for the 1972 ERA resolution reached thirty-eight. The three-state strategy was refined in 2011–12 when United for Equality of Washington, D.C., had members of Congress introduce in both houses new resolutions to remove the time limit from the original 1972 ERA resolution. These new resolutions were intended to address the practical problem faced at the state level when campaigners for the ERA, in a classic double bind, have constantly to deal with the objection that the ERA is dead because of the time limit. The perceived viability of this proposed measure is based on the fact that the time limit in the 1972 ERA resolution was only in the preamble to, and not included in, the actual wording of the proposed amendment.[23]

In the second decade of the twenty-first century, as the centenary of the suffrage victory approaches, Alice Paul's counterpart to the Nineteenth Amendment, which also represents the completion of the unfinished business of the Civil War, remains in limbo. The moral force of the pro–ERA argument comes not only from the exigencies of justice—though, in the case of women's history justice has been thin on the ground—but also from the fact that in 1979 even thirty-five ratified states represented a huge proportion of the population. It will be interesting to see if the ERA will be ratified in time for the 2023 centenary of its introduction by Paul in 1923.

CHAPTER 9

Intended Consequences

After the November 2 general election in 1920, some daily newspapers reported on the culmination of the United States' peaceful revolution of the day before. On this first day after women all across the country were finally able under law to help choose their elected representatives equally with men, often lengthy features told of women crowding the polls, using their maiden names and carrying their dogs to the polls. Others reported apparently deliberately insensitive poll workers asked women their age and shouted it out. Soon, life and death appeared, with an aged suffragist dying three days after casting her vote and a woman missing the opportunity to vote because she was giving birth.[1] Some of the stories referred to the "woman vote" affecting the poll numbers[2] and others dismissed it.[3] Local issues, however, often took priority over the effect of this culminating act of the peaceful national sex revolution in voting, partly because women had previously won equal voting rights in some states, while elsewhere, both previously and during the NWP campaign, they had won unequal voting rights. Whether the voting rights were equal or unequal, women's presence at the polls had already become so much a part of normal life that it was not newsworthy.[4] There could easily have been another reason for this: suffrage was ignored at that point not only because had it won, but also because it pertained to women. And, as American history has so amply demonstrated, women can be ignored.

So insignificantly does women's ingress to the voting booth seem to have featured in official minds across the nation, in spite of the 72-year struggle to win this one advance, that few records were kept distinguishing men and women voters. As a consequence of the neglect of this pivotal juncture in United States history, statistics are mostly unavailable to gauge accurately what the female vote in the 1920 elections might signify. The country had to wait until December 19 for an estimate of the total, which came up at between 28 million and thirty million votes cast. Although we lack a proper count, women voters were estimated to have voted at three-fifths of the male rate,[5] low given the huge and terrifying specter that the prospect of votes by women had raised in debates during the preceding years, a specter used repeatedly as a reason to deny suffrage. Such numbers and the continued nonemergence in the 1920s of the huge threat of a voting bloc of women helped politicians, newsmen, observers and historians in the ensuing decades to start, and continue, to ignore or write off this new piece of national history as not being worth all the fuss. These failures haunt the truth of suffrage history even today, as scholars, if they do not actually ignore the amendment, continue to dismiss its importance in spite of the monumentality of the achievement.[6] Yet, among the huge range of truths about votes by women waiting to emerge over time, one specific truth of the significance of the win of suffrage for women had already begun to emerge in the time between ratification and the general election. In keeping with so much of American history, this began—and already had begun—in unequal voting states to appear at the local level: the impact of suffrage on the black community. This is a part of the history of woman suffrage that, in the convenience of dealing with race and sex separately because of the complexity of the histories, has been too easily ignored. The day after the general election a story on one contest leaps out: "Little interest was taken in the election, except for the constable's race, although the vote was larger than it was thought it would be. Many women voted. In one polling place it was said that about 50 negro women but only one white woman voted."[7]

In the perspective of modern history which says that black people could not vote until the 1960s, this anecdote is tantalizing. Given the time and place—North Little Rock, Arkansas—and given the general assumptions about black history, it raises many questions, such as how black women got to vote. There are more: How did the racial disparity come about? What were the issues or circumstances that brought them out? Did they appear at the polling place as a bloc? What exact polling place? Who estimated the numbers? Why was there "only one white woman"? How could the black women afford the poll tax? What were the voting numbers at other polling places? How did the women affect the outcome of that election race?

From the perspective of a century after 1920, the result, or even the candidate's name, hardly matters,[8] for the story even in its vague outlines is startling to say the least. Given the history of the South, the very fact of black men exercising their right to vote would often be significant on its own. The fact of a large number of black *women* voting at one polling place so soon after ratification, however, is startling. And, whatever the answers may be to the questions the story raises, they reveal an extremely important fact: equality of opportunity in voting after the Nineteenth Amendment applied to women of both major races in the nation.[9] This equality is exactly what the original suffragists intended to achieve when votes for ex-slaves were mooted even before abolition, but circumstances had led to the postponement of that dream by the politicking of men, both black and white, after the end of the Civil War. The history is long and convoluted.

Back in the 1820s, when women first began to emerge publicly as active in reform—and when reform in a national sense essentially meant abolition— many of them appreciated that reform much more comprehensive than pure abolition was necessary. Many individual women, and an increasing number of them, saw that slavery was not only an institution to be abolished, but also a symbol of all the institutionalized inequalities in America's supposedly equal society. In particular, women's lack of legal, social and civil freedom in the society, specifically their almost legal, social and political nonexistence except as the quasi-property of their husbands and fathers, led to the often-used analogy of the slavery of women.[10] If women's own lack of freedom was tied to the paradigm of slavery, women in time saw also that their own emancipation was tied to that of the slaves. This view arose not only because so many women worked for abolition, but also because abolitionism based on an argument for justice and equality must also extend logically to the status of women. In time, in the minds of some key male abolitionists such as William Lloyd Garrison, Wendell Phillips and Frederick Douglass, it did so.

Early suffragists—women like Elizabeth Cady Stanton, Susan B. Anthony, Lucretia Mott and Lucy Stone—seemed to assume, or had even been promised, that after the Civil War the justice of the abolition of the institution of slavery would also extend to that other institutionalized inequality, much larger numerically, which slavery symbolized: that of women, especially to reward women for giving up their own struggle for equality during the war. Women, however, were bitterly disappointed. That women, having supported the war and fought for black freedom during its course, faced yet another struggle for rights for themselves alone emerged clearly in a speech by Wendell Phillips as the new president of the American Anti-Slavery Society in 1865, when he declared,

> I want to have another amendment passed which shall read thus: no State shall at any time make a distinction of civil privileges between the children of parents living on or born on her soil, either of race, condition or color.... I hope some day to be bold enough to add "sex." However, my friends, we must take up but one question at a time, and this hour belongs exclusively to the negro. Let us see

to this, that no State shall make a distinction among its citizens either of race, color, or condition, and when ... we have achieved that, we will have ... put the negro in the full enjoyment of his liberty.[11]

This statement made clear the one-sex meaning that Phillips gave to the word "negro." Following the Declaration of Independence's murky "all men are created equal" statement, he meant males only: women were expendable. Even at this crucial turning point in the history of the nation, with Phillips unilaterally determining publicly that the equality of women was inopportune, he refused to recognize, in spite of his professed beliefs, that with the end of the Civil War this could be the moment to eradicate legal and civil inequality not only of race, but of sex and to complete the Revolution of 1776. Subsequently, to the shock and horror of suffragists at the time, the Fourteenth and Fifteenth amendments not only excluded women, but also clearly and legally institutionalized women's subordinate status in American society, for the Constitution now for the first time specified that "men" did indeed equal "male" only. Suffragists had reason to be bitterly disappointed by the behavior of their erstwhile colleagues, who so swiftly abandoned them to support votes for freedmen only—the more expediently, the men argued, to ensure passage of the amendments.

Women's history, understandably, accords Wendell Phillips notoriety for saying at the time that "this is the Negro's hour," if not so succinctly.[12] The betrayal of women at the same time by Frederick Douglass receives less notice. This is due partly to recognition of his crucial support of suffrage at Seneca Falls in 1848. Yet, to maintain Douglass on his woman's rights pedestal ignores the fact that he betrayed women during Reconstruction—and like Phillips and many others helped to delay woman suffrage for more than fifty years. In addition, he had laid the groundwork for his obstructionism towards women since the early 1850s when, changing his position on slavery from justice to expediency by abandoning moral abolitionism to support political abolitionism in order to garner financial support for his own newspaper, he began attacking anyone who did not support him. In fact, from 1851, he obviously felt he could dictate to others in the abolitionist camp that they should act according to principles that he defined, including expediency. Leading female abolitionists such as Lucy Stone and Abby Kelley became two early targets of his attacks because they dealt not solely with abolitionism but also with the rights of women, a dual focus which was then anathema to Douglass.

With Stone already attacked in 1853 for not standing on what Douglass perceived as principle in a racially charged situation during a speaking tour in the upper South in 1855, it was Kelley's turn to feel Douglass's wrath when, in a speech that he gave at the Ladies' Anti-Slavery Society of Rochester—an organization founded to help finance his newspaper—he blamed Kelley for the 1840 American Anti-Slavery Society split. This split had come about ostensibly because of William Lloyd Garrison's inclusion of Kelley in a key committee. In fact, the Kelley situation was simply the excuse to make the long-festering split a reality, leading to the creation of a separate political abolitionism group. Douglass, however, did not spare Kelley, but his condemnation of her was worse than blaming her only because of her dual focus: it was also a condescending, patronizing and demeaning dismissal of woman's equality. The split, he said, was due to "a very minor question": "Shall a woman be a member of a committee in company with men? ... How beautiful would it have been for that woman, how nobly would her name have come down to us in history, had she said: 'All things are lawful for me, but all are not expedient! While I see no objection to my occupying a place on your committee, I can for the slave's sake forego the privilege.'"

This attack put clearly on show the slippery nature of Douglass's version of equality even while elevating himself to a higher plane than other abolition workers: in his attacks on both Stone and Kelley he demanded that the women stand on principle, unless it was more expedient not to. This put women in an impossible position. Douglass maintained his view of the relative merits of equality for former male slaves and equality for women during the controversy over the Reconstruction amendments. In a letter in September 1868 to a Miss Griffing of Rochester refusing an invitation to speak on woman suffrage, Douglass wrote that black male suffrage was "more urgent" than women's "because it is life and death to the long-enslaved people of this country.... While the Negro is mobbed, beaten, shot, stabbed, hanged, burnt, and is the target of all that is malignant in the North and all that is murderous in the South his claims may be preferred by me without exposing in any wise myself to the imputation of narrowness or meanness towards the cause of woman...."[13] Douglass demonstrated no concern for what female ex-slaves might go through as free people in the United States, while he clearly shows his prejudices against white women. Sojourner Truth had already pointed out the duplicity of people such as Douglass regarding her sex during her address to the first annual meeting of the American Equal Rights Association in New York City on May 9, 1867, when she said, "[I]f colored men get their rights, but not colored women theirs, you see the colored men will be masters over the women and it will be just as bad as before."

Stanton and Anthony made a stand against this prioritization of equalities, campaigning in Kansas in 1867 in favor of votes for women. They were vilified for doing so. In a classic moral dilemma, the two long-term suffragist-abolitionists found themselves fighting against an amendment that secured black men the vote, not because they were against enfranchising them, but because they were against an amendment that excluded women. The public conveniently forgot the prodigious abolitionist work of the women in the years leading up to and during the Civil War and branded them racist. By 1869, they were ostracized for their unyielding stand against the Fifteenth Amendment, which, now that male citizenship was secured through the Fourteenth, would lock into the Constitution voting rights for males only. Refusing to make some inequalities more equal than others, Anthony argued at the annual meeting of the American Equal Rights Association in May 1869 that the Fifteenth Amendment "put 2,000,000 colored men in the position of tyrants over 2,000,000 colored women." She went on: "The question of precedence has no place on an equal rights platform." In an early reference to the intersection of race and sex, she heatedly fired back at Douglass, after he proclaimed the greater urgency of black men's vote over equal rights for all women, "When he tells us that the case of black men is so perilous, I tell him that even outraged as they are by the hateful prejudice against color, he himself would not today exchange his sex and color with Elizabeth Cady Stanton."[14]

The monumental betrayals by Phillips and Douglass and that of their supporters launched new inequalities. After the Civil War, black men were legally freed with what amounted to a right to vote. Female slaves were legally freed, but with black men over them. Black and white women had seen their freedom curtailed within the continued subordination of all women in society, now by all men, by the addition of the word "male" to the Constitution. All these changes impinged on the position of the norm—white men—but these still held most of the power in society.

These events had an effect on how women had to present their arguments in favor of suffrage. When men had decided to use expediency and set the terms of the debate by capturing the rhetoric of "universal suffrage" to mean male suffrage only, women had to follow. It is impossible to argue for reform or to defend a position on grounds of justice against arguments of expediency, for they represent two different languages. This led women who had previously worked for reform on the principle of justice to stray into racially divisive territory. Stanton and Anthony argued, for example, that if there was to be institutionalized discrimination in voting matters, it should not be on grounds of sex, but on grounds of education. Informed voters were more valuable to the polity than uneducated voters demagogues could easily sway. An educated vote by definition would have included educated white women at the expense of uneducated freedmen—a position simple to slur as racist. For Stanton and Anthony, it was manifestly unjust, however, that educated white women should be excluded from the franchise while uneducated black men were admitted to it. The same sense of manifest injustice permeated their arguments against uneducated male immigrants unversed in the American way being given the vote—or actually voting without citizenship, which Anthony herself saw—when American-born white women were excluded from participation in their own government.

Stanton and Anthony were human beings like everyone else, tossed in an ocean of partisan and expedient rhetoric not of their making: anger and bitterness would be only natural. In spite of their decades of hard work for equality, their own rhetoric degenerated, allowing them to be slurred as racist. Anthony in particular is still excoriated today by historians who sit in judgment but fail to appreciate the real temper of those times and see nothing of women's new reality behind some apparently remarkably restrained comments. How many times, for example, did Anthony encounter arrogant men—recently freed partly because of her work, in the enjoyment of that freedom, having the vote and therefore being legally superior—who denigrated her to her face because she was a woman and white? A hint of such appears in Anthony's comparison of Douglass's position with that of Stanton in 1869: would he indeed have changed race and sex with her in that climate?

Little allowance is made in these condemnations either for how frantic both Stanton and Anthony must have felt as they saw the only opportunity in several generations to win the vote for all women slipping away fast. Stanton was correct, short of two years, in anticipating how long it would take to nullify the word "male" in voting rights in the Constitution. In view of their impeccable credentials, calling either woman racist is unjust. Casting racial slurs and undermining character rather than addressing the issues was an easy out during Reconstruction. Looking back from a twenty-first century hair-trigger politically correct perspective, it is very easy to conclude racism.[15]

In the long "Age of Expediency" that took power during Reconstruction, antiblack sentiments featured regularly in suffragism, reflecting the national trend. These sentiments became more visible when southern women began to reemerge,[16] and the situation required extreme delicacy when women of North and South tried to cooperate in that postwar clime. Diplomatic tiptoeing desperately attempted to reconcile irreconcilables when racism accusations muscled their way in during the planning for the women's building project of the 1893 Columbian Exhibition.[17] Later that decade, black women, who were increasingly focusing on suffrage as the means to resolve racial problems, accused white suffragists of expediency and of denigrating blacks. In 1898, Helen A. Cook, president of the black Washington Woman's League, exhorted Anthony in an open letter "to signalize the end of the first half century of effort, and the beginning of a new and brighter era by leaving behind the old formula and basing the claims of women wholly on right and justice."[18] Miss Cook and others who followed up on her letter seemed unaware how men of both races had thrown out the women's attempt at justice in favor of expediency during Reconstruction. Given how women's history is repeatedly forgotten, this was perhaps understandable. Racism is always assumed the worse crime. Yet history should result in more than judgment: it requires some appreciation of the culture of its era. To demand higher standards from white women surrounded by a racist culture when they are pursuing redress of their own inequalities is once again applying the double standard that has bedeviled all of the female sex. As Anthony's biographer stated, while a male leader like Douglass could unquestionably put his interests ahead of others, women have never been allowed to do so.[19] Douglass gets away with it even though he betrayed the women who supported him and his cause to the detriment of their own. Cook unfortunately ignored the long history of denigration of white women in their pursuit not only of woman suffrage but of freedom and equality for blacks—just as many people today ignore it.

It would have been easy to derail the cause of women's rights by such incidents, which too frequently threatened the primary thrust of the women's cause. Yet women of any race could have called on Frederick Douglass's wisdom to stop it, for in 1855, he gave them the template for winning women's rights. While attacking Kelley, Douglass said the "slave's cause" was "already too heavily laden" to deal with anyone else's problems. He continued: "The battle of Woman's Rights should be fought on its own ground."[20] Applying Douglass's own argument, women's struggle was "already too heavily laden" and should be left unencumbered with complications that could derail it. In other words, within the women's cause, race should take a back seat, just as women's rights did for black rights.

Such was easier to say than to do, for the relationship between the two races was fraught, not just in the society at large but also among women. Even Alice Paul, aware of the delicate relationships she had to maintain for southern suffrage support, very quickly encountered the problems of reconciling justice on account of race with that of women in practical politics. During the planning of the Great Suffrage March, black women pressed for racial integration of participants, ultimately with the clout of Ida B. Wells-Barnett, the famous antilynching crusader, journalist and a founder of the NAACP.[21] This could jeopardize southern women's support, which was crucial for a federal amendment. Perhaps they pressed for participation, innocent of the politics that Paul had to deal with. Perhaps, unaware of Douglass's admonition, they simply determined to include race in woman suffrage because black women expected to fight for suffrage as if integration had already occurred. Perhaps they determined to foist race publicly on woman suffrage to expose racial inequalities and upstage the prime concern of the march. They did this early in 1913, when seven more arduous years, it was to prove—longer than the Civil War—would still be required to transform opposition to suffrage into congressional support. Even in 1919, suffrage was still up in the air there, while in the last debates some members of Congress still attempted to limit woman suffrage to white females only.[22] In the end, however, the ratified amendment basically added to the Fifteenth Amendment, and despite many attempts to compromise it the new amendment resolved the worst failure of Reconstruction politics by finally including the word "sex" in the Constitution in voting, without exclusion by race. The Nineteenth Amendment could not have excluded blacks anyway: discrimination on account of race had been unconstitutional since the 1860s—if only in theory—because of the Reconstruction amendments.

CHAPTER 10

Woman Suffrage and Civil Rights

A Changed Racial Dynamic

The significance of the opportunity that the Nineteenth Amendment opened up for black women emerged in the 1920 election, the Arkansas incident[1] being only one example of many black women voting nationally. In fact, from promulgation of woman suffrage on, the emergence of black women voters as distinct from white women voters was covered as newsworthy. An interesting impression to emerge was that black women seemed more aware than white women of the potential of their vote. One story just about summarized what happened across the South: "Negro women are registering in large numbers ... and Democratic leaders ... are surprised at the indifference of white women and the insistence of negro women on qualifying to vote."[2] Indeed, black women registered in many places, causing quite a stir. Kentucky, South Carolina and Texas women besieged the registrars to enroll. In Alabama, in 1920 after ratification, women furious about discriminatory registration requirements contacted the NAACP for help, saying they wanted to sue. In Norfolk, Virginia, two African American women actually won a case against the city's registrar for the unfair literacy tests.[3] Then, on the day of the general election throughout Georgia, where women were not allowed to vote because registration had closed before ratification, African American women crowded the polls and tried to vote anyway: "Negro women were refused ballots at the voting places in Savannah today. Many negro women have registered here since the suffrage amendment became effective, but the election judges ruled that they were not entitled to vote because of a state law which required registration six months before an election. No white women presented themselves at the polls."[4]

Here again black and white women behaved differently. In Georgia, white women may have been meekly acting on the judges' decision or on a combination of respecting the law and indifference to the vote. Black women, however, seem actively to have chosen to challenge that judicial decision by appearing at the polls. They might get to vote, but if rejected, they could cry discrimination. Whether they intended to demonstrate discrimination on account of sex or on account of race is not clear.[5] This event seems akin to what happened in North Little Rock, Arkansas, where many more black than white women turned up at one polling place. There, the only apparent legal factor to hold back newly enfranchised women in Arkansas was the poll tax, in force according to regular rules in 1920 because women had obtained primary voting rights in 1917. If women felt any interest in voting, they could have registered for the primary and automatically qualified to vote in the general election. The tax applied to both races. The only factor, all other things being equal, to exclude women from voting was not having paid the poll tax.[6] Like Georgia, the question therefore arises: Why did so many black women appear at this polling place and there was hardly a white woman?

All these incidents were significant enough to be newsworthy before and after the election and they indicated the reach of suffrage under the new amendment across the female color line. To anyone at the time taking note, they indicated the future. Yet the potential impact of the amendment was more than the ability of women of both major races to vote in elections. Before voting even began that November 2, in Arkansas the "future" had already happened: "For the first time in the history of the state, the name of a negro will be submitted to the voters of Arkansas for the governorship. J.H. Blount, negro, of Forrest City...."[7] This was huge. With Reconstruction, the South had elected black officials, a practice later ended with the onslaught of Jim Crow laws and the ever tighter grip of the Democratic Party machine. The real significance of J.H. Blount emerges in a later story: "[With] complete organization of the Negroes ... [it is] possible [that] the Negro men and women of the state can roll up a bigger majority than the Democrats at the general election." Here it is now clear that it was the *combination* of male votes with those of newly enfranchised women that allowed the notion of a black governor.[8] The woman suffrage movement had been watched eagerly by black activists for years, and black women had contributed to that cause. Now that black women had some political leverage, they were wasting no time in capitalizing on it for their own cause. In other words, for the black community, votes for women meant that the racial dynamic had changed.

Moving Center Stage

The racial dynamic had changed because when women won the vote finally on August 26, 1920, many historical events took place, not just the promulgation of the Nineteenth Amendment. That day also, a decades-long national debate affecting half the population finally cleared the table. When women won the vote, it meant that if they wished, they could now consider new departures, such as moving into the political system to promote reforms that they wanted. Many of them did so, choosing to work for employment reforms for women and children or else to campaign for an end to the poll tax. Others worked for more comprehensive reform like the ERA. The promulgation of the vote for women, however, signified a different new possibility for African Americans: it represented an opportunity to press their own claims for participation in the polity and for legal reforms to remove racial discrimination. Specific injustices against blacks had been instituted and enforced for decades, even after the abolition of slavery. In matters of voting, even though half of the black population was supposed to be included in voter rolls under the Fourteenth and Fifteenth amendments, black men had been excluded for years from the polity by state measures later anchored securely by key national judicial decisions in the 1870s. These measures, in fact, emerged not just from a swift retrenchment from the heady and recriminatory atmosphere of Reconstruction, but from an inbred and institutionalized discriminatory outlook sanctioned by law. The Supreme Court gave this behavior its official stamp of approval, swiftly following on its decision not to include women as eligible to vote under the Fourteenth Amendment, which women argued for before the justices in 1875. In *Minor v. Happersett* that year the court held that even if women were citizens, voting rights did not apply to them, for voting rights were not a privilege of citizenship.[9]

In the period before her own trial after she was charged with the crime of voting, Anthony had anticipated the repercussions of such a legal decision as the Supreme Court made in Minor's case. She declared in speeches across two counties, "If we once establish the false principle that United States citizenship does not carry with it the right to vote in every state in this Union, there is no end to the petty freaks and the cunning devices that will be resorted to, to exclude one and another class of citizens from the right of suffrage."[10] Anthony was right: a gigantic restriction on the right of citizens to vote having been already established through women, it was then relatively easy to turn on the much smaller group black men represented and also to extend discriminatory restrictions beyond the vote. A year after Minor's case the Supreme

Court began to limit the Fifteenth Amendment's restrictions on discrimination against freedmen. This represented a major impetus to emerging Jim Crow laws, for once black men could be excluded from the vote and power by various means not relating to race, they could be excluded officially from anything.

These injustices were still in force in much expanded form in 1920 and had been reinforced by further exclusions such as the white primary; but in 1920, with women's exclusion from the vote finally removed and with the national agenda finally cleared of this one huge domestic controversy, a vacuum now waited to be filled. For African Americans, the end of the woman suffrage debate meant the opportunity for their concerns to take center stage. It meant more, however. For a fight, they had increased clout, for the number of black voters had potentially doubled, and if not doubled, women represented to black men the thin end of the wedge for ending discrimination against them in voting rights.[11] Further, this could work both ways: if black men *and women* were denied the vote even though the Constitution purportedly now protected both race and sex from discrimination in voting rights, the peaceful revolution of 1920 would signify a doubled injustice if black men *and women* were *actually* denied access to the voting booths. This new dynamic, therefore, pointed not only to a potential doubling of the number of foot soldiers willing to fight, but also an even bigger goal to shoot for. For the black community, in spite of continuing segregation and discrimination against them, suffrage represented a win-win opportunity, even if winning took a long time.

For anyone who had eyes to see, therefore, the twentieth century's central controversy in the United States had already emerged and could be discerned from newspaper reports of the actions of African Americans and specifically those of black women after the suffrage victory. It was exactly what some antis in the South had predicted: a potential transformation in politics and the ultimate breakdown of the segregated South. The only question for antis who were focused on race was how long it would take and what might be done to prevent or forestall it.

In sum, the point when women won the vote was pivotal not only in national but also in African American history, when the curtain came down on the old act and rose on the new one. With woman suffrage settled, the nation could move onto something else. This would not have occurred in 1920 without the campaign of Paul and Burns, which projected the huge suffrage cause onto the national stage, finally clearing the decks of a 72-year-old struggle and making space for other controversies to take over. No matter how the issue is looked at, the victory in woman suffrage meant not only a huge step forward for women, but also the opening of a new chapter for African Americans.

The fact of such a direct result of the success of the woman suffrage campaign is rarely acknowledged. In particular, historians of black civil rights, except perhaps for specialized studies of black women's campaigning, have failed to accord to the amendment its significance for black history overall. In fact, there has been a distinct propensity in most histories to write off woman suffrage as insignificant, and too often there has been a failure to recognize its key role as part as part of the evolution of black civil rights' emergence and success on the national stage in the 1960s. The victory of the woman suffrage movement resonates today throughout the fabric of national life, not just through its effects for women at the present time, but also for its effects on the black community. Yet, to read the histories, the impact of the woman suffrage movement on that community does not exist or is difficult or impossible to discern, except in the specific area of women's history, which like suffrage a century ago awaits comprehensive integration into national history.

Indeed, not only have the suffragists received virtually no credit where it is due, but they have also been attacked for so-called racism. After promulgation of the Nineteenth Amendment, in a repeat of the Anthony and Stanton experience, race was again injected into women's rights and turned against the women who had won valuable legal rights for black women. In spite of what Alice Paul and others had gone through for the Nineteenth Amendment, in the 1920s Paul's actions in particular angered black women. This was, specifically, her decision to focus on the ERA to secure equal rights for all women under the law instead of working to end exclusions of black women from the vote. Paul argued that such exclusion was race discrimination, not sex discrimination. Her words may have been upsetting, but she was correct in the statement of fact. Her position has been frequently characterized as racist, which it may have been. However, it is equally possible to argue she was frustrated at the diversion from a focus on equal rights for all women. It is hard to believe that Paul did not know of Douglass's admonition to fight "the battle of Woman's Rights ... on its own ground," for she read everything about the vote she could find while working on suffrage. Besides, focusing on a single issue was her way, and the only issue for her was woman's rights. Moreover, Paul's aim was to secure the fundamental right of equality for women under the law. Without that equality, to try to enforce a specific right—even the vote—now that it had been obtained, was a diversion, because the latter could not occur without the former. In this perspective, Paul was anything but racist: the truth of this lies in the fact that her work on the Nineteenth Amendment and for the Equal Rights Amendment applied, or would apply, to all women, no matter their race.[12]

Establishing a Precedent

Indeed, it often seems that too much consideration is given to perceived discrimination perpetrated by Alice Paul against the black community and too little to what Paul and the NWP contributed to that struggle. The fact is that Paul and the NWP had not simply won African Americans the formidable weapon of equal suffrage, both as a tool and even as a battleground larger than what had existed before women won the vote; they had also established a precedent for African Americans for campaigning for equal rights, and the latter had the advantage of having seen it win victory. The components of this model were the same groundbreaking characteristics, already surveyed, that made the suffrage campaign so powerful. First, it claimed a position in the public space to imprint the grievances front and center on the public mind. In the suffrage case, it was one specific grievance that had to be dragged through seven decades and more. Second, it targeted the president directly. Third, Paul moved into Washington permanently, making the nation's capital the main stage, focus and center for suffrage activities. Fourth, the NWP created a nationwide campaign of women who also repeatedly rallied in Washington from all across the country.

Fifth, the women used every type of means to highlight the cause—automobile, railroad, airplane, the telephone and movies, plus traditional methods such as the newspapers and the theatre. Sixth, they lobbied interminably, turning every crisis and challenge into an opportunity to push suffrage while campaigning everywhere, including political conventions and following the president around. During the final crucial days of ratification, Paul had the NWP set up temporary headquarters in both Tennessee and Ohio to lobby the 1920 presidential candidates, Harding and Cox, both of Ohio, and win their endorsement of suffrage to help in the crucial final legislative showdown in Nashville. Seventh, through the women's innovation of the party-in-power campaign, they actively used what leverage they had to the maximum effect, both for publicity and to win practical political benefits for the cause. Eighth, the women pushed themselves to the limit, enduring prison, hunger strikes and force-feeding in pursuit of their cause.

Parades, picketing, prison and hunger strikes made up the wide range of tactics that Paul and the NWP employed for suffrage victory. They were the major components of a campaign with countless smaller details, employed within a nonviolent philosophy to win suffrage. Although the term "militant" applied to Paul and the NWP, that did not mean violent. It simply meant being forceful and asserting a right to their demands. Hunger strikes and the torture of force-feeding were part of the process of pushing to the limit what an individual could do and endure without fighting back. Paul came to the suffrage scene in the United States with experience of the complete range of tactics she could choose. In her commitment to nonviolence, she eschewed the actual violence the WSPU later used. Paul and the NWP won suffrage without loss of a single life, while all injuries were due to attacks by fellow citizens or deliberately contrived torture by the administration on women who were demonstrating peacefully.

This victory was a remarkable achievement, the first of its kind in the history of the United States. This largely unrecognized nonviolence was central to the campaign for woman suffrage. The accolade as the national leader of nonviolence in this country, however, usually goes to Martin Luther King, Jr., with the lineage of the philosophy for King tied to Gandhi.[13] Gandhi, however, gained much of his own philosophy through observing and learning from the early WSPU in London, the British organization that Paul worked with. Like the NAWSA's response to the NWP before suffrage victory, Gandhi distanced himself from the later WSPU and contrasted himself to his benefit with their methods.[14] Ultimately, however, the development of modern nonviolent political activism points directly back to the women. Paul and the NWP were the first to use nonviolence successfully in pursuit of a political aim in the United States. The black community owes them a huge debt.

CHAPTER 11

The Long-Term Influence of Paul's Campaign

Parades and Cultural Celebrations

Although its influence has been largely ignored, Paul's campaign for woman suffrage created the first successful civil rights movement in the United States in the twentieth century. It had a lasting impact on the nation, particularly on groups with civil rights aims.

While the influence of the NWP campaign is rarely if ever mentioned and a direct connection may be difficult to pin down, it is hard to believe that the women did not influence men such as Marcus Garvey, who immigrated to the United States in 1916 and founded the all-black Universal Negro Improvement Association (UNIA). He used, like the women did, elaborate pageantry, but for promoting the black cause, using themes devised from the history of people from Africa. In 1920 thousands lined the streets of Harlem to see him and his followers, outfitted in military styles of various lineages, march to the opening of the UNIA First International Convention displaying banners proclaiming, "We Want a Black Civilization" and "Africa Must Be Free." Mainstream black leaders heaped ridicule on Garvey for his daring so-called overreach of normal black behavior, a replay of what the women themselves had experienced for their daring first parades of women less than a decade before.[1]

As significant as Garvey's adoption of the women's proven techniques soon after the women won is the fact that every single tactic, or versions of them, that Paul and the NWP used reappeared in later decades in the black civil rights movement. The right to picket the White House was used, for example, in Lafayette Square—exactly where the suffragists had introduced it twenty years before—by black protesters during the 1930s picketing to free the Scottsboro Boys of Alabama, who were sentenced to death during their initial trials for allegedly raping two white women in 1931. Those trials were ostensibly rushed to avoid riots and lynchings, which said much about law enforcement at the time and raised the ire of the black community. The long-running appeals and retrials continued until 1938.[2] Picketing the White House for many different kinds of causes has continued to this day. Major events such as the Journey of Reconciliation by the Congress of Racial Equality in 1947 to challenge southern states' continued segregation in buses in interstate commerce and the Freedom Rides organized in 1961 echo the suffragists' use of the transcontinental trains for campaigning for the vote. The Selma to Montgomery march of 1965 echoes the women's pilgrimage from New Jersey to Washington, D.C., in early 1913 to publicize suffrage and the Great Suffrage March. The black civil rights movement, therefore, was able to take, and build on, the major elements of the campaign in which women finally claimed public space for themselves and for their own political aims as a minority group pressing against the establishment for reform.[3]

Mass Demonstrations

A further echo of the legacy of the tactics of the NWP campaign for black civil rights took place in 1963 with the March on Washington for Jobs and Freedom, at which Martin Luther King, Jr., delivered his "I have a dream" speech. This most famous of national marches owed its legitimate right to take place where it did directly to what the women had done fifty years before—specifically the Great Suffrage March of January 1913, when women demanded and commandeered through the use of Pennsylvania Avenue the nation's capital as the citizens' place of registering their wishes and bringing them to public notice. The National Mall, where King delivered his speech, was largely only a dream when Paul demanded for women the right to march where the men marched.[4] By 1963 the Mall hosted the great rallies, but Pennsylvania Avenue hosted marches then as it does today. The suffragists pioneered this. The link between marches for black civil rights in Washington and woman suffrage history is direct, even if the actors in black civil rights in 1963 were unaware of the debt they owed to women. The same is true for marches against other political grievances.

It may be a huge task to document the direct connection, but it is important to note that the NWP's public position in such methods of campaigning did not stop outright with their suffrage victory. The suffragists continued to employ the same methods, if not in Washington then elsewhere, through the 1920s, particularly with a huge event at Seneca Falls in 1923 for the launch of the ERA, which was preceded by motorcades decked in the purple, white and gold of suffragism. The same kind of pageantry occurred later the same year at the Garden of the Gods in Colorado. Even as late as 1933, the NWP continued to display full pomp and ceremony for very public activities, such as the funeral of sponsor Alva Belmont that February, and another that July at the Washington Monument to commemorate Belmont and other suffragists who had passed.[5] Although the less intense post-victory era had reduced the impact of such displays, these techniques maintained a public presence long afterwards. Indeed, protesters against the civil war in Ireland, and others demanding political amnesty early in the 1920s, mimicked what the suffragists had done outside the White House. In sum, all these examples of the continued use of the NWP's methods and the memories of the NWP campaign not only did not fade instantly with ratification, but both the original tactics and the later ones established the ideas of the whole process of civil rights campaigns for later generations as an example to follow.

Freedom of Assembly and Freedom of Speech

The failure to make the connection between the black civil rights movement and the woman suffrage movement has also led to the failure to recognize the constitutional influence of the suffragists and their public protests in Washington on civil rights activism. By their work, the women made secure for such protests the constitutional rights on which such campaigns are based: the First Amendment rights of freedom of assembly and freedom of speech. During their campaign, the suffragists found that they had to fight not only for the right to vote but also for the right to use the tactics that made the fight possible. They secured the right to use these tactics by court challenges to the administration's overreach against the citizens' right to picket the president peacefully.[6] If the women had not secured these rights, no group, even African Americans marching in and on Washington, could have done what they did without having to fight that fight. National protests against the Vietnam War would have had a very different character also.

The women won for succeeding groups, therefore—of which the black community is the most visible—key legal strengths that the groups could use to their advantage: a constitutional ban on discrimination in voting not just on account of race, but also on account of sex, and the right to freedom of assembly and freedom of speech, which made marches and rallies possible.

CHAPTER 12

Civil Rights Cross-Pollination

For their contribution to changing the voter dynamic, the national agenda and the strategy and tactics for protest for civil rights—for all these reasons—the woman suffrage campaign and victory was the pivotal battle in the struggle for civil rights in the United States. Unlike the Civil War, which was enjoined to preserve the union and ended up freeing the slaves and enfranchising black men, woman suffrage was won relatively peacefully, with injuries sustained only by women. Paul and her colleagues deserve national accolades for bringing to a conclusion the first and only successful nonviolent civil rights movement in U.S. history,[1] for its impact is still felt today any time U.S. citizens picket or march in Washington, D.C., to demand action of their government. It is important not to underestimate not only woman suffrage, but also American women's unique contribution to this area of United States political life and to incorporate this achievement in the national historical consciousness.

Suffrage women did not have an effect on the emerging black civil rights movement only by the methods outlined. They also helped by campaigning for black rights, action which, in the case of new recruits after the suffrage victory, was due to the hunt of many suffrage women for a cause as worthy as the one they had just fought for. Black women, very naturally, had mostly focused on black rights, including suffrage, all along. The powerful educator Mary McLeod Bethune, as president of the Florida chapter of the National Association of Colored Women, worked against KKK threats, registering black voters in spite of the obstacles of Florida voter laws. Ida B. Wells Barnett, the crusading journalist who launched the antilynching campaign, was founder of the National Association of Colored Women and active in suffrage from early in her work.[2] Mary Burnett Talbert from Oberlin, Ohio, crusaded against lynching and racism generally and helped establish the Niagara Movement, a precursor of the NAACP. Supporting votes for women, she addressed the Symposium of Leading Thinkers of Colored Women in Washington, D.C., in 1915 and featured in the early–1920s controversy when former suffragists attempted to focus Paul and the NWP on the rights of black women.

But if black women bridged the suffrage-race divide, white women did so as well, just as abolitionist women had done fifty years and more before. Several years before she became the main financial support of the CU/NWP, Alva Belmont worked to bring black women into the suffrage campaign in New York.[3] Elizabeth Freeman—one of the participants in the New Jersey to Washington, D.C., pilgrimage in 1913—campaigned against lynching in addition to working for suffrage. In fact, her work arose out of her suffrage campaign trip to Texas in 1916. Shocked on hearing about the horrible public lynching in Waco of a retarded black boy, seventeen-year-old Jesse Washington, just two days after the lynching she interviewed witnesses and reported on the event to publicize the horror and began to campaign against lynching forthwith.[4] As a suffragist with such a dual role, she likely encountered suffragist Florence Kelley, whose commitment to causes ranged far and wide, including involvement in the antilynching crusade. At one time a vice president of the NAWSA, Kelley was a founding member of the NAACP and one of the individuals behind the controversy in the early 1920s that erupted over the involvement of the NWP in issues relating to black women. Although not a member of the NWP, Kelley was another suffragist who formed a bridge between women's rights and the rights of the black community.[5]

Former supporters of votes for women also helped the black community by working to create opportunities equal to those that whites had, even if convention deemed they be separate. Such an individual was Adolphine Fletcher Terry in Little Rock, Arkansas. An executive council member of the NWP, Terry stood by the suffragists during the darkest days of opposition to their methods during the force-feeding of Paul, even though in Little Rock her position in a family of German background was difficult because of strong local anti–German sentiment during the war. Terry, who had known Lucy Burns at Vassar, had her eyes opened to racial discrimination in an exchange with Burns while a student, an experience that stayed with her for the rest of her life. After suffrage, Terry contributed to black equality by helping in the 1920s to create a black YWCA in the Arkansas capital.[6] All these women, each involved in her unique way in suffrage, brought to a black-rights movement, which had found new impetus because of the woman suffrage victory, the experience and knowledge of the suffrage campaign and thereby helped to enrich the black-rights movement in its coming challenges.

Not only did women work for black rights, but blacks and whites also worked after the suffrage victory against poll taxes. This reform would benefit both groups, for the additional tax on a single household for a wife to vote was prohibitive for lower income groups, so repeal was important to both races. Yet the real facts about poll taxes are not necessarily how they are perceived, which is that only blacks had to pay them. Poll taxes were just as much about controlling the electorate and even if poorer whites were only collateral damage to enactment of these laws, restricting them too conveniently meant even greater control of the electorate. The sweeping effect of poll taxes became especially important after ratification, for white women were hit disproportionately by these taxes on voting, and not just because there were generally more white women than black. White men tended to be threatened by the woman vote and the increased cost represented a useful excuse to prevent a wife from voting. Black husbands saw the female vote as a step towards racial equality, while in those states where cumulative taxes when previously unpaid were levied, they deferred to their wives' registration because, as new voters, the women had no back poll taxes to pay.

Campaigns of both women and blacks during this period were not completely successful and the poll tax was ultimately banned across the nation only by the Twenty-Fourth Amendment to the United States Constitution in 1964. The anti-poll tax movement, however, demonstrated clearly the new political dynamic, not just with a significant women's campaign in Alabama in the 1930s against the tax, but also later in the same decade when the NAACP had a fleeting period of near success. In fact, the women's campaign in Alabama, where cumulative poll tax regulations amounted to a prohibition on voting for many people, the campaign of white women achieved notoriety when it began to expand its focus to include race rights.[7] The benefit of the Twenty-Fourth Amendment for anyone other than African Americans rarely features.

These poll tax campaigns, however, which centered on winning the same reform—although for different reasons—reflected the fact that, with the vote, the two major races in the United States could already, and would, work together for civil rights. In Hot Springs in 1927, for example, three thousand black Arkansans helped to vote in a new mayor who promised them a fair deal, and "white men and women carried Negroes to the polls."[8] Other significant progress in this new era—albeit likely slower than the individuals affected might have wanted—was the election in Chicago of the first northern black congressman to the House of Representatives in 1928, while in the 1930s, a large group of African Americans became what was unofficially called Roosevelt's Black Cabinet to provide the administration with advice on race issues.

A woman, significantly—Mary McLeod Bethune—was behind this. Having already been an advisor on race relations to President Coolidge, she served as one of thirty-five African Americans Roosevelt appointed to the National Youth Administration (NYA) in 1935. She became the highest black federal government female official in 1936 as director of the NYA. In 1936, almost as close as anyone could be to the first couple, Bethune became Roosevelt's race relations advisor and that year organized the Federal Council on Negro Affairs, which held two conferences on race issues in Washington, D.C., in 1937 and 1939.[9]

In succeeding decades, black women continued to work for equality of blacks.[10] Rosa Parks, refused voter registration twice in the early 1940s, from then on was active in the cause of civil rights. She rattled the Montgomery bus codes in 1943 by entering a bus at the front instead of the back, but she shattered them in the mid–1950s by refusing to give up her seat for a white *man*, a double transgression. Parks was convicted for doing so, and the Montgomery bus boycott began, which led via the Supreme Court decision[11] to desegregation of the city's bus system.[12] In Arkansas, Daisy Bates, the wife of L.C. Bates, a black newspaper publisher in Little Rock, became active in the NAACP and ultimately spearheaded the contentious school desegregation movement which, in 1957, led to President Eisenhower's decision to send federal troops to Arkansas for the first time since Reconstruction. Bates aggressively pursued desegregation by advising and guiding the black students who had enrolled in the high school there during the standoff. It is questionable whether making those young people run the gauntlet, day after day, of the aggression they encountered was good for them, but desegregation in Little Rock, which had already been proceeding in other locales in the state, followed upon this national crisis. Bates' national profile, because of her contribution to the progress of black civil rights through this Arkansas crisis, was significant enough that she addressed the rally at the Lincoln Memorial during the March on Washington of 1963,[13] the only woman to do so.

White women also continued to contribute to black civil rights in later years after ratification of the Nineteenth Amendment. Suffragist Adolphine Fletcher Terry featured in the Little Rock desegregation crisis when she rallied other white women against Little Rock's school segregation and closure during the state's long-running standoff against the federal troops.[14] Ten years later, she drew the parallel between what suffragists had done fifty years before with the recent black civil rights movement and other contemporaneous protest movements. Speaking of the suffrage campaign on the fiftieth anniversary of Arkansas' ratification of the amendment, she said, "The Negroes ... are using the same tactics today. It's funny, but you just have to do it. 'Ladies' and 'Uncle Toms' don't get anywhere."[15]

Some white women who contributed to the cause of blacks are largely unknown. Educator Nelle Morton devoted the first part of her career to advocating for the disadvantaged she saw around her, first in Tennessee and later in New York. Her commitment extended to the racially downtrodden and she represents one example of a woman who worked against racism during later decades following the suffrage victory and helped with the emerging black rights movement. In 1945, when racial discrimination had begun to become the major issue the nation needed to deal with and racial inequalities were becoming more prominent with increasingly ominous overtones, she assumed the key role as executive secretary in the Fellowship of Southern Churchmen (FSC). Committed to creating "opportunities for people to unite on the basis of common interest rather than on the basis of race, class, religion, or nationality," Morton redirected the work of her organization, the Fellowship of Southern Churchmen. Previously it had linked together individuals concerned about race relations across the South. With Morton's reorganization, it now established local cells of people with the same concerns so that if and when difficulties arose, networks and organizations already existed to tackle them productively. During her tenure as executive secretary in the FSC, she was a key behind-the-scenes organizer and participant in the 1947 freedom ride in North Carolina. Morton's work blazed trails for later black rights activists, but the cells she organized disbanded with the expansion of civil rights organizations and the emergence of new black leaders after the Montgomery bus boycott.[16] Another of these less prominent white women was Myrna Copeland of Huntsville, Alabama, who was an active helper with food counter sit-ins, one of the few white women to march from Selma to Montgomery in 1965, and one who discussed strategy with Martin Luther King at his home during planning for the Birmingham civil rights demonstrations that started in 1963.[17]

CHAPTER 13

The Inequalities of Inequalities

The involvement of white women in the black rights movement in the 1960s led to a huge shot in the arm for women's rights, not only because some women became activists for the first time in the movement but also because of how they were treated by men within it. Martin Luther King has today an image somewhat akin to, if not greater than, that of the nineteenth-century Frederick Douglass. There was good reason, however, that Daisy Bates of Arkansas was the only woman to speak at the Lincoln Memorial rally during the March on Washington in 1963: sexism within the black civil rights movement, sexism in which King played a part. In fact, most women in black civil rights up to that time were shunted aside for the 1963 rally in spite of their protests, including the wives of the leading marchers. Although it is not clear how it came about, Bates was drafted as a speaker only at the last minute to silence the protests of the women. Neither Bates, however, nor any other woman was included in the meeting with President Kennedy at the White House after the rally, while the fact of Bates' address has been almost completely forgotten. Due to the sexism of the leaders of the black civil rights movement, black woman, therefore, encountered the fact that, below race, there existed sex discrimination.[1]

White women working for black civil rights not only encountered the racism of new black leaders determined to make their movement a black movement, but the sexism of black leaders also. The experience of sexism in the black civil rights movement has been credited along with New Left politics with the emergence of Women's Liberation in the late 1960s, which Sara Evans wrote about as an insider.[2] Apart from recording her own experiences, Evans relates how two white women activists in the Student Nonviolent Coordinating Committee (SNCC), Mary King and Casey Hayden, produced in the fall of 1965 the first discussion paper, which they called "a kind of memo," comparing their treatment as women to blacks' treatment under white domination. History seemed to be repeating itself, as women in the abolitionist movement in the 1830s and 1840s found the same problems. Just as in the 1830s and 1840s, this twentieth-century discussion and exposure of sexism blossomed. Meanwhile, the explosion of the Black Power outlook was pushing whites, including women such as King and Hayden, out of the black rights movement, at which point they often linked up with the New Left. This, for a time, was a somewhat more congenial ground for women activists. But even there, sexism reared its ugly head, and, with the realization by women that they encountered sexism everywhere, this development evolved into the national Women's Liberation Movement (WLM).

Such facts are well known but they have been for a long period ignored and have eroded the equally important fact that many women never stopped working for women's rights and that even since ratification of suffrage women had pushed and made strides for women's rights. Paul, in fact, died while still campaigning for the ERA in 1977, more than fifty years after she had launched it, while succeeding generations of women contributed in various ways towards establishing the equality of women in every decade. All of this challenges the notion that what is known as "second wave" feminism grew out of black civil rights. That fact was true in many individual cases, and it is true that the WLM emerged largely from the black rights movement and the New Left and launched women's rights as a mass movement issue in the late 1960s. It also imparted to women's issues a burst of energy similar to what Paul and Burns had brought to suffrage in 1913 and which Paul had been waiting for ever since the launch of the Equal Rights Amendment in 1923. The ERA needed the momentum to win passage in Congress and the states and the appearance of the WLM raised the prospect of ratification. The emerging limitations of the Fourteenth Amendment approach to women's equality, which itself had emerged from the black rights movement, had now projected the ERA to prominence as the most appropriate means of establishing a blanket philosophy across the nation on account of sex.

This new impetus, emerging to women's rights like nineteenth-century women abolitionists emerging to women's rights from opposition to slavery, and with influences from the New Left, also brought to the forefront analyses of women's oppression that were radical new departures for most observers. Yet this apparently new departure actually brought back old ideas with a prestigious lineage and catapulted them to modern national prominence. The new fundamental questioning represented a replay in modern times of an old stream of feminism, the one that Elizabeth Cady Stanton personified in the

1890s, but whose roots lay decades before in Frances Wright and Mary Wollstonecraft. In Stanton's later personification of feminism, she had stretched far beyond demands for legal and educational reforms for women and reached into an analysis of women's oppression that spread far, wide and deep.[3]

The WLM did the same, most women not knowing, because of the dearth of women's history at the time, that nothing they dug up was new. If it existed, Stanton and other women of the nineteenth century had already found it. Both the Stanton analysis and that of the WLM were well-grounded, but philosophy initially lacks the specificity to allow the immediate development of solid continuing practical politics. More important, this approach also represented a threat to values and outlooks which had a deep and abiding hold on the American psyche, both female and male. The WLM approach therefore produced a backlash specifically against the ERA. This indicated the fundamentally revolutionary nature of Paul's proposal even if it seemed reformist to some because it worked within the Constitution.[4] The ERA failed for many reasons, but partly because of the fears that the WLM's fundamental challenge raised for relations in society. This stream of feminism proved a double-edged sword in the sixties and seventies of the twentieth century just as it had done in the nineteenth.

When the ERA failed ratification it was consigned to political limbo. Even if women contributed to the work and success of black rights in the 1960s, today women in the United States still do not have equal rights under the Constitution. Discrimination on account of sex still does not receive the same level of scrutiny in courts of law that is accorded to race discrimination. Prohibitions on discrimination on account of sex, therefore, still have a way to go before inequalities before the law are removed, specifically in the shape of a constitutional prohibition on account of sex equal to that on account of race that Reconstruction introduced. Yet, in spite of many women, including white women, working for black rights all along, the black community tends largely to ignore the rights of women. In fact, the prioritizing of inequalities so clearly articulated by Frederick Douglass and Wendell Phillips more than 150 years ago still blatantly operates, while that philosophy of the inequality of oppressions has thoroughly infiltrated the psyche of women concerned about women's inequality. The impact of accepting this philosophy in an unexamined fashion appears every time it is stated that black women are more oppressed than white women or where the combination of inequalities—the intersection of race and sex—are said to add up to worse for black women than what white women face. These approaches may be valuable ways of looking at a complex issue, but they still represent a prioritization of the eradication

From early January 1919, to keep the pressure on a president whose interest was consumed with democracy abroad and the mechanism for permanent international peace after the end of the Great War, the NWP began 24-hour firelight vigils they called "watchfires for democracy" outside the White House, relighting them whenever the police managed to stamp them out. The accompanying banners excoriated Wilson for his hypocrisy, the one in this photograph reading, "President Wilson is deceiving the world when he appears as the prophet of democracy. President Wilson has opposed those who demand democracy for this country. He is responsible for the disfranchisement of millions of Americans. We in America know this. The world will find him out" (Library of Congress Prints and Photographs Division, Washington, D.C., Harris & Ewing Collection, 1918, Digital ID: http://www.loc.gov/pictures/item/hec2008008277/).

of inequalities, which is a fundamental contradiction in terms and objectionable in itself.

The faults inherent in prioritizing inequalities become evident from an opposite perspective. Black rights leaders rely on statistics to promote reforms, especially affirmative action. To adapt this approach to women's inequalities and view the situation objectively within the long history of the subjugation of all United States women for most of its history, the argument can be advanced that as white women have represented, and still represent, the largest oppressed group in the nation, collectively they have been more oppressed than black women. The power of such an argument emerges from historical facts. For example, the granting of suffrage to men simply because they were black and freed did represent discrimination against women deliberately excluded from the vote because of their sex. Based on the 1860 census, 875,877 freedmen 21 and over were potential voters. Including all free black males— 115,391 enumerated in 1860—the total of potential new black male voters was 991,268 with the Reconstruction amendments. Females over 21 comprised 6,371,734 whites, 131,758 free blacks and 858,674 former slaves in 1860. These women constituted 48 percent of all voting age citizens, totalling 15,324,540

In March 1918, the first appeals of the suffragists against their imprisonment for picketing peacefully were successful, establishing the legality and constitutionality of the NWP's tactics in picketing the president even during wartime. This picket against British treatment of the Irish in Ireland from April 1920 demonstrates the direct influence of the suffragists' work, not only at the White House but also at the Capitol, where Capitol police had had their work cut out to prevent the picketers getting inside (National Photo Company Collection, Library of Congress Prints and Photographs Division, Washington, D.C., Digital ID: http://www.loc.gov/ pictures/item/nps200700453/).

persons, whereas black males represented only 6.47 percent.[5] All these women represented a bloc at that time of more than seven million individuals in the nation, about eight times the number of freedmen enfranchised, with white women being the overwhelming majority. These numbers only increased over the more than 50 years after Reconstruction that winning the vote required.

To present this argument is not to support it blindly: it is to demonstrate that numbers can advance any agenda. With them, it is easy to generalize, to emphasize the experience of some individuals and to eradicate the relevance of that of others. This argument also demonstrates how a collective history can advance an agenda, allowing the application to modern individuals the experience of people long gone and even long after a complaint has been addressed as comprehensively as any law and legal system can continue to do. To present the statistics of white women to support women's history is also to point out the weaknesses of others using numbers for purposes which put the rights of women behind the rights of others. It is important to remember, however, when talking about discrimination and inequality that ultimately statistics are less important than individuals' experience. Yet statistics do present insights. Because white women are attached to the white male power structure it has been very easy to dismiss them. This is a large number of women to dismiss. As Frederick Douglass said long ago in a statement pointed at white women—for he already ignored black women in supporting "universal" suffrage—"As you very well know, woman has a thousand ways to attach herself to the governing power of the land and already exerts an honorable influence on the course of legislation...."[6] Douglass could argue whatever he wanted, but it was still not equality.

The National Women's Conference held in Houston in November 1977 demonstrated this race problem clearly. Congress's law for this conference mandated a racial balance reflecting society's makeup at that time, yet officials found such major racial underrepresentation among the 2,000 elected delegates that delegates-at-large had to be drafted to fulfill the law's requirements. At that conference in 1977, white females constituted only 64.5 percent of elected delegates, while the white female population represented 84.4 percent of women of all races.[7] Today, white females constitute 33 percent of the whole population and, without equality under the law, represent the largest minority group in the nation that is discriminated against. Black and Hispanic women are only about 7 percent and 8 percent, respectively.[8] These facts and the application of them will appeal to or enrage a reader, depending on their sympathies. The facts do, however, demonstrate that two different, equally strong arguments can arise from using the same sources differently to advance each side. To point this out is not to argue in its favor, however. It is only to show that to do so adds to the problem of the current inequalities of inequalities, or, to put it another way, the problem of prioritizing inequalities.

Another problem for the rights of women is that, while race has always been an additional factor in the oppression of certain women, race has impinged on and invaded the issue of women's rights not just repeatedly, as Anthony and Paul found out, but does so to the exclusion of white women, even today. In about six months of a year's subscription to *Ms.* magazine during 2008–09—a magazine about women's rights—not one out of six *Ms.* Foundation ads that appeared featured a white woman. Yet sexism is still rampant: in 2012, a new Web site was quickly inundated with reports of sexist incidents that mostly women, but some men, experience every day.[9] This Web site originated in the United Kingdom and spread swiftly elsewhere in the world, although not, apparently, to the United States. The prejudice reported may be largely hidden from public view, yet the Web site and ensuing book illustrate the fact that sexism consists often of factors beyond the public arena. Legislation, perhaps, cannot deal with it effectively, while political correctness can too often extend into a prohibition on free speech. The point is, however, if racism still exists, so does sexism. An extreme example is domestic violence or the subordination of women in some religious régimes today.

This situation raises questions as to whether today's analyses of inequities are well founded. If it is correct, as many an analyst argued with the rise of the WLM, that race and sex discrimination have the same root in patriarchy, with the former a manifestation of sexism, then the general apparent acceptance of the argument that racism is an evil worse than sexism is misplaced.[10] In this approach, in fact, the eradication of sexism requires the more fundamental transformation. If the patriarchal argument is correct, women's equality will be much harder and take longer to achieve than racial equality. The history of women in the United States seems to support this idea. Yet, whatever the origin of what seems to be a natural inclination of the human psyche— for some people to put others down in whatever fashion so that they themselves are elevated—with all its horrific manifestations, from domestic violence to slavery to poverty to war—at bottom, no matter what the oppression, they all cause unimaginable pain to the individuals experiencing it.

Nelle Morton, a theologian as much as an educator by profession, later in life departed from her concern for everyone else's oppression to come to an understanding of her own and that of other women. She applied her erudition to traditional theology and as such was heralded as a leader by women in that field. From the understanding she had gained through her contributions to the eradication of all manner of oppressions throughout her life and with the added appreciation of women's oppression from her own experience, she captured the problem succinctly. Within a context of individuals arguing that the oppression of women, especially in the Western world and the United States in particular, was not as bad as the oppressions of race, class and colonialism, Morton stated that the pain of sexism is the same pain as the pain of racism.[11]

Morton's statement provides an illuminating framework for examining the differences bedeviling the various women's movements. Reducing oppression of whatever nature to the common denominator of the pain it causes to individual human beings demonstrates that the prioritization of the resolution of inequalities, and the arguments over which oppression is worse or which combination of oppressions make some people worse off than others is misplaced. Morton's profound statement provides understanding and potential for mutual empathy so that antagonisms may be laid to rest. We are not, however, at that point yet: conflict over prioritizing oppression and jockeying for a higher position among them is something in which women as women usually lose.[12]

Two major streams have characterized American history, the one of women, much larger than the black one, and the one of African Americans, which has had much greater presence than that of women. They have always existed together and they have been woven together as movements against oppression from early in their histories. Women of both races, from Lucretia Mott, Frances Wright and the Grimké sisters to Maria Stewart, Harriet Tubman and Sojourner Truth, fought for abolition. Later generations of American women fought for the end of Jim Crow and for equality of African Americans in the modern nation, while women of both races have fought for the emancipation of women. Men of both races have fought for abolition and black equality, and many have also argued for the equality of women ever since William Garrison began to promote women's rights along with abolition, men such as Miles Langley of Arkansas, who tried, but failed, to have woman suffrage included in the new state constitution in 1868, and the various congressmen who originally and repeatedly introduced what later became known as the Susan B. Anthony Amendment, and those who first introduced the ERA to Congress in 1923.

Along the way, the histories usually tell it, women were given the vote in 1920 even though women's victory is a feat which should rank with the Reconstruction amendments for establishing equality under the law. It is, however, never accorded that status. Yet its import—the enfranchisement of 50 percent of the population—resonated resoundingly for African Americans at the time, and it did so not only in the political potential it represented for blacks but also in the tactics that Paul and the NWP had introduced in their campaign. It is still, therefore, important today, even if its contribution is unknown. Throughout the histories of the two inequalities the work of ending the two oppressions has been inextricably woven in an ever more complex pattern. It is within that pattern that prioritization reared its ugly head.

In sum, the perennial dilemmas of the two movements for the end of the oppressions of race and sex is that, while the one cannot be understood without the other, the histories of both are so complex that they require separate treatment to capture the narrative and create understanding. Such an approach honors the distinctiveness, the richness and the uniqueness of each history. However, the problem raised by treating the two histories separately is that it has been too easy to downgrade and ignore the distinct history of women, to lose it both as a separate entity and in the treatment of the nation's history as a whole and to relegate the women's cause to nothingness. Yet again, if the two oppressions of race and class are dealt with together under the common subject matter of civil rights, women again get lost, usually today subordinated to the unspoken assumption that race oppression is more significant. This is a problem which happens particularly in public discourse today.

CHAPTER 14

Woman Suffrage
and the Prioritization
of Inequalities

When women won the vote in 1920, they won a stunning victory with major ramifications still affecting not just women but the whole of American society today. It was stunning in spite of its limitations, which women knew well: they continued to campaign to remove them and women still work for equality a century on.

Iron Jawed Angels, the 2004 HBO movie commemorating Paul's trail-blazing campaign, aired during the 2008 election campaign and sparked this writer's interest in those events and ultimately provided the impetus during a visit to Washington, D.C., in 2010 to find suffrage sites, in particular the actual building where Paul had displayed the NWP's victory flag. The assumption was that not only would the building be marked clearly, but also that other important suffrage locations in Washington would be marked and books with the information would be easy to find. To summarize a long story, only the Sewall-Belmont House Museum was identified with the struggle for votes for women during the National Woman's Party's campaign in the nation's capital. That building became the NWP's headquarters only in 1929, but its NWP artifacts are stirring. Further afield, the new Occoquan museum in Lorton, about twenty miles to the south in Virginia, and Alice Paul's family home in Moorestown, New Jersey, were both easy to locate and very satisfying.

Multiple searches on the Web during that visit to D.C. produced only a brochure of women's history sites from the National Woman's History Museum (NWHM), a useful summary of the suffrage struggle but one lacking key details.[1] My dissatisfaction led to a month of solid research on the Web and through any available books on the history of the final campaign in D.C.

to pin down events and people to places. The month ended in another quick trip to Washington to locate and photograph the actual locations. That tour was disturbing: few of the places of this revolutionary political activism remain. What is worse, no plaques marked where the women headquartered their struggles.

This state of affairs was deeply saddening. In fact, it was shocking to discover that the most important campaign for civil rights for women—the first successful nonviolent civil rights campaign in United States history—was all but wiped out where it happened. Given the history, this should not have been so, yet such a trajectory for women's history was acted out for all to see soon after victory. Ratification disappeared rapidly from the news, except for challenges to it. During the 1920 election, stories appeared about the potential influence of women's votes and of candidates Cox and Harding meeting with the new voters in their presidential campaigns. Then it was all but gone: it was as if some collective decision emerged that, with the controversy over, women could and would just disappear.

The official handling of the start of the new era has contributed to the neglected fate of suffrage history. Few tallies were kept of separate male and female voting statistics, creating difficulties for future historians trying to assess the effect of the woman vote in the 1920 general and subsequent elections.[2] The suffrage monument tells the story clearly. The monument, with Lucretia Mott, Elizabeth Cady Stanton and Susan B. Anthony, stood for one day in February 1921 in the Rotunda Hall of the Capitol and then was quickly removed to the crypt. It was only in 1997 that it was returned—and that was after a campaign of many women's groups that the NWHM successfully spearheaded.[3] The history of the NWHM itself is a symbol of the status of women in the United States. The museum is an invaluable resource, but as yet it exists only on the Internet, while women's attempts to have Congress allocate a place in D.C. for a building have been long stalled. A further example is the lowly status of Women's History Month. It began as Women's History Week in California in 1978, but only a few celebrate it today. Few know, either, of Women's Equality Day, August 26, first promulgated in 1979. Yet women still comprise just over 50 percent of the population. In the United States, it is sad to note, recognition of women's history is seriously lacking.

The treatment of black civil rights history and its icons such as Martin Luther King presents a major contrast. King has his special day and February is Black History Month. A statue commemorating King stood in Statuary Hall for nearly a decade before the women's groups managed to have the Suffrage Monument reinstated. The National African American Museum of Black History and Culture is slated to open on the National Mall in 2015. All of this is just. Yet what remains unjust is the neglect of women and their campaigns for equality. These examples are a measure of how far women in the United States have still to travel before equality as a basic principle is an accomplished fact. Meanwhile, the work of the black civil rights movement, both in time and in tactics, was not the originator of the model for success in such modern movements: it only followed in the footsteps of the NWP.

This hierarchy of black and women's civil rights history pertains across the board, both academically and in popular culture. Almost any search on the Web for civil rights will produce countless links to African American history and very little about women, although the two have consistently had to struggle for very much the same things. This disparity should be surprising, for the two movements are not discrete entities. Yet they are generally treated as such or, if linked, women's campaigns are appended to that of black civil rights and usually are said to have emerged from the latter.

One of the most disturbing examples of what seems to be the exclusion of women from a survey of civil rights in the United States emerged with the imprimatur of public history authorities in a 2009 brochure from Cultural Tourism of Washington, D.C. The brochure, entitled *Civil War to Civil Rights: Downtown Heritage Trail*, comprises several walking tours in the United States capital, with frequent stops where civil rights events occurred.[4] Along with familiar national landmarks such as the Treasury Building and Ford's Theater, stops in this brochure include the Willard Hotel, where Martin Luther King, Jr., worked on his "I have a dream" speech in 1963. Also featured are the headquarters of the National Council of Negro Women. The brochure refers to the "lady clerks" a shorthanded administration was forced to employ at Treasury during the Civil War. Photographs of President Lincoln's wife; Harriet Beecher Stowe, author of *Uncle Tom's Cabin*; and Clara Barton, founder of the American Red Cross, also appear. All these had a role to play in the events around the Civil War which led to the abolition of slavery, but women emerging into the workforce or working for the rights of a minority group cannot necessarily be described as campaigning for women's rights per se. Such involvement is often only tangential. The stop at the boardinghouse owned by Mary Surratt, convicted as a coconspirator in Lincoln's assassination, is particularly ironic: Surratt was hanged even though no woman was equal with men under the law.

The women's actual struggle for the vote appears in the brochure, at last, with a photograph of a parade of women captioned, "A woman's suffrage march on the avenue, 1913." This is actually a photo of *the* Great Suffrage

March that Paul and Burns organized for March 3, 1913, when the final and successful campaign for the vote for women began. It fails to mention that the march ended in an anti-woman riot—the kind that blacks faced—and led to a Senate investigation. It also fails to identify it as only the first event in a grueling, nationwide campaign which ultimately would win women the vote after a period of 72 years. The brochure does not say the photograph has major import for women, blacks and the nation at large.

This Washington, D.C., civil rights brochure demonstrates the highly specialized meaning and exclusive nature that the term "civil rights" has acquired. It reflects what "universal suffrage" meant during Reconstruction: suffrage for all, not defined by race, as long as voters were male, for in mainstream civil rights histories, black women's separate struggle after the Reconstruction amendments for inclusion in the polity is rarely given its due. The development of this exclusion has had many causes, one being the tendency of the media and academe to define the term narrowly, while women themselves adopted the name "Women's Liberation" when the latest wave of women's rights burgeoned in the late 1960s. This gave women's concerns their distinct identity, while the much narrower term "civil rights" was inadequate to describe what women were pursuing.

A major practical reason for this exclusion of women from the definition of civil rights is because women as a group are generally ignored and subordinated to race struggles. Also, when the linkages between the black struggle and the woman struggle are made, the history becomes so complex that it is almost impossible to handle. A major technological reason for excluding women from civil rights, however, is the simple fact that the black civil rights movement occurred during the television age. In fact, it was made for television as much as television seemed to be made for it and it was watched right inside people's homes. It also occurred within the living memory not only of the protagonists but also of observers.

The women's struggle for the vote occurred only during the silent film era, when live images of the struggle were available largely only as newsreels seen in public places. Most recordings of the suffrage events—largely ignored by newspapers until the final years in Washington, D.C.—were in print. The writing until late in the struggle was shallow, critical and dismissive, photographs scarce. The suffrage events also took place a century ago and the protagonists are gone. Primary retellings are available only as books. Oral histories were recorded long after the fact; film, although it exists, is scarce. Second- and thirdhand memories of daughters, granddaughters, great-granddaughters, nieces and the like are helpful but inadequate sources. While the black civil rights movement still lives today in miles of footage that resonates with many viewers because they saw it when it happened, such is not the case with votes for women. The women's struggle for the vote long ago passed into the past, so much so that it is not unusual to hear women express surprise, sometimes for the fact that women were allowed to vote much later than men and sometimes because they had to struggle hard to win the vote and were tortured in the process.

Another important fact is that "liberation" goes much further than a struggle for external changes to the defining civic circumstances in which people operate within a society, such as the right to participate, to vote and to work, and the responsibilities attendant on these rights—such as to be informed, to take part in less welcome activities such as jury service, to obey the law and to accept equal—in other words, to not demand or expect preferential—treatment under the law. "Liberation" refers to much more than this. It refers to an individual—every individual ultimately—freeing the psyche of the more subtle imposed and internalized limitations on one's potential as a human being. It also means to transcend negative emotions such as anger, hatred and the tendency to dominate and pay back that so often accompany the experience of the struggle to break free from injustices and to remove the limitations a society has imposed structurally. In these two contrasting interpretations, it is possible for anyone to be *free* once those societal struggles and limitations have been removed. To be liberated, however, is a much deeper internal struggle within an individual which leads to transcending the narrow focus and behaviors of the former.

Partly because the modern black civil rights movement came later, therefore, following in time and tactics what the women did and with greater technological resources, black leaders have been more successful than women in claiming visibility for themselves and their movement's victories. As a group, however, African Americans are much more vocal and have demanded their place in the pantheon of national heroes and history—a logical goal for them and their struggles. As a group, African Americans, at less than 15 percent of the population, also benefit from comprising a very visible and discrete group with a common cause within the polity. Women, on the other hand, comprising all races, are much more amorphous: being half of all, they often seem not to belong to any group in particular and are easily lost in the whole. Many individual women also strive to deny any special identity as women, while women's issues seem not to matter for large numbers of them. Further, comprising 50 percent of the population, they are harder to unite behind a goal, while women historically have never been united on women's position in society, the vast majority of them living and working, perhaps, without deep reflection on their world. Only numerical minorities among them, of all races, have fought for the rights of women, while other numerical minorities have fought against any change. During the last campaign for the vote, the NAWSA claimed two million members.[5] At its peak the NWP had about 70,000.[6] Even combined, this is a minuscule representation of the 26,500,000 potential female voters counted in the 1920 United States census.

Apart from the one brochure on civil rights sites in D.C., the NWHM Web site information and the now-you-find-it-now-you-don't Tailored Tours brochure of women's history on the Web, no other book or pamphlet devoted to the places of the final woman suffrage campaign in the nation's capital emerged from this author's research in 2010. Not available at that time but available now on the Web is the brochure "Women Who Made History: A Guide to Women's History Sites in Washington, D.C."[7] This was published originally in 2000. There is some overlap between this brochure and the NWHM brochure, the 2000 brochure mentioning fewer sites but including a useful map of central D.C. with the locations marked. Both include the Sewall-Belmont House and place it within the context of the woman suffrage and ERA campaigns. Yet another brochure, about the Capitol Hill Historic District,[8] also mentions the Sewall-Belmont House and Museum but contains little content about woman suffrage. Since this author's original research into the NWP's specific campaign locations, the White House Historical Association has linked to the Web information about protest at President's Park, which surrounds the White House and includes Lafayette Square. The only date to appear on this document—2007—is in the text.[9] Only one section deals with woman suffrage. Unsatisfying in itself, the treatment also fails to identify the Lafayette Square campaign with the NWP, or even with the correct dates. It also fails to appreciate the groundbreaking significance of the NWP campaign.

Yet the real history clearly reveals that the NWP virtually owned Lafayette Square from January 1917 until February 1919, when the last D.C. suffrage demonstration occurred there. They owned it not only because of the picketing, but also because crowds hung around to see what might happen to the occupants, and mobs gathered or may have been rented to ensure that arrests would occur. Visitors to the nation's capital at that time would go out of their way to witness these events: the NWP campaign turned Lafayette Square into a tourist destination at a time when a major episode in American history was playing out. Equally significant, from the arrival of Paul and Burns in D.C. before the Great Suffrage March of March 1913—the one designated as "a" suffrage parade in the *D.C. Walking Tour* brochure—there began a period that lasted until ratification in 1920, when Washington was the center of so much activity that the women placed it on the map in an unprecedented way. They transformed the "tomb" into the stage for a monumental national struggle. There, a group of young women arrived in late 1912 and until 1920 stared down the president of the United States in order to force a successful conclusion to the campaign for votes for women, which had been ongoing since 1848. It is a remarkable story of determination, brilliant local and national strategic planning, innovative tactics without end, wins and losses, the president riding roughshod over citizens' rights, official hardheadedness and brutality, physical hardship and the political use by the women of nonviolence in order to win what remains today a stunning victory. The victory was so unquestionable that some people in the twenty-first century are unaware that such a struggle took place: witness the male librarian who said emphatically to this author that American women have had the same history as American men and the female librarian who said she had thought that American women had always had the right to vote.

In failing to recognize this fundamental fact, all these existing brochures are seriously lacking in historical accuracy. In particular, they fail to accord to civil rights for women the kind of almost exclusive focus that the Washington, D.C., brochure on civil rights devotes to African American civil rights.

The reason for this failure emerges from the study of civil rights history sites that the National Park Service Historic Landmarks Program produced in 2000 and revised in 2008.[10] While not devoted exclusively to Washington, D.C., it gives insight into the contrast between the treatments of the two subjects. *Civil Rights in America: A Framework for Identifying Significant Sites* is probably the clearest and most comprehensive overview of the recognition of civil rights in the United States. For the purposes of women's history research, it is valuable because it includes women as distinct from "minorities" worthy of historical landmarks. It notes "the civil rights struggle for women is a window on changing definitions of citizenship.... The clearest narratives are found in the campaign for the right to vote and the subsequent debates over the Equal Rights Amendment."

This study has serious shortcomings, however, because it also makes the cause of women's civil rights face multiple ways at one time. It states that the civil rights struggle for women "has been shaped by gender, race, and class.... Because women constitute half of every racial, ethnic, religious, or regional group, their story is difficult to tell in isolation.... It is important to tell this story in a way that renders visible the full diversity of the participants and links the women's civil rights struggles to those of other groups and to clarify the different perspectives and priorities that profoundly affect the implicit meanings of that ambiguous word 'equality.'" This is one way of looking at women's history, even women's suffrage history specifically. But the statement is shot through with assumptions that beg to be challenged. One fact it does not take into account is that women as a group in the United States constituted less than 50 percent of, and were truly in a minority in, the nation's population until the 1950 census. All women combined, that is to say, in spite of their size as a group, were in a numerical minority, not a minority with its acquired, modern, meaning of race and ethnicity. At some time in the 1940s, the balance tipped from men to women, but men, from the founding until 1950, were in the majority. The struggles of women as women—and their achievements, such as the Nineteenth Amendment—become more significant in light of this fact.[11]

This study's statement also, in spite of identifying women as a group that was historically discriminated against, nevertheless goes on to emphasize that their struggles and achievements should be linked to other groups defined by race and class. This is the perfect formula for confusion. Worse, it enables the subordination to others of the struggles that women had to fight as a separate group and the victories that they won. It also means the loss of women's distinctive history, for when they are included within groups not primarily focused on civil rights for women, men and other issues such as race or class invariably take over, producing inaccuracy by essentially downgrading women's history. Such problems emerge clearly within this study. Whereas in the introduction the authors cite women separately in the pantheon of civil rights issues, they later have a difficult time not slipping into the modern, exclusionary, meaning of civil rights to determine historical time frames and topics. The assumption is that the movements for civil rights of women should be tempered by every "minority" movement: it is never analyzed with the movements for civil rights for racial and ethnic minority groups subsumed in the history of American women.

To deliberately link women's history with all other groups is a hard balancing act and the practical results are clear: "Of the National Historic Landmarks identified ... thirty-three are associated with African Americans, sixteen with American Indians, fifteen with women, six with Asian Americans, one with Hispanics, and one with the gay and lesbian movement. National Park Service units and National Historic Trails that interpret civil rights include nine associated with African Americans, three with American Indians, two with women, and two with Asian Americans." By one perspective, these results are laudable. By another, it is a cause for concern, for by comparing these numbers with current United States population statistics, African Americans, who comprise less than 15 percent of the population, are overrepresented by a huge margin, while women, who represent today slightly over 50 percent of the total population, are significantly underrepresented. Another cause for concern is that this determined pursuit of rendering diversity visible—to adapt the words of the report—has rendered white women invisible in comparison with the scope of the work they did. Because of the obvious bent of the landmarks program, it is unclear from the statistics, for example, who or what exactly is being represented with those associated with women. Is it women's civil rights or is it the struggles of race or class? Is there double counting going on? These are important questions. The inclusion of a leading woman from a racial minority, for example, is historically truthful and important. However, if it is done at the exclusion of an equally important white woman or as a convenient way of achieving two results in one it is less than historically accurate. It also simultaneously discriminates against white women who, numerically, were in the vanguard of the campaigns for civil rights for women.

Class consciousness and bias is also clearly evident in the writing of the National Park study: "Although educated, predominately white, and mostly middle-class women led the various movements, success depended on coalitions and alliances with working class and minority women."[12] Once again, this statement is historically correct and important as far as the description of the participants is concerned. Identifying all strata of leaders and participants is important for uncovering the history of previously forgotten women and for the goal of historical accuracy. The statement, however, is shot through with prejudice against the "predominantly white and mostly middle-class women who led the various movements." Some of this cast is understandable in the light of the recognition such women tended to receive automatically because of their wealth and station in life, for women of lower social position and economic status are more likely, and more easily, lost to history. However, it is important to temper this class-conscious approach to the history of women, because it was the very wealth and station of these "predominantly white and mostly middle-class women" which provided the greatest shock value to the various women's movements, not just during the last decade of the campaign for suffrage. It emerged clearly again during Women's Liberation, when women's complaints about inequality were often dismissed as unreasonable middle-class female bellyaching. The reason it is important, in terms of women's history, to avoid this class prejudice is precisely because wealth and economic status are constantly used as weapons *against* women when women fight for their civil rights. Elizabeth Cady Stanton pegged it concisely:

The coarser forms of slavery all can see and deplore, but the subjection of the spirit, few either comprehend or appreciate. In our day women carrying heavy burdens on their shoulders while men walk by their side smoking their pipes, or women harnessed to plows and carts with cows and dogs while men drive, are sights which need no eloquent appeals to move American men to pity and indignation. But the subtle humiliations of women possessed of wealth, education, and genius, men on the same plane cannot see or feel, and yet can any misery be more real than invidious distinctions on the ground of sex in the laws and constitution, in the political, religious, and moral position of those who in nature stand the peers of each other?[13]

While it can be argued, therefore, that it is important to elevate the contribution of working-class women at the expense of that of wealthy women—for this is the unfortunate result of this overt class-consciousness approach—it can equally be argued, for several reasons, that wealthy and socially prominent women were the key to the evolving women's struggle. The details of discrimination may have been different, but women were unequal whether they were poor or rich; and wealthy women led the struggle for women's rights, not just in the historical time line but also in resources, including time and money. Their wealth also stripped away all other arguments for discrimination against women and laid bare clearly that discrimination against women—their exclusion from the polity, general legal discrimination and restricted earning potential—was on account of sex, pure and simple. At some level, such discrimination has been economic, excluding women from jobs because of fear of wage dilution, for example; but with prominent women's wealth and social position, it was the reverse. It was less because they had no wealth that they experienced discrimination; it was more because they did. As many tales in the nineteenth century of women who started out wealthy reveal, a wealthy woman losing her identity, fortune and earnings within marriage was in a worse legal position than a woman with nothing on entering marriage. In a society in which wealth defined all, the former had much to lose and a lot to fight for. Poor women's struggle, if it was an economic one, was more about not having anything ever.

In fact, it can be argued that by some measures, it was a greater injustice for upper-class women to be excluded from the vote than it was for poor women. Likely better educated, owning wealth and paying high taxes, such women could compare themselves with men. The comparison was often unfavorable, for they saw men who often had no money or education, who often could not speak English and who were not even native-born, with political power over them. An individual's ideology will color a reader's understanding here. Upper-class women today, however, are excoriated for being privileged.

They have been excoriated, in fact, for not being poor, as if being poor is the only injustice in the world. Conflation of distinct but related issues such as wealth and class has led to this distortion. But the perspective of wealthy women is understandable if their own, instead of a lower class-conscious perspective, is adopted in understanding them. In this way of looking at things, poor women had a lot less, if nothing at all, to fight for—and with. A poor background or a world of scrabbling for existence took all energies and time, and from abject economic circumstances it is easy to identify the problem not as one of sex discrimination but as one of economics and poverty. No airs and graces were expected of them, although they were still confined by their sex. Women wealthy or of comfortable means had to break down artificial boundaries that only their class had to face. The Declaration of Sentiments of Seneca Falls of 1848 covered all women. However, no matter what the original intentions of those women might have been in the struggle for reforms, including the vote, no matter how narrowly they might have considered interpreting the reach of the reforms they worked for, the results have flowed far beyond the wealthy. Many others have benefited from the reforms that wealthy women have won, including having the right to vote. This additional perspective needs to be considered when remembering the struggle for civil rights in the United States. Again, a reader's preferences will determine whether to examine the idea dispassionately or not.

In sum, the National Park Service Historic Landmarks Program's *Civil Rights in America: A Framework for Identifying Significant Sites* is important for what it reveals of historic sites and the place of women within them, but it is flawed for its treatment of women in that context. And, while its contents are insightful, in terms of the significant suffrage sites of the NWP campaign in Washington, D.C., its importance is negligible. In fact, the list it includes of potential civil rights sites for recognition at the time of its revision in 2008 bear such a strong resemblance to the contents of the Washington, D.C., civil rights walking tours brochure that it is hard to avoid the conclusion that the National Park brochure is the precursor to the brochure that all but ignores women's struggle for the vote. In other words, the problems implicit in the rush for diversity to which the cause of women is subordinated has clearly and unavoidably resulted in ignoring, if not downgrading, the true and significant value of the woman suffrage campaign in the nation's capital.

The statistics, terminology and overall approach in the brochure demonstrate one fact clearly. The profoundly different characterization of the two main civil rights movements and their consequent position in the hierarchy has led to the distortion of history. It is normal in the twenty-first century to talk of civil rights and to automatically exclude or subordinate a huge part of the struggle. It is this outlook that led to the historically untruthful caption attached to the photograph of the 1913 march in Washington, D.C., in the D.C. *From Civil War to Civil Rights* brochure and to the almost complete exclusion of women from a brochure that should by rights have acknowledged their struggle and its central contribution to the whole. This situation has also failed to acknowledge not only the key role that women have played in the expansion of civil rights and democracy in the United States but also their leading role in this matter. The most innovative leaders, who laid the groundwork for the rest of the twentieth century and beyond, were Alice Paul, Lucy Burns, Mabel Vernon, Doris Stevens and the countless other members of the NWP fighting against what evolved into a dictatorial Democratic administration during the First World War. All the men—of whatever color or class—who challenged that administration at that time for their own reasons or challenged industry in the pursuit of better conditions and pay—all had a *right* to participate in their own governance under the United States Constitution. They had that right by inbuilt assumptions at the time of the founding, through the expansion of that right, or through the Fourteenth and Fifteenth amendments. Whether that right was enforced or not at state level or through Supreme Court decisions or by federal law is another matter entirely. At that same time, while many women had equal or limited voting rights due to hardwon victories at the state level, none of those who campaigned anywhere, picketed, went to prison, went on hunger strike or were forcibly fed had any right under the United States Constitution to their own governance. For this fact alone, the history itself and the public recognition of that history need correcting as the centenary of the women's struggle progresses and the centenary of its victory approaches.

Equally important is the need to correct the perception about the history of nonviolence in the pursuit of civil rights in the United States and to place it where it belongs, with the women of the suffrage movement and specifically with the women of the NWP. As the victors in the first nonviolent civil rights campaign in the nation's history, Alice Paul's statue should long ago have been commissioned and placed in the National Statuary Hall of Congress, while major thoroughfares in cities should have already commemorated Alice Paul, or at least individual state suffragists, as this seems to be the standard procedure for commemorating civil rights leaders. Plaques or markers placed in key Washington, D.C., locations would also be appropriate. Such belated recognition of the women's first in the nation would be a laudable goal for the centenary of women's victory in the struggle for the right to vote.

Marking the trail is an important goal. History is about place. For women in the United States, it is about many places largely forgotten and mostly gone. Even a plaque in an isolated location can resonate with a casual reader, helping some find out more about who did what where, when and why. Historic markers can spark an interest for some and lead to a search for greater knowledge. Commemorative plaques would definitely help to repair the forgetfulness or ignorance of past generations and also ensure that future generations will not continue to remain ignorant. To know where to put such markers, however, requires the facts, and for that, it is time to set out on a woman suffrage—a women's civil rights—tour of Washington, D.C.

CHAPTER 15

Neglected Civil Rights Sites
in Washington, D.C.

To stand in Lafayette Square in Washington, D.C., today is to stand at the epicenter of a revolution in American politics. With the White House—the home of the president of the United States and the locus of every United States administration's power—just across the street, the stage is set for understanding the most important civil rights struggle in United States history. That struggle was of 50 percent of the population—women—for the vote, which would finally win them the right to consent to their own governance. Begun in 1848, the endgame of this struggle for entry to the polity took place here a century ago.

At that time, President Wilson was in power. In this square, a small group of determined women gathered to zero in on the man who had staked a claim for the centrality of the presidency in the United States Constitution. Here those women focused their energies with the intention of holding him to that claim. Through holding Wilson to his own words that the president was a channel of the people's wishes, they intended to have him use his influence and power to win Congress around to pass an amendment to the Constitution that would finally remove blatant and explicit sex discrimination in all voting laws across the nation. The successful result of their struggle was the largest enfranchisement in the history of the United States, that of 26,500,000 women. With the fundamental law of the land behind women, the doors were open to their right to vote in any election in the land.

Yet nobody, if just strolling through, or even taking in, the White House on a visit to the capital, could know the role that Lafayette Square played in United States history, for there is nothing to be found to commemorate this historic revolution found in the nation's past. Yet, within easy view of the

Continuing in the path of the suffragists, this political amnesty picket at the White House on December 1, 1922, picked up on the precedent that the suffragists had set, even to the direct address to the president on her banner (National Photo Company Collection, Library of Congress Prints and Photographs Division, Washington, D.C., Digital ID: http://www.loc.gov/pictures/item/2001706320/). The tactics that women had introduced to win civil rights for all women were soon used by black groups for civil rights for oppressed African Americans. A photograph of a group protesting the trial and imprisonment of the Scottsboro Boys, six young men arrested in northern Alabama and sentenced to death for the purported rape of two white women is available at http://www.whitehousehistory.org/presentations/the-half-had-not-been-told-me/white-house.html (accessed May 19, 2014).

White House the National Woman's Party led the struggle from this square. It was here that members of that party were the first to use picketing the president as a brand-new tool of American political activism. It was here that they fought to protect citizens' rights of freedom of assembly, freedom of speech and freedom to petition. It was here that they orchestrated a groundbreaking political lobbying campaign. It was here that they exposed the president's hypocrisy by using his own words. It was here that they stood or marched in all types of weather in the face of national opprobrium and direct physical attacks in order to prevail against a wartime president in their cause of freedom and justice for women. It was here they were arrested and taken to court, refused to recognize *man*-made justice, went to prison, introduced hunger strikes, were tortured—and finally won. And it was here that they met to honor their heroes and to celebrate their ultimate victory. All these tactics of political activism are still in use today in the United States. Some are, admittedly, transformed sometimes through the constant ebb and flow of power between the people and the people in power and sometimes by the evolution of Washington, D.C., itself as over time it has grown and changed and sometimes by the adoption of differing philosophies. But it was here in Lafayette Square that women established the model for American political activism of the twentieth century and beyond. To cap it all, they did so peacefully, bringing about the first successful nonviolent civil rights victory in the history of the United States.

A spot in Lafayette Square facing the White House reveals the stage of some of the most contentious suffrage battles of a century ago. The White House itself was the scene of countless delegations from the NWP and the NAWSA to President Wilson in their attempt to bring him to the side of suffrage. The sidewalk in front of those famous gates is where, with Alice Paul's leadership, the National Woman's Party broke new ground with political activism, first picketing for suffrage and then standing their ground against a president who, when the United States declared war on Germany, had become primarily commander-in-chief. The women continued their protests for months. Crowds vilified and physically attacked them and police arrested them here although they stood in protest peacefully with banners held high, that in itself an innovation in this context. This is also where they lit fires for their twenty-four-hour vigils. In exactly the same spot but facing the square, however, is revealed the rest of the stage of this national revolution: four more locations where momentous women's history occurred.

To the right, at number 21 Madison Place, is the Benjamin Ogle Tayloe House, in the teens of the twentieth century known as Cameron House. This became the headquarters of the National Woman's Party in November 1915 and the women remained there until late in 1917. A plaque relates that Tayloe built the house in 1830 and it became quite a "social center" during his time; that Garret A. Hobart, James D. Cameron and Marcus A. Hanna also lived there; and that it became known as the "Little White House" when President McKinley frequently visited Mr. Hanna there. There is nothing, however, telling of Cameron House's more important, more recent role in the advance of American democracy, when the National Woman's Party occupied it and decided on the first-ever picketing of the chief executive of the United States after yet another dismissive meeting with him about suffrage for the fourth year in a row. The picketing began on January 10, 1917, for finally the women had experienced enough of Wilson's political slipperiness: the immoveable object that was Wilson had finally encountered the irresistible force that was the NWP.

That morning, the first picket of twelve women, complete with banners calling for liberty and the vote and with pennants with the NWP's colors of gold, white and purple held high, emerged and walked down the sidewalk and across the road to place themselves at the gates of the White House in what turned out to be a long-drawn-out phase of the struggle in which women upped the ante several times. They were accused of not being womanly, even though they stood peacefully holding their delicate, hand-sewn silk messages aloft—silent sentinels to the continued unequal treatment of the whole of their sex across the nation and the refusal of the self-avowed leader of public opinion to influence reform of this glaring inequity. This act took a deter-mined act of courage by the participants. By it, the women claimed their place in public and, therefore, in the public sphere. Well educated and usually from the middle class and above, the appearance of women of such stature had an intrinsic shock value, for women of class were not supposed to act in such a manner. Yet, even though they were stonewalled, they had the courage to cross very deliberately the invisible line that had previously held them back and intentionally out of the limelight. They stood their ground continuously from that point on.

It was from Cameron House that several hundred women walked to picket, many of them to be imprisoned, others to go on hunger strike and several, including Alice Paul herself, to be forcibly fed. With women having so emphat-ically invaded the public sphere under the leadership of Paul and the intractable determination of the NWP, it was only a matter of time when they would finally, if painfully, extract suffrage from an unwilling but ultimately resigned Congress and thirty-six states. The women trod this east side of the square between Cameron House and the White House countless times from 1915 until late in 1917 when the all-male Cosmos Club beside them, tired of the troublesome women on their doorstep, bought their building, forcing them out. The Cosmos Club then at least devoted a section of the house to women.

Also on Madison Place, from 1895 until 1965, stood the Belasco Theater, in the location of today's United States Court of Claims Building on the corner directly opposite the White House grounds. The NWP held public meetings here, especially important ones being held in May 1914 during the two succeeding weekends of great demonstrations across the nation of all suffrage workers that concluded in D.C. on May 9. Another momentous meeting took place after the authorities released the suffragists from prison en masse in November 1917. The meeting was held here to honor with a public rally the courage of the former prisoners, to further promote the cause and to emphasize the administration's high-handedness. It was on this occasion that the NWP presented the suffragist prisoners with their commemorative pins in the shape of a "grated door."

Close by, on the southeast corner of the square, stands the monument to the Revolutionary War hero Lafayette. It was at this monument, and sometimes on it, that the NWP chose to highlight yet again the president's dissembling. After his half-hearted yet influential endorsement of the suffrage amendment before the first successful vote in the House of Representatives in January 1918, his only subsequent action was a grand silence while success in the Senate remained blocked. In August 1918, therefore, the women once again poured out of their headquarters, assembled at the statue of Lafayette and began to speak Wilson's words. Yet the police stopped them. Forty-eight were charged with holding a meeting on public grounds or climbing on the statue. Twenty-six received jail terms.

Here also, that September, the NWP again upped the ante when members congregated to read and then burn Wilson's own words about democracy, which had resounded as stirring rhetoric during the jingoism of a nation at war in the name of freedom and democracy. They sounded empty, meaningless and worthless, however, to the women of America, who continued to encounter the president's intransigence and the increasingly hard line of his administration.

These fires that first burned Wilson's empty words evolved into the Watchfires for Freedom, which the NWP instituted on January 1, 1919, at the White House gates in a special urn. Originally lighting the fire with wood from a tree from Independence Square, Philadelphia, and placed directly in line with the White House front door, the NWP introduced these Watchfires to maintain the suffrage campaign in the public eye as, increasingly, Americans refocused their lives on postwar disruption and opportunities which relegated suffrage to the level of the trivial and the forgotten yet again. The NWP also continued to burn the president's words in these fires. Changing watches of suffragists all day kept the fires burning in spite of repeated attempts to extinguish them, while from the NWP headquarters a bell rang at each change and those times when Wilson's words went up in flames.

The irony of the women's campaign compared with contemporaneous foreign affairs was not lost on participants and observers. January 13, 1919, was the day the peace conference convened with the president's participation at Versailles to decide on the democratic administration of post–World War I Europe. Yet that day, twenty-three American women were arrested outside the White House for their continuing demand for democracy for themselves at home. It was during this latest stage of the campaign that the women inflamed not only anti-suffragists but many of their supporters when they burned a black-and-white drawing of Wilson, an event reported as "burning in effigy," described as "a huge doll stuffed with straw and slightly over two feet in height" and blown out of proportion by a hysterical media.[1]

From this same spot on Lafayette Square it is also worth contemplating two other locations connected with the last suffrage campaign, although neither is visible from the square. The climax of women's 72-year struggle for the vote—fifty-two of these for a federal amendment to remove sex discrimination in voting—took place at 8:00 a.m. on August 26, 1920, at 1507 K Street Northwest, the home of President Wilson's secretary of state. Bainbridge Colby signed the proclamation of the Nineteenth Amendment there "without ceremony of any kind," while "the issuance of the proclamation was unaccompanied by the taking of movies or other pictures, despite the fact that the National Woman's Party ... had been anxious to be represented by a delegation of women and to have the historic event filmed for public display and permanent record."[2] The failure to record the event was a huge loss to suffrage history. This treatment contrasts starkly with the great fanfare when President Johnson signed the Civil Rights Act in 1964. Then, black leaders surrounded the president while TV beamed the event across the nation. American history has a movie record of that momentous occasion[3] to play again and again. Women have none.

Still further afield in this general area was located the second headquarters of the National American Woman Suffrage Association in D.C. from late 1916 at 1626 Rhode Island Avenue NW. The building, formerly the French embassy, was a gilded-age mansion suitable not only for the official daily business of a political campaign but also for housing suffragists visiting the city and for large meetings and formal entertainments. Jeannette Rankin, the first woman elected to Congress in 1916, for Montana, spoke from the balcony here in 1917. The building—reminiscent of the status of, but far more opulent than, Cameron House—signified also the startling evolution in the public visibility and the importance nationally of woman suffrage since Alice Paul and Lucy Burns had entered the scene in late 1912. Such a high-class headquarters also demonstrated the pressure that the NAWSA felt from the NWP's emergence as the pacesetters for all aspects of the campaign, for the latter's move into Cameron House at the end of 1915 gave them headquarters that reflected their national leadership. At a distance of more than a mile from the NWP location, the new NAWSA headquarters in D.C., clearly set the two organizations apart, while the distinct distance from the president and Congress also pointed to the differences between the tactics of the National and the NWP, the former still espousing a much more restrained and conventionally ladylike approach to winning the vote. Out of sight of the White House—and more easily and likely out of mind—the new headquarters of the NAWSA was located straight up 16th Street from the White House to Scott Circle and left onto Rhode Island Avenue, about three miles from the other key center of activity for suffrage work, the United States Capitol.

Jackson Place on the west side of the square now becomes the center of attention. It was here at number 14 that the NWP opened its third headquarters in February 1918 in an even more historic house in Washington, D.C. Since they had lost Cameron House, they had operated out of temporary and inadequate offices on Connecticut Avenue three blocks from Lafayette Square. It "is one significant block nearer the Executive Offices," wrote the *Suffragist* almost exultantly, emphasizing its tactic of targeting the president.[4] It was from here that the NWP continued its campaign, focusing on the Lafayette monument, burning the president's words, and maintaining the freedom fires. It was on the balcony above the main entrance they rang the changes of the various activities associated with the Watchfires. This is where Alice Paul directed the campaign for the final victorious votes in Congress and later the campaigns for the thirty-six state ratifications. Specifically, it was onto the balcony above the columned entrance that on August 20, 1920, Alice Paul emerged to drape over the balustrade the Victory Flag to the cheers of the party's victorious members below. The flag, in the NWP's colors of gold, white and purple, was spangled with thirty-six stars representing the ratified states.[5]

The Jackson Place headquarters had become a center for women supporting the cause, where they could stay while in D.C. or meet in the welcoming tearoom, the Grated Door. This pointed and irreverent reference to Wilson's repeated imprisonment of the suffragists would not have been lost on congressmen or newspaper reporters who would often drop in on the hunt for a story.[6] This headquarters remained the hub of the group's activity until the NWP moved to its fourth location in 1922. Fourteen Jackson Place stood approximately where number 722 stands today. As for the whole of Lafayette Square, its sidewalks, the White House, the Lafayette monument, Cameron House and the locations of the Belasco Theatre and 14 Jackson Place were such key places of suffrage activity that, for those aware of the history, it still vibrates with the imprint of that relentless and victorious campaign of a century ago.

The nonstop Lafayette Square activity from 1915 had intensified and ultimately concluded the women's campaign to refocus the Constitution towards the president in the cause of woman suffrage. That campaign had begun on January 2, 1913, with the opening by Alice Paul and Lucy Burns of their first headquarters in Washington, D.C. Even at that early point they had zeroed in as closely as they could to the White House, and that first headquarters of what later became the NWP is just a short walk away around the Treasury Building to F Street where the Willard Office Building now stands beside the Willard Hotel. The original office of the Congressional Committee of the NAWSA, which Paul started with Burns when they first began their campaign, was located in the basement of the Kellogg Office Building at 1420 F Street. Soon, the group had expanded into the upper floors, while by November 1913, editorial offices for the new publication *Suffragist* had also been established in 1416 F Street.[7] This first headquarters was demolished in 1917. Meanwhile, very quickly—although only during the planning of the Great Suffrage March of March 1913—the National Association Opposed to Woman Suffrage opened an office just over a block away on the opposite side of the road at 1307 F Street. The NWP remained at the F Street location until November 1915, when they moved to Cameron House.

All around this area are further key locations of the women's final struggle for the vote. The Willard Hotel, then known as the New Willard Hotel, was the scene of much suffrage activity, for the women often met and socialized here, likely taking advantage of the separate women's entrance on F Street. The precursor to the NWP, the Congressional Union, held a great fund-raising ball there in April 1914.[8] The next year, the Willard hosted the forty-seventh annual convention of the NAWSA from December 14 to 19, with 546 accredited delegates attending, the largest number on record. The convention occupied the whole tenth floor and the ballroom of the hotel for its activities.[9]

These events occurred nearly fifty years before Martin Luther King refined his "I have a dream" speech in the Willard.

A quick walk along F Street and a turn left on 15th Street leads to the steps nearby of the Treasury Building, where Alice Paul staged the pageant of women's history and achievements during the Great Suffrage March. Beyond the far side of the White House on 17th Street NW is located the Continental Hall of the Daughters of the American Revolution, at that time recently built, where, after the Great Suffrage March riot, the suffragists, having intended simply to hold a rally, conducted a fiery protest meeting of enraged participants. Also on the far side of the White House, at 1925 F Street, is the former home of Representative William Kent of California and his wife, Elizabeth. Mrs. Kent had effectively been the NAWSA's Congressional Committee until Paul and Burns took it over. A year later, Mrs. Kent hosted in her home the Congressional Union's first meeting as an organization completely separate from the NAWSA. This was where Paul laid out her plans for the nationwide suffrage demonstrations for May 2, 1914, and the D.C. demonstration for May 9 and also launched her revolutionary "party in power" campaign. Mrs. Kent hosted NWP meetings repeatedly during the next ten years, continuing her support into the era of the Equal Rights Amendment. Built in 1849, the house is today the official residence of the president of George Washington University. For many years, from 1933 on, it housed the prestigious 1925 F Street Club and is also known as the Steedman-Ray House or the Alexander Ray House.[10]

The Great Suffrage March of 1913 followed Pennsylvania Avenue from the Capitol, turned beside the Treasury Building up 15th Street, passed the White House at 1600 Pennsylvania Avenue and ended up at Continental Hall. The history of the first great march for a political cause held in the nation's capital, organized by women in the cause of woman suffrage haunts all the streets around here. To walk from the White House to the Capitol is to follow the route in reverse: yet many times during the eight years after that first great march, suffragists of the NWP, not only those based in D.C. but countless numbers of them converging from around the nation, would march in both directions for suffrage, leading delegations to Congress, delivering petitions and meeting with fellow campaigners. Along the route to the Capitol after early 1914 these delegations would pass by the NAWSA's headquarters, which was located in the former Munsey Building at 1329 E. Street NW, a street now lost in Freedom Plaza, today commemorating Martin Luther King, Jr. The office in the Munsey Building was the 's first national headquarters in the capital as the older organization scrambled on the tail of Alice Paul's strategy to adjust to the rapidly evolving suffrage landscape.

Further southeast along Pennsylvania Avenue and to its north lies the judicial district of Washington, D.C., where more suffrage activity took place. Much action occurred at the District Police Court at 6th and D streets NW, where the first picketers were tried. Here they were sentenced to jail for exercising their constitutional rights of peaceful assembly and free speech. The penalties imposed led to the night of terror at Occoquan, to other imaginative tortures by authorities of the campaigning women, to hunger strikes, forcible feeding, and to the women's victory and vindication when they were freed en masse in November 1917. The trials and sentencing that took place in 1918 of the women who burnt the president's words, an act that led to their imprisonment in the disused workhouse—specially prepared to take them pending the outcome of their deliberately delayed trials—occurred in the federal police court. Appeals against the sentencing of the women occurred in the courts in this area.[11]

More roads to the northeast further along Pennsylvania Avenue en route to the United States Capitol lead to Union Station, which opened in 1907 during consolidation of rail stations in the nation's capital. Union Station became a focus of suffrage activity when the women began fanning out across the country in 1914 for the first boycott of the party in power during the midterm elections that year. Two years later, the repeat country-wide 1916 boycott campaign started off once more from here that April 9, with a stunning rendition of Paul's publicity skills. On this occasion, large crowds of women cheered the arrival of cars bedecked with flowers and purple, white and gold banners and packed with suffragists including Lucy Burns and Inez Milholland, ready to start out to spread the word. A band struck up the "Marseillaise," while a huge chorus followed with renditions of "Onward Christian Soldiers" and "America." A bugle fanfare then accompanied the suffragists' march towards the train, and soon the Suffrage Special—a complete chartered train with ten carriages, two drawing rooms and business offices—pulled out of the station for a six-week tour to carry the message of votes for women across the country.[12]

Past those streets leading to the courts and to Union Station and in front of the Capitol, the Great Suffrage March assembled at the Peace Monument, with Inez Milholland on a white horse at its head. It was around here that the Suffrage Pilgrims—the group of women who started in February 1913 to walk from New Jersey to D.C. in the freezing cold to take part in the parade, having entered the capital on Maryland Avenue—met with pilgrims who had arrived earlier and were joined by Alice Paul. An impromptu parade along Pennsylvania Avenue to the CU office followed. This spontaneous event attracted spectators who, mysteriously appearing out of nowhere, crowded the pilgrims and suffrage headquarters. Alerted to potential trouble on the day of the official parade, Paul began asking for protection from the D.C. police force, a request that was ignored, with scandalous consequences.[13]

The United States Capitol was the location of constant suffrage activity. It was the destination of countless parades, both from within Washington and from across the country. It was the focus of intense and innovative lobbying and of picketing. Suffrage activity there led to suffragist arrests. Suffrage work also led to the presentation of petitions, to House and Senate committee meetings, to the introduction of resolutions on votes for women, to congressional votes taken and congressional votes lost, to Wilson's appearance before the Senate on September 30, 1918, to finally making a—failed—plea for a yes vote on woman suffrage as a war measure. The United States Capitol was also where Congress received Wilson's final, grudging telegram from France, urging a yes vote. It was here also in May and June 1919 that finally Congress fell into line—and here that the votes for the Susan B. Anthony resolution were tallied and won.

But the United States Capitol was the occasion of much more than official and direct political action. Besides the parades, petitions and arrests, it was here, during Wilson's post-reelection speech to Congress in December 1916, that one group of five women led by Mabel Vernon, supported by another group of five led by Lucy Burns, upended all protocol. Having established their positions early, when the president spoke of extending suffrage to the territory of Puerto Rico even as he still refused to acknowledge votes for women, the women audaciously unfurled over the balustrade of the visitor's balcony a banner demanding, "Mr. President, What Will You Do For Woman Suffrage?"[14] It was also here on Christmas Day 1916 that the NWP decked out the Statuary Hall with suffrage colors for what Alice Paul said, to her knowledge, was the first time "the Capitol has ever been given for a memorial meeting for anyone who is not a member of Congress."[15] The colorful and moving memorial service was for Inez Milholland, who had died while on the campaign trail that November 25. It was also in the United States Capitol that the Woman Suffrage Monument depicting Lucretia Mott, Elizabeth Cady Stanton and Susan B. Anthony was presented to the nation in February 1921—deliberately in an unfinished state to refer symbolically to the unfinished story of women's emancipation in the United States and to other past and future participants in the struggle.

The story of suffrage in Washington, D.C., however, does not end at the Capitol. To its east where the United States Supreme Court building now stands, at the Old Brick Capitol there was once located the fourth headquarters of the NWP. The strategic significance of this new location, which opened in 1922, was clear. With women now able to vote, the NWP had a new agenda: equality under the law regardless of sex. In fact, during the next ten years the NWP worked for about 600 pieces of state and national legislation, winning about half of their proposals.[16] It was while here that the NWP reconfigured its organization and launched the Equal Rights Amendment. The NWP lost this headquarters in 1929 with the plan to build the Supreme Court building. Through eminent domain they received $299,200, although they estimated that their building was worth $750,000. Today, on that spot, the pediment of the Supreme Court proclaims, "Equal Justice for All"—incongruously, when no equal rights on account of sex exist in the Constitution even today.

Far in the distance from this point in Washington, D.C., more than two miles away along Independence Avenue at 19th Street close to the RFK Stadium, stood until the 1970s the District jail where the hunger-striking Alice Paul and Rose Winslow were force fed. Close by was located the condemned and unsanitary workhouse where the women arrested for protesting at Lafayette's statue in August 1918 were incarcerated.

Near the Capitol, at 144 Constitution Avenue NE—at what was originally called 144B Street NE—the fifth and final headquarters of the National Woman's Party is located. Known originally by its women occupants as the Alva Belmont House after the woman who was the party's long-term benefactor and who bought the house for them, this historic site is today known as the Sewall-Belmont House Museum. The NWP moved here in 1929 after displacement by the plans for the Supreme Court building, and it was here that Alice Paul lived for much of the rest of her life, conducting her still-incomplete campaign for women's equality under the law and specifically for the Equal Rights Amendment.

The foregoing is not an exhaustive list of all the locations in Washington, D.C., associated with suffragists or where the NWP fought for votes for women a century ago. It would be satisfying, however, after a century of neglect, to see this history commemorated on official markers, such as the black civil rights movement has. To have even a few places recognized would be gratifying. One particularly appropriate would be an additional plaque on Cameron House to recognize the crucial role of that building in expanding democracy and revolutionizing political activism in the United States through women's work to win the vote when women introduced picketing to American political life. A plaque to mark the spot of the NWP's headquarters at 14 Jackson Place on the west side of Lafayette Square, which the women occupied at ratification, would also be appropriate and recognize its equally crucial role in the history of the United States and its women. Given the national historic role of Lafayette Square, this should be relatively easy. Likely more difficult would be to have a historic plaque installed at the location of the first head-quarters of the NWP's trail-blazing campaign, which currently remains unmarked and forgotten under the Willard Office Building. However, it should not be so difficult to have a marker to commemorate at the Supreme Court the location of the fourth headquarters of the NWP, where women, now nationally enfranchised through their momentous personal struggles down many years, not only orchestrated a huge and significantly successful legislative program for reform of laws affecting women during the 1920s, but also launched the Equal Rights Amendment in 1923. The installation of per-haps another plaque might be possible on the house at 1925 F Street, currently the home of the president of the University of Washington. Although never a headquarters of the NWP, it housed for many years NWP activist Elizabeth Kent and hosted several key NWP events, including the meeting in January 1914 when Paul called for the May 1914 national suffrage demonstrations and announced the revolutionary party-in-power policy of the CU. The house also hosted the major NWP meeting of 1921 when the future of the party after the suffrage victory was debated. The mansion at 1925 F Street deserves a plaque if only because it is one of three significant extant homes with great age and historic connections in D.C. which were associated with suffrage activ-ity. Too many others have long succumbed to the wrecker's ball. Only in the case of the Sewall-Belmont House is the direct link to woman suffrage rec-ognized, and the NWP moved there a decade after the suffrage victory. It is sad in terms of women's history that only these three buildings remain. At least, however, they do remain: too many other historic suffrage locations are long gone.

Given the number of significant woman suffrage sites in Washington, D.C., and the contribution of this stunning victory to the advance of all civil rights in the United States, to have these five places marked does not seem unreasonable. Given the intricacies of bureaucracy, it might be more difficult than it seems, but it would be a great triumph if they were in place before the actual centenary of the great suffrage victory of August 26, 1920. And if the Equal Rights Amendment were ratified before the centenary of its introduc-tion in 1923, that would also be a great triumph. If this book helps in that purpose, it will have been worth all the challenges encountered while research-ing and writing it.

Chapter Notes

Preface

1. Authors Donald M. Jacobs, Arvarrh E. Strickland and F.C. Barton (*The Rise and Struggles of American Civil Rights* [Chicago: United States History Society, 1970]) include women in their survey up to that time.

Chapter 1

1. Unidentified, no date, "Miss Paul Tells of Tube Feeding in English Prison," http://sites. bergen.org/ourstory/resources/Suffrage/news clips/Tube_Feeding_2_1910.pdf (accessed November 21, 2013).This news report likely came from the *Philadelphia Inquirer* of January 21, 1910.

2. Robert P.J. Cooney, Jr., and the National Women's History Project, *Winning the Vote: The Triumph of the American Woman Suffrage Movement* (Santa Cruz, CA: American Graphic Press, 2005).

3. "Statement Issued January 3rd by the Congressional Union for Woman Suffrage," *Suffragist,* January 10, 1914, p. 4; January 17, 1914, p. 6.

4. Carrie Chapman Catt and Nettie Rogers Shuler, *Woman Suffrage and Politics: The Inner Story of the Suffrage Movement* (New York: Scribner's, 1923; Seattle: University of Washington Press Americana Library, 1969), 245–8. The *Suffragist's* weekly editions from December 27, 1913, to March 28, 1914, repeatedly discussed the party-in-power tactic, the CU's opposition to the Senate vote in March 1914 and to the proposed Shafroth-Palmer Amendment.

5. "Demonstration Plans Maturing," *Suffragist,* February 28, 1914, p. 2.

6. Catt and Shuler, *Woman Suffrage and Politics,* 489–491. The treatment that Catt and Shuler described from politicians is virtually the same as that which Equal Rights Amendment campaigners experience even today.

7. See "Opening Meeting for 1914 of Congressional Union," *Suffragist,* January 17, 1914, pp. 5–7 at 6; "Notes of the Week," *Suffragist,* February 21, 1914, pp. 2, 3. The *Suffragist* reported on the progress of this cross-country organizing regularly, both before and after the successful May 9 rally in Washington, D.C. With the call for the rallies made in January 1914, it signaled the first step in the CU's nationwide organization plan. If not intended as a direct challenge, the NAWSA could easily take it as such. Given subsequent events and the NAWSA's political maneuverings over the suffrage amendment, Paul's call and early organizing work proved extremely valuable.

8. Mary Walton, *A Woman's Crusade: Alice Paul and the Battle for the Ballot* (New York: Palgrave Macmillan, 2010), 110. This author is indebted to Walton's modern comprehensive narrative of Paul's crusade for the timing of many details of the campaign in this chapter.

9. Katherine H. Adams and Michael L. Keene, *Alice Paul and the American Suffrage Campaign* (Urbana: University of Illinois Press, 2008), 135–8; Walton, *A Woman's Crusade,* 125, ch. 10.

10. Terry spoke of this many years later. See Stephanie Bayless, *Obliged to Help: Adolphine Fletcher Terry and the Progressive South* (Little Rock: Butler Center Books, 2011), 84. For the cemetery story, see Linda J. Lumsden, *Inez: The Life and Times of Inez Milholland* (Bloomington: Indiana University Press, 2004), 1–2.

11. Walton, *A Woman's Crusade,* 140.

12. Doris Stevens, *Jailed for Freedom: The Story of the Militant American Suffragist Movement* (New York: Schocken Books, 1976), 47.

13. See Blatch's letters to the editor, *New York Times,* August 18, 22, December 7, 8, 9, 1909. See also the Women's Freedom League's newspaper, *Vote* 1, no. 2 (November 4, 1909).

14. Catt to Frances M. Lane, February 14, 1917, National Woman's Party Papers, in Walton, *A Woman's Crusade*, 153–4.

15. Stevens, *Jailed for Freedom,* 78 and 79.

16. "Believes That Arkansas Women Will Soon Vote," *Arkansas Gazette,* April 2, 1916, p. 21.

17. Ida Husted Harper, *History of Woman Suffrage, 1900–1920*, vol. 6 (New York: National American Woman Suffrage Association, 1922), 19. Women won presidential suffrage or its near equivalent in five states between 1913 and 1918. See Walton, *A Woman's Crusade*, 208. New York women won full suffrage in November 1917.

18. Stevens, *Jailed for Freedom*, 83, 84.

19. "Her Pressure on Congress: Suffrage Lobbyist's Card Index Keeps Tabs on Members' Home, Influences, Financial Backers, and Even Golf Partners," *New York Times*, March 2, 1919.

20. Walton, *A Woman's Crusade*, 166.

21. Ibid., 178, 181.

22. See Turning Point Suffragists Memorial, http://www.suffragistmemorial.org/About_Us.html (accessed May 24, 2014) for specific suffragist prisoners.

23. Walton, *A Woman's Crusade*, 185, 189, 191.

24. Midge Mackenzie, *Shoulder to Shoulder: The Stirring History of the Militant Suffragettes* (New York: Vintage, 1988), 112.

25. The article, "Miss Alice Paul on Hunger Strike," *New York Times*, November 7, 1917, states she had already been on hunger strike for 24 hours as of November 6.

26. "Suffrage Women Threaten Wilson," *New York Times,* November 12, 1917.

27. Walton, *A Woman's Crusade*, 198–200. The most direct depiction of this whole campaign is director Katja von Garnier's movie *Iron Jawed Angels* (2003). While scripted for dramatic effect, the movie's treatment of Paul and the militant suffrage campaign is essentially true.

28. Inez Haynes Irwin, *The Story of Alice Paul and the National Woman's Party* (New York: Harcourt, Brace, 1951; Washington, D.C.: National Woman's Party, 1964, 1977), 301. "Frosty Reception for Miss Vernon: Local Suffragists Disapprove of Visit Here of Woman's Party Organizer," *Arkansas Gazette,* November 9, 1917, p. 1.

29. "Miss Jane Pincus Has Small Crowd: Gives History of Woman's Party and Tells of White House Picketing," *Arkansas Gazette,* November 11, 1917, p. 27; "Chilly Reception, Just as Forecast: Picket-Orators Arouse Little Enthusiasm in Small Audiences," *Arkansas Gazette,* November 21, 1917, p. 14.

30. Mrs. T.T. Cotnam, Josephine Miller and Gertrude Watkins. See "Greatest Victory yet for Suffrage," *Arkansas Gazette,* November 14, 1917, p. 4. For Miller see Bernadette Cahill, "'Young people think women always had the right to vote': Josephine Miller and the Arkansas Woman Suffrage Campaign," *Pulaski County Historical Review* 61 (Spring 2013): 11–15.

31. Lynda G. Dodd, "Parades, Pickets, and Prison: Alice Paul and the Virtues of Unruly Constitutional Citizenship," *Journal of Law and Politics* 24, no. 339 (Fall 2008): 339 at 411–2.

32. In 1920, the estimated number of female voters in New York was 3,000,000. At the 1920 election, only about 1,100,000 voted, but this was still a significant number (see William L. Chenery, "One in Three Women Vote," *New York Times,* December 19, 1920).

33. Correspondence of Judge Mullowney, 26, 27 November 1917, National Woman's Party Papers, in Walton, *A Woman's Crusade*, 207, 271, n. 50, 51.

34. "Congress Warned by Suffrage Leader," *New York Times*, December 14, 1917.

35. "Woman Threatens Wilson: Mrs. Baker Says Reprisals Will Be Taken if Suffrage Is Beaten," *New York Times,* January 3, 1918.

36. "It is difficult to express our gratification at the President's stand. For four years we have striven to secure his support for the national Amendment for we knew that it and perhaps it alone, would insure our success," they responded. See "Wilson Backs Amendment for Woman Suffrage," *New York Times*, January 10, 1918, pp. 1, 3.

37. See, for example, *Wiley v. District of Columbia*, 47 App. D.C. 412 (1918) and *Hunter v. District of Columbia*, 47 App. D.C. 406 (1918).

38. "Answers Suffrage Plea: Tumulty Says President Can't Do More Than He Has for Amendment," *New York Times*, May 25, 1918.

39. "Wilson Presses Suffrage," *New York Times*, June 6, 1918; "Wilson Spurs Fight for Women's Vote," *New York Times*, June 14, 1918; "President Urges Suffrage on Senators," *New York Times*, June 25, 1918.

40. "President Wilson's Speech at Mount Vernon Declaring There Can Be No Half-Way Peace," *New York Times*, July 5, 1918.

41. "President Asks Vote for Suffrage," *New York Times*, July 31, 1918; "Again Urges Suffrage," *New York Times*, August 3, 1918; "Would Let Suffrage Wait," *New York Times*, August 8, 1918.

42. "Suffrage Disorders: Comment on the Recent Disturbances at Washington," *New York Times*, August 8, 1918, p. 22.

43. Walton, *A Woman's Crusade*, 222.

44. "Plan Suffrage Campaign," *New York Times*, September 2, 1918.

45. "Militants Angry at Reply to Conservatives, Voice Protest Near White House," *New York Times*, September 17, 1918.

46. "President's Words Burned as Suffragists Protest in front of White House," *Suffragist*, September 28, 1918, pp. 6–8, at 7.

47. "Wilson Makes Suffrage Appeal, but Senate Waits," *New York Times*, October 1, 1918.

48. "Defend 'Liberty' Fires: Mrs. Brannan and Mrs. Rogers Say White House Patrol Will Stay," *New York Times*, January 10, 1919.

49. "Police Stop Demonstration Before White House on Eve of Amendment Vote," *New York Times*, February 26, 1919; "Arrest 22 Militants," *New York Times*, February 25, 1919; "New Suffrage Proposal Drafted to Meet Southern Views," *New York Times*, March 1, 1919; "For Suffrage Compromise," *New York Times*, March 2, 1919; "Congress Ends; Big Bills Killed by a Filibuster," *New York Times*, March 4, 1919.

50. "New Fight for Suffrage," *New York Times*, February 4, 1919.

51. "Suffragists Off in 'Prison Special,'" *New York Times*, February 16, 1919; "Six Suffragettes Put Under Arrest," *New York Times*, March 5, 1919; "Militants Demand a Special Session," *New York Times*, March 11, 1919.

52. "Congress Called by President to Meet May 19," *New York Times*, May 8, 1919; "Suffrage Majority Assured in Senate," *New York Times*, May 23, 1919; "Ranks Wilson with Lincoln," *New York Times*, May 30, 1919; "Suffrage Wins in Senate, Now Goes to States," *New York Times*, June 5, 1919.

53. "Women Organize in West," *New York Times*, May 7, 1919.

54. "Federal Woman Suffrage," *New York Times*, June 6, 1919.

55. "Gov. Smith Calls Suffrage Session," *New York Times*, June 10, 1919; "Three Governors Call Special Sessions," *New York Times*, June 15, 1919; "No Special Session in Jersey,"

New York Times, June 14, 1919; "Suffragists Hail Texas," *New York Times*, July 6, 1919; "Arkansas for Suffrage Amendment," *New York Times*, July 29, 1919; "Arkansas Ratifies," *Woman Citizen*, August 9, 1919, 246; "Alabama Senate Rejects Suffrage," *New York Times*, July 18, 1919; "Wilson in Suffrage Plea," *New York Times*, July 17, 1919.

56. "Elated Over Political Outlook," *Woman Citizen*, July 26, 1919, p. 195.

57. Walton, *A Woman's Crusade*, 241.

58. Irwin, *The Story of Alice Paul*, 14, 6.

59. NAWSA had forty-four state auxiliaries and two million members at the end of 1915 when Carrie Chapman Catt took over (Sara Hunter Graham, *Woman Suffrage and the New Democracy* (New Haven & London: Yale University Press, 1996), 86).

Chapter 2

1. "Colby Proclaims Woman Suffrage," *New York Times*, August 27, 1920.

2. Walton, *A Woman's Crusade*, 244.

3. Dora Lewis to Caroline Katzenstein, 4 March 1919, in Walton, *A Woman's Crusade*, 233.

4. "Suffragists Reach Paris: Will Go to Geneva Today Representing 'Unenfranchised' Nation," *New York Times*, June 1, 1920.

5. "Colby to Proclaim Suffrage Promptly," *New York Times*, August 19, 1920, p. 1.

6. "26,500,000 Women in U.S. Eligible to Vote: Census Bureau Estimates 31,500,000 Men Will Go to Polls," *Arkansas Democrat*, October 8, 1920, p. 8.

7. Derived from Joseph C.G. Kennedy (superintendent of the census), *Population of the United States in 1860; Compiled from the Original Returns of the Eighth Census Under the Direction of the Secretary of the Interior* (Washington, D.C: Government Printing Office, 1864), 592–597. The white male population in the eighth census was 13,844,537. The 21-and-over white male population was 6,971,106.

8. *General Population Statistics, 1960, United States Summary* (Washington, D.C: U.S. Census Bureau, 1961), Table 46, at 1–151, http://www2.census.gov/prod2/decennial/documents/09768103v1p1ch4.pdf (accessed November 1, 2013).

9. Ibid., Table 52 at 1–160.

10. Terminology used in the U.S. Census Summary includes other ethnicities.

11. Derived from *General Population Statistics, 1960*, Table 52 at 1–160.

12. Data for ages from only 21 and above were not available. The U.S. census southern population includes three regions: South Atlantic, East South Central and West South Central. Together, they comprise Delaware, Maryland, Washington, D.C., Virginia, West Virginia, North Carolina, South Carolina, Georgia, Florida, Kentucky, Tennessee, Alabama, Mississippi, Arkansas, Louisiana, Oklahoma and Texas, omitting Missouri, a former slave state.

13. From a speech by President Nixon at a signing ceremony on July 5, 1971: "The reason I believe that your generation, the 11 million new voters, will do so much for America at home is that you will infuse into this nation some idealism, some courage, some stamina, some high moral purpose that this country always needs" (see Carl M. Cannon, "Youth Vote: Dems' Secret Weapon 40 Years in the Making?" Real Clear Politics, March 2011, http://www.realclearpolitics.com/articles/2011/03/25/youth_vote_dems_delayed_time_release_capsule.html#ixzz30eoWYl1v (accessed May 3, 2014).

Chapter 3

1. *Virginia Gazette*, 26 July 1776; *Virginia Gazette*, 18 July 1777, cited at James R. Heintze, "The First Celebrations" at http://www1.american.edu/heintze/fourth.htm#Beginning (accessed November 3, 2013).

2. Labor Day Parade, Union Square, N.Y. Photograph, Robert N. Dennis collection of stereoscopic views, New York Public Library's Digital Library, digital ID G91F182_006F, http://digitalgallery.nypl.org/nypldigital/dgkeysearchdetail.cfm?strucID=624181&imageID=g91f182_006f (accessed November 3, 2013).

3. Lisa Tichner, *The Spectacle of Women: Imagery of the Suffrage Campaign 1907–14* (London: Chatto & Windus, 1987), 57.

4. Emmeline Pankhurst, *My Own Story* (London: Eveleigh Nash, 1914), 64–5.

5. Tichner, *The Spectacle of Women,* 74–75.

6. Ellen Carol DuBois, *Harriot Stanton Blatch and the Winning of Woman Suffrage* (New Haven and London: Yale University Press, 1997), 101–3; Cooney, *Winning the Vote,* 105.

7. Holly J. McCammon, "Out of the Parlors and into the Streets: The Changing Tactical Repertoire of the U.S. Women's Suffrage Movements," *Social Forces* 81, no. 3 (March 2003): 787–818 at 794 (University of North Carolina Press).

8. Cooney, *Winning the Vote,* 105.

9. Christine Mastalio (project manager), *Boone Parade,* "Women's Suffrage in Iowa: An Online Exhibit," http://sdrc.lib.uiowa.edu/exhibits/suffrage/1890parade.html (accessed November 13, 2013).

10. Mrs. S.S. Wassell, "History of Equal Suffrage Movement in Arkansas: An Account of the Patient, Persistent Efforts for the Emancipation of Women, from Pioneer Days to the Present," *Arkansas Gazette,* February 9, 1919, p. 30. This story is without sources and as yet unconfirmed. It was written when parades had featured in suffrage campaigns for a decade or more. It is not hard to imagine Little Rock suffragists discussing them and that one of the several suffragists of the 1880s and 1890s who were still around or who knew those campaigners related the story either when Mrs. Wassell wrote in 1919 or when the parades began.

11. Women marched through Hillsboro, Ohio, in 1873 stopping at every saloon to pray for the barkeepers and the imbibers within. By 1875, well over a hundred communities had witnessed such marches (see http://www.ohiohistorycentral.org/w/Temperance_Movement?rec=560 (accessed November 19, 2013).

12. Cooney, *Winning the Vote,* 105, 127.

13. "Suffragette Tells of Forcible Feeding," *New York Times,* February 18, 1910. This article focuses on the force-feeding that Paul experienced and does not mention parades.

14. "Committee History," Joint Congressional Committee on Inaugural Celebrations, http://www.inaugural.senate.gov/about/history (accessed May 3, 2014). This Web site contains much less detail than Wikipedia, "United States Presidential Inauguration," http://en.wikipedia.org/wiki/United_States_presidential_inauguration (accessed November 3, 2013), which references further sources. For further anecdotes and more details, see Jim Bendat, *Democracy's Big Day, 1789–2013* (iUniverse Star, 2012) and Paul F. Boller Jr., *Presidential Inaugurations* (Orlando, Florida: Harcourt, 2001).

15. Adams and Keene, *Alice Paul and the Suffrage Campaign.*

16. Alice Paul to Mary Ware Dennett, January 6, 1913, National Woman's Party Papers, in Walton, *A Woman's Crusade,* 54–8, 258, n. 13.

17. *Suffrage Parade: Hearings Before a Subcommittee of the Committee on the District of*

Columbia, United States Senate, Sixty-third Congress, vol. 1 (Washington, D.C: Government Printing Office, 1913), 461.

18. Adams and Keene, *Alice Paul and the Suffrage Campaign,* 99.

19. To see how Paul made Washington, D.C., a stage, see "Program for Week, Washington, D.C.," *Suffragist,* November 29, 1913, p. 18, listing many street meetings during the NAWSA National Convention.

20. World Digital Library, Confederate Veterans Convention, Jacksonville, Florida, 1914, http://www.wdl.org/en/item/4051/ (accessed November 3, 2013).

21. "Washington as a Suffrage Center," *Suffragist,* May 23, 1914, p. 6.

22. Irwin, *The Story of Alice Paul,* 483.

23. "Suffrage Disorders: Comment on the Recent Disturbances at Washington," *New York Times,* August 8, 1918, p. 22.

24. Extracts from Woodrow Wilson, "Constitutional Government in the United States" (New York: Columbia University Press, 1908), in *The U.S. Constitution: A Reader,* Hillsdale College Politics Faculty (Hillsdale, MI: Hillsdale College Press, 2012), 649–660 at 652.

25. Wilson, "Constitutional Government," in Hillsdale College Politics Faculty, *The U.S. Constitution,* 649–660 at 652.

Chapter 4

1. Lucy C. Barber, *Marching on Washington: The Forging of an American Political Tradition* (Berkeley: University of California Press, 2002), 11, ch. 1.

2. Mary Gray Peck, *Carrie Chapman Catt: A Biography* (New York: H.W. Wilson, 1944), 83–4.

3. See, for example, the extensive analysis of the presidential vote in "The Suffrage Issue in the Next Election," *Suffragist,* April 8, 1916, p. 8; and "Four Million Woman Voters," at 6.

4. Cooncy, *Winning the Vote,* 105.

5. "Suffrage Cheers for Mrs. Pankhurst," *New York Times,* October 21, 1909.

6. "Arrest 41 Pickets for Suffrage at White House," *New York Times,* November 11, 1917; Oregon Public Television, *The Suffragists* (2012), http://www.opb.org/television/programs/oregonexperience/segment/the-suffragists/ (accessed April 23, 2014).

7. "Women's Political Union Joins Congressional Union," *Suffragist,* January 22, 1916, p. 2.

8. "20,000 Women in Great Parade: Fifth Avenue a River of Fire," *New York Times,* November 10, 1912; Cooney, *Winning the Vote,* 181.

9. Elizabeth Cady Stanton, Susan B. Anthony and Matilda Jocelyn Gage, eds., *History of Woman Suffrage, 1861–1876,* vol. 2 (New York: Fowler & Wells, 1882), 407–520.

10. Susan B. Anthony, *The Trial of Susan B. Anthony* (Amherst, New York: Humanity Books, 2003). For women who voted in Anthony's time in protest against exclusion from the vote in the Reconstruction amendments, see "Women Who Voted, 1868–73," Rutgers University, Elizabeth Cady Stanton and Susan B. Anthony Papers Project, sorted by state, http://ecssba.rutgers.edu/resources/wompolls.html (accessed November 14, 2013).

11. *Minor v. Happersett,* 88 U.S. 162 (1875).

12. Dodd, "Parades, Pickets, and Prison," 339.

13. Irwin, *The Story of Alice Paul,* 430–477, and Peck, *Carrie Chapman Catt,* 315–343.

14. Carrie Chapman Catt, "Letter to Auxiliary Presidents of the Enfranchised States," 12 January 1916, Library of Congress, NWP Papers: Group 1, the Suffrage Years, Reel 23, cited at *CU/NWP Documents Which Chronicle Division Between NAWSA and CU/NWP,* http://www.oocities.org/emilyc_25/cunwp_split.html (accessed April 24, 2014).

15. Stevens, *Jailed for Freedom,* 13.

16. Peck, *Carrie Chapman Catt,* 325.

17. See transcript of suffragist Mrs. T.T. Cotnam's article, "History of Woman Suffrage in Arkansas," originally published in the *Arkansas Gazette* in its centenary special of 1919, http://www.arkansasties.com/Special/History ofWomensSuffrage.htm (accessed November 14, 2013).

18. Irwin, *The Story of Alice Paul,* 459.

Chapter 5

1. "Suffragists Burn President's Words," *New York Times,* September 16, 1918.

2. Irwin, *The Story of Alice Paul,* 486.

3. Cooney, *Winning the Vote.*

4. "Her Pressure on Congress: Suffrage Lobbyist's Card Index Keeps Tab on Members' Home Influences, Financial Backers and Even Golf Partners," *New York Times,* March 2, 1919.

5. The *Suffragist* of 1916 repeatedly refers to the campaign against the party in power. See, for example, "Opposing Democrats," *Suffragist,* August 19, 1916, p. 6, and "Democratic Excuses," *Suffragist,* August 26, 1916, p. 6.

6. Little Rock suffragist and later black civil rights supporter Adolphine Fletcher Terry was quoted in Kay Koehler, "Woman Suffrage: Pioneers Recall the early Days—and Look Ahead," *Arkansas Gazette*, June 22, 1969, p. 5D, as saying, "We acted like complete hellions to get the vote. We of the 'lady' class had always been on a pedestal ... beauteous womanhood, all that kind of junk. The men had looked up to us, idolized us. They changed their attitude when we tied ourselves to telephone poles and did the most unseemly and unladylike things to attract attention to our cause." This is the closest this researcher has come to mention of American women adopting this tactic of the British suffragettes. There is no evidence of such activity in Little Rock during the suffrage campaign.

7. Adams and Keene, *Alice Paul and the Suffrage Campaign,* 30–33.

8. Doris Stevens, "The Militant Campaign," *Suffragist,* July 19, 1919, pp. 8–9.

9. "Democrats Aroused by Woman's Party Campaign," *Suffragist,* October 21, 1916, pp. 7–9.

10. The exact words of the second quotation are: "Uncompromising thought is the luxury of the closeted recluse" (see "The Leaders of Men," Wilson's speech at the University of Tennessee, 17 June 1890, in August Heckscher, *The Politics of Woodrow Wilson* (New York: Harper & Brothers Publishers, 1956), 74 and 75).

11. Adams and Keene, *Alice Paul and the Suffrage Campaign,* ch. 2.

12. For a thorough examination of Paul's leadership style, see Dodd, "Parades, Pickets, and Prison," at 379–382 and n. 178–187.

13. Stevens, *Jailed For Freedom,* xxxv.

14. Vivian Pierce, "Susan B. Anthony, Militant," *Suffragist,* March 3, 1917, p. 7.

15. For the story of how, once again, males betrayed women when they came to their aid in organizing the 1876 centennial celebration in Philadelphia and the full background for her protest on July 4, 1876, see Jeanne Madeline Weimann, *The Fair Women: The Story of the Woman's Building, World's Columbian Exposition, Chicago 1893* (Chicago: Academy Chicago, 1981), 2–4.

16. Stevens, *Jailed for Freedom,* 7.

17. "Women Who Voted, 1868–73," Rutgers University, Elizabeth Cady Stanton and Susan B. Anthony Papers Project, http://ecssba.rutgers.edu/resources/voters.html, sorted by date (accessed November 18, 2013).

18. "Early Suffrage Protests," *New York Times,* July 11, 1915.

19. *Constitution of the Women's Freedom League* (London: Women's Freedom League, 1909), by permission of the British Library Board, Shelfmark 08415.f.14(2), http://www.bl.uk/learning/images/21cc/society/large1218.html (accessed November 19, 2013).

20. "What We Think," *The Vote* 1, no. 1 (October 30, 1909).

21. Elizabeth Crawford, *The Women's Suffrage Movement: A Reference Guide, 1866–1928* (London: Routledge, 1999, 2001), 720–724.

22. Alice Stone Blackwell, "An Obstinate Briton," *New York Times,* December 7, 1909.

23. Nora Blatch DeForest, "Militant Methods," *New York Times,* December 10, 1909. DeForest the next year was chair of the Pageant Committee of her mother's (Harriot Stanton Blatch) Equality League of Self-Supporting Women, later the Women's Political Union of New York.

24. The upscale women's magazine *Designer* even defended the WSPU's militancy. "The militants are destroying property for precisely the same reasons that our American ancestors destroyed tea in Boston Harbor," the author wrote. "The uprising of woman indicates the greatest political revolution the world has ever seen" (see Raymond S. Spears, "What Does the Militant Movement Mean?," *Designer*, September 1914, pp. 10, 47). Ironically, this article appeared the month after the war broke out in Europe, at which time the WSPU had stopped its suffrage campaign and begun a recruitment campaign. The WFL had suspended its campaign, but resumed it in 1916.

25. "Winning the Last Trench for Woman Suffrage," *Suffragist,* December 7, 1918, p. 9. Note that in Britain, only those women over the age of thirty who were householders, owned property or were married to a householder won the right to vote. British women would not win equal suffrage until 1928.

26. Stevens, *Jailed for Freedom,* 184–6.

27. See F.W. Pethick-Lawrence, *The Treatment of Suffragettes in Prison* (London: Women's Social and Political Union, n.d. (WSPU Leaflet no. 59), WSPU Collection, Museum of London, in Kevin Grant, "British Suffragettes and the Russian Method of Hunger Strike," *Comparative Studies in Society and History* 53, no. 1 (2011), 113–143 at 114, n. 3.

28. In Linda J. Lumsden, *Rampant Women: Suffragists and the Right of Assembly* (Knoxville:

University of Tennessee Press, 1997), 130–1, 236, n. 136.

29. "Mr. Upton Sinclair's Hunger Strike," *Glasgow Herald,* May 1, 1914, p. 9.

30. In Catherine J. Lanctot, "'We Are at War and You Should Not Bother the President': The Suffrage Pickets and Freedom of Speech During World War I," *Villanova Law/ Public Policy Research Paper,* no. 2008-16, 64 pages, at 47–8, n. 245, http://dx.doi.org/10. 2139/ssrn.1126806 (accessed November 19, 2013).

31. "Irish and American Political Prisoners," *Suffragist,* October 6, 1917, p. 3. See also Michael Biggs, "The Rationality of Self-Inflicted Sufferings: Hunger Strikes by Irish Republicans, 1916—1923," *Sociology Working Papers,* no. 2007–03, Department of Sociology, University of Oxford, England, http://users.ox.ac. uk/~sfos0060/SWP2007-03.pdf (accessed November 22, 2013).

32. Unidentified, no date, "Miss Paul Tells of Tube Feeding in English Prison"; see also, "Alice Paul Returns Home," *New York Times,* January 21, 1910, a story filed from Philadelphia.

33. "Suffragette Tells of Forcible Feeding," *New York Times,* February 18, 1910.

34. Adams and Keene, *Alice Paul and the Suffrage Campaign,* 17.

35. "Won't Try to Start Suffrage War Here," *New York Times,* January 2, 1910.

36. Unidentified, no date, "Miss Paul Tells of Tube Feeding in English Prison."

37. Walton, *A Woman's Crusade,* 200–201.

38. Luke 23:34.

39. Grant, "Russian Method of Hunger Strike," 114, n. 3.

40. See Adams and Keene, *Alice Paul and the Suffrage Campaign* and Walton, *A Woman's Crusade.*

Chapter 6

1. "Sees New Hope in Woman Suffrage," *Arkansas Gazette,* October 9, 1920, p. 1.

2. "Seems Ladies Now Have All Men's Rights," *Arkansas Gazette,* September 9, 1920, p. 14.

3. Lorraine Gates Schuyler, *The Weight of Their Votes: Southern Women and Political Leverage in the 1920s* (Chapel Hill: University of North Carolina Press, 2006), 3–6.

4. *Woman Citizen,* August 23, 1919, p. 1.

5. Catt and Shuler, *Woman Suffrage and Politics,* 107.

6. Carrie Chapman Catt, "Doubting Thomases," *Woman Citizen,* May 1, 1920, p. 1201.

7. "Ask Action in Maryland," *New York Times,* August 25, 1920; "Seek Assembly Session," *New York Times,* August 27, 1920; "Asks Suffrage Law in Maine," *New York Times,* August 31, 1920; "State Rulings Aid in Women's Voting," *New York Times,* September 5, 1920.

8. "Wants New Suffrage Act: Woman's Party Will Urge the Passage of an Enforcement Measure," *New York Times,* November 6, 1920.

9. "26,500,000 Women in U.S. Eligible to Vote: Census Bureau Estimates 31,500,000 Men Will Go to Polls," *Arkansas Democrat,* October 8, 1920, p. 8; "Making Indians Citizens," *New York Times,* June 7, 1924. The Indian Citizenship Act was also known as the Snyder Act, which President Calvin Coolidge signed into law on June 2, 1924; Asian American Democracy Project, http://aaldef.org/programs/voting-rights/ (accessed October 24, 2013).

10. Michael J. Klarman, *From Jim Crow to Civil Rights: The Supreme Court and the Struggle for Racial Equality* (Oxford: Oxford University Press, 2004), 28–39. This is an excellent analysis not only of disfranchisement of black men supported by legal decisions, but also of the courts' barring black men from jury service and the courts' support of segregation generally and discrimination in education in particular.

11. Schuyler, *The Weight of Their Votes,* 69.

12. "Says Women's Poll Tax Receipts May Be Invalid," *Arkansas Gazette,* April 9, 1917, p. 4.

13. "Women's Right to Vote Is Assailed," *Arkansas Gazette,* November 18, 1917, p. 1.

14. "Says Women Don't Need Tax Receipt to Vote" *Arkansas Democrat,* October 2, 1920, p. 2; "Judge Protects Women," *Arkansas Gazette,* November 2, 1920, p. 14; "Tax Receipt Not Needed by Women," *Arkansas Gazette,* October 27, 1920, p. 8.

15. See Alexander Keyssar, *The Right to Vote: The Contested History of Democracy in the United States* (New York: Basic Books, 2000), 368–89.

16. Schuyler, *The Weight of Their Votes,* 46.

17. "Only One Woman Voted in Georgia," *Arkansas Gazette,* November 5, 1920, p. 10.

18. "New Woman Member of Congress Fought Suffrage," *New York Times,* November 5, 1920.

19. Elizabeth Stephens Summerlin, "'Not Ratified but Hereby Rejected': The Women's Suffrage Movement in Georgia, 1895–1925," MA thesis, Georgia College and State Univer-

sity, 2007, http://athenaeum.libs.uga.edu/bit
stream/handle/10724/11730/summerlin_eliza
beth_s_200912_ma.pdf?sequence=1 (accessed
October 29, 2013).

20. "Ida Joe Brooks to Run for Superintendent of Public Instruction," *Arkansas Democrat,*
August 21, 1920, p. 1; "Women Not Eligible for
Office," *Arkansas Democrat,* October 11, 1920,
p. 6.

21. "Move to Make Women Eligible for Office in Massachusetts," *New York Times,* December 7, 1920.

22. "Only One Woman Voted in Georgia,"
Arkansas Gazette, November 5, 1920, p. 10.

Chapter 7

1. "Who's Who in the Day's News," *Arkansas Democrat,* August 30, 1920, p. 4.

2. The caption to a photograph of the first
New Jersey all-female jury in Bayonne. *New
York World,* November 4, 1920, p. 10, reported
the story.

3. An article headlined, "Women Jurors
Assess $50 Fine on Milk Dealer," *Arkansas De-
mocrat,* September 1, 1920, p. 1, stated that this
was believed to be a first. The jury comprised
"six society women" who were also "political
leaders."

4. Helen H. Gardener, "The First All-
Woman Jury," *Woman Citizen,* February 7,
1920, p. 810.

5. "Declares Women Are Not Liable for
Jury Duty," *Arkansas Democrat,* October 5,
1920, p. 8.

6. "Republicans Join Democrats to Aid
Three Amendments," *Arkansas Democrat,* October 20, 1920, p. 1; Proposed Amendment 14
provided for woman suffrage in Arkansas.

7. "Tax Receipt Not Needed by Women,"
Arkansas Gazette, October 27, 1920, p. 8.

8. "Women and Juries Again," *Suffragist,*
January 25, 1919, p. 4.

9. See the letter of Judge Howe to Myra
Bradwell on women's exemplary role in juries
in early 1870 in Elizabeth Cady Stanton, Susan
B. Anthony and Matilda Jocelyn Gage, eds.,
History of Woman Suffrage, 1876–1885, vol. 3
(Rochester, NY: Susan B. Anthony, 1886),
736–7.

10. The story headlined, "Here's How Man
May Profit by Woman's Victory," *Arkansas
Gazette,* August 23, 1920, p. 1, noting Chicago's
"unenviable record of jury leniency towards
women murderers and husband killers in particular," reported that a local judge had stated

that female jury duty would come with woman
suffrage and that women would "vote to con-
vict a guilty woman every time and we intend
to make Chicago safe for husbands."

11. Mary Summer Boyd, "Jury Service—by
Sufferance or by Law," *Woman Citizen,* May 29,
1920, pp. 1330–1. In spite of the early jury history in Wyoming, the author here states that
the attorney general in Wyoming soon excluded women from jury service.

12. Burnita Shelton Matthews, "The Woman
Juror," *Women Lawyers' Journal* 15, no. 2 (January 1927), http://wlh.law.stanford.edu/wp-
content/uploads/2011/01/the-woman-juror-
15wlj151927.pdf (accessed October 29, 2013).
For a thorough analysis, see McCammon, *The
U.S. Women's Jury Movements,* 34, 41–2.

13. "Women of Arkansas Cannot Be Notaries," *Arkansas Democrat,* September 14,
1920, p. 6.

14. "Bills in Congress Relating to Women,"
Suffragist, April 1920, p. 44.

15. "As to Dangerous Legislation," *Woman
Citizen,* July 26, 1919, p. 186.

16. "Changes in Wages During and Since
the War, September 1914–March 1920," National Industrial Conference Board, Research
Report No. 31, September 1920, New York, 7,
Table 1, http://books.google.com.do/books/
about/Changes_in_Wages_During_and_
Since_the_Wa.html?id=S3svAAAAYAAJ (accessed May 3, 2014).

17. National Industrial Conference Board,
"Changes in Wages," 6, Diagram 1.

18. "Shall Women Give Up Their Jobs?"
Woman Citizen, July 5, 1919, pp. 142–3 at 142.

19. Fred Smith Hall and Elisabeth W. Brooke,
*American Marriage Laws in Their Social As-
pects: A Digest* (New York: Russell Sage Foundation, 1919).

20. "The Book Stall," *Woman Citizen,* June
7, 1919, p. 23.

21. Tiffany K. Wayne, *Women's Roles in
Nineteenth Century America* (Westport: Greenwood Press, 2007), 6–9.

22. Alice Paul, editorial, *Suffragist,* January–
February 1921, p. 339.

23. "Colby to Proclaim Suffrage Promptly:
Will Announce Validity of the Amendment on
Receipt of Tennessee Certification" *New York
Times,* August 19, 1920, pp. 1–2 at 2.

24. Alice Paul, editorial, *Suffragist,* January–
February 1921, p. 339.

25. Alice Paul, editorial, *Suffragist,* January–
February 1921, p. 339.

26. Michael B. Dougan, "The Arkansas

Married Woman's Property Law," *Arkansas Historical Quarterly* 46, no. 1 (Spring 1987): 3–26, at 12–13. The author states that Arkansas was the first in the nation, "with the possible qualification of Florida," without further explanation of the statement. See also Carole Shammas, "Reassessing the Married Women's Property Acts," *Journal of Women's History* 6, no.1 (Spring 1994): 9–30, for an analysis of how beneficial the acts were. The Law Library of Congress Web site, *American Women,* http:// memory.loc.gov/ammem/awhhtml/awlaw3/ property_law.html (accessed June 27, 2013), includes a short summary of the history of the laws and a guide to further resources.

27. See the Law Library of Congress Web site, *American Women,* for its short summary of similar laws, http://memory.loc.gov/am mem/awhhtml/awlaw3/property_law.html (accessed June 27, 2013).

28. "Soon Will Have Woman Notaries," *Arkansas Gazette,* August 29, 1920, Part II, p. 12; "Women of Arkansas Cannot Be Notaries," *Arkansas Democrat,* September 14, 1920, p. 6.

29. J. Morgan Kousser, "Poll Tax," in Richard Rose (ed.), *International Encyclopedia of Elections* (Congressional Quarterly Press, 2000), chapter pages available as pdf file, http://www. hss.caltech.edu/~kousser/dictionary%20en tries/poll%20tax.pdf (accessed March 1, 2014).

30. *Breedlove v. Suttles,* 302 U.S. 277 (1937).

31. The historical analyses of the post–World War I campaigns against the poll tax have considered it primarily as a movement of African Americans. This discounts women's long-standing concerns that the poll tax stopped women voting. Women's activism to repeal the tax after they won the vote, when they found themselves facing huge obstacles because of the tax, was instrumental, if little known, in the repeal of the tax (see Sarah Wilkerson-Freeman, "The Second Battle for Woman Suffrage: Alabama White Women, the Poll Tax, and V.O. Key's Master Narrative of Southern Politics," *Journal of Southern History* 68, no. 2 (May 2002): 333–374, and Ronnie L. Podolefsky, "The Illusion of Suffrage: Female Voting Rights and the Women's Poll Tax Repeal Movement After the Nineteenth Amendment," *Columbia Journal of Gender and Law* 7 (1997–8): 185–237.

32. *Harper v. Virginia Board of Elections,* 383 U.S. 663 (1966).

33. *Woman Citizen,* May 29, 1920, pp. 1322–1332.

34. "Recommendations on Uniform Laws Approved by National League of Women Voters February 1920 at Chicago Convention," *Woman Citizen,* May 29, 1920, p. 1321.

35. "Bills in Congress Relating to Women," *Suffragist,* April 1920, p. 44.

36. Walton, *A Woman's Crusade,* 247, states that during the 1920s the NWP drafted 600 pieces of legislation, of which 300 passed.

37. Dorothy M. Brown, *Setting a Course: American Women in the 1920s* (Boston: Twayne, 1987), 52–7.

38. See the outline of Women's Bureau history from the Department of Labor, http:// www.dol.gov/dol/aboutdol/history/dolchp01. htm (accessed March 8, 2014).

39. Caroline J. Gleason, *Report of the Social Survey Committee of the Consumers' League of Oregon on the Wages, Hours, and Conditions of Work and Cost and Standard of Living of Women Wage Earners in Oregon with Special Reference to Portland* (Portland: Keystone, 1913).

40. Oregon Public Television, *The Suffragists.*

41. Rosemarie Zagarri, "The Rights of Man and Woman in Post-Revolutionary America," *William and Mary Quarterly* 55, no. 2, 3rd series (April 1998), 203–230; Omohundro Institute of Early American History and Culture, http://www.jstor.org/stable/2674382 (accessed February 22, 2013); Zagarri notes (214–6) that the Jeffersonians in the new Republic favored the Lockean ideas, whereas the Federalists, wary of unleashing unbounded freedom among all levels of society, favored the Scottish enlightenment philosophy. These differences manifested in the party political battles of the early republic. However, when it came to the rights of women, the differences all but disappeared. She states (224) that this Scottish enlightenment-based definition of rights and duties recognized that as human beings women and men were equal in "dignity and moral standing." She also examines the late eighteenth-century debate about the rights of women, including the benefits and the impact of this debate over time. One benefit was that such a debate opened up the question of woman's rights.

42. John Thomas McGuire, "The Most Unjust Piece of Legislation: Section 213 of the Economy Act of 1932 and Feminism During the New Deal," *Journal of Policy History* 20, no. 4 (2008): 516–541.

43. Deborah M. Thaw, "The Feminization of the Office of Notary Public: From *Femme*

Covert to *Notaire Covert*," *John Marshall Law Review* 31, no. 3 (Spring 1998), 703–734.

44. Bernadette Cahill, "Congressional Medal for World War Two Granite Falls Woman Pilot," *Women's History Month Spotlight, High Country Press,* March 11, 2010, http://www.highcountrypress.com/weekly/2010/03-11-10/womens-history-month-spotlight.htm (accessed March 21, 2014).

Chapter 8

1. Cynthia Harrison, *On Account of Sex: The Politics of Women's Issues, 1945–1968* (Berkeley: University of California Press, 1988), 15–38.

2. Catherine E. Rymph, *Republican Women: Feminism and Conservatism from Suffrage Through the Rise of the New Right* (Chapel Hill: University of North Carolina Press, 2006), 18, 24.

3. Martin Gruberg, *Women in American Politics: An Assessment and Sourcebook* (Wisconsin: Academia Press, 1968), 26.

4. Harrison, *On Account of Sex,* 7.

5. Schuyler, *The Weight of Their Votes.*

6. Rymph, *Republican Women*, 4, 40–67.

7. Harrison, *On Account of Sex,* 109–111.

8. *American Women: Report of the President's Commission on the Status of Women* (Washington, D.C: Women's Bureau of the Department of Labor, 1963), 44–48.

9. *Minor v. Happersett*, 88 U.S. 162 (1875).

10. Harrison, *On Account of Sex,* 98–105.

11. See, for example, Charles Whalen and Barbara Whalen, *The Longest Debate: A Legislative History of the Civil Rights Act* (Washington, D.C: Seven Locks Press, 1985, commemorative ed. 2010), 115–118. These authors repeat the content of the original edition of this history of the Civil Rights Act in their 2010 edition, even though the original appeared in 1985, three years after Cynthia Ellen Harrison, in "Prelude to Feminism: Women's Organizations, the Federal Government and the Rise of the Women's Movement, 1942–68," PhD diss., 2 vols., Columbia University, 1982, in vol. 2 at 469–476, gave the true history of this amendment. This demonstrates clearly the dichotomy between the history of black civil rights and that of women's civil rights. Harrison's published version of the thesis is, unfortunately, truncated.

12. Harrison, "Prelude to Feminism," vol. 2, pp. 475–476.

13. *Reed v. Reed*, 404 U.S. 71 (1971).

14. Bernadette Cahill, "Some Women 'Out of Touch' as U.S. Congress Breaks Again on Fairness and Equal Pay," Women's News Network, June 27, 2012, http://womennewsnetwork.net/2012/06/27/women-out-of-touch-u-s-congress/ (accessed March 21, 2014).

15. For the history of these developments, see Mary Becker, "The Sixties Shift to Formal Equality and the Courts: An Argument for Pragmatism and Politics," *William and Mary Law Review* 40, no. 1 (1998): 209–277; Serena Mayeri, "Constitutional Choices: Legal Feminism and the Historical Dynamics of Change," *California Law Review* 92, no. 3 (May 2004): 755–839; and Serena Mayeri, "A Common Fate of Discrimination: Race-Gender Analogies in Legal and Historical Perspective," *Yale Law Journal* 110, no. 6 (April 2001): 1045–1087.

16. Poll conducted for the ERA campaign by Opinion Research Corporation Caravan Services, http://2passera.org/survey.shtml (accessed March 21, 2014).

17. *United States v. Virginia*, 518 U.S. 515 (1996).

18. The Originalist: "Justice Antonin Scalia," *California Lawyer,* January 2011, http://www.callawyer.com/clstory.cfm?eid=913358 (accessed March 21, 2014).

19. *Ledbetter v. Goodyear Tire and Rubber Co.,* 550 U.S. 618 (2007).

20. Hazel Greenberg, ed., Anita Miller, project director, The Equal Rights Amendment Project, *The Equal Rights Amendment: A Bibliographic Study* (Westport, CT: Greenwood Press, 1976), xx–xxii.

21. Allison L. Held, Sheryl L. Herndon and Danielle M. Stager, "The Equal Rights Amendment: Why the ERA Remains Legally Viable and Properly Before the States," *William and Mary Journal of Women and the Law* 3, no. 1 (1997): 113–136.

22. Archivist of the United States, "Memorandum Opinion for the Counsel to the President," May 13, 1992, http://www.justice.gov/olc/congress.17.htm (accessed May 3, 2012).

23. For a summary of the history of these two strategies and a review of young people's perception of the ERA, see Bernadette Cahill, "Some Women 'Out of Touch'" as U.S. Congress Breaks Again on Fairness and Equal Pay," Women's News Network, June 27, 2012, http://womennewsnetwork.net/2012/06/27/women-out-of-touch-u-s-congress/ (accessed March 21, 2014).

Chapter 9

1. See *New York World*, November 3, 1920, pp. 6, 7, 8; November 4, 1920, p. 16; November 5, 1920, p. 1.

2. See "Chicago Vote a Record Breaker," *Arkansas Gazette*, November 3, 1920, p. 6, and the Memphis story, "Three Women Elected to School Board," *Arkansas Gazette*, November 4, 1920, p. 11.

3. See the story about the League of Nations and the "failure" of the "feminine" vote in *New York World*, November 4, 1920, p. 1.

4. The full picture was complex. Washington, Oregon, California, Montana, Idaho, Nevada, Wyoming, Utah, Arizona, South Dakota, Colorado, Kansas, Oklahoma, Michigan and New York had full suffrage before ratification. The other states had various measures of unequal suffrage, such as presidential suffrage, primary suffrage, primary suffrage in some cities, municipal suffrage in some cities, school, bond or tax suffrage, various mixtures of partial suffrage, or no suffrage at all. Most of the states without any woman suffrage were former colonies (see Keyssar, *The Right to Vote*, 400–402).

5. William L. Chenery, "One in Three Women Vote."

6. Schuyler, *The Weight of Their Votes*, 3.

7. "Campbell Leading in Constable Race," *Arkansas Gazette*, November 3, 1920, p. 14.

8. No follow-up story has emerged.

9. Some women were excluded from the vote because of race even with the Fifteenth and the new amendment, including about 60,000 American Indian women and 8,607 Chinese and Japanese women. Women were also "deprived of the ballot under state statutes in harmony with constitutional provisions," while American women married to aliens had no vote, which soon became a reform demand (see estimates of Census Bureau, "26,500,000 Women in U.S. Eligible to Vote," *Arkansas Democrat*, October 8, 1920, p. 9).

10. Tracy A. Thomas, in "Elizabeth Cady Stanton and the Notion of a Legal Class of Gender," in Tracy A. Thomas and Tracey Jean Boisseau, eds., *Feminist Legal History: Essays in Woman and Law* (New York and London: New York University Press, 2011), 142, outlines the history of the analogy of women's subordinate status, especially within marriage, to slavery from the time of Mary Wolstonecraft in the eighteenth century, through Elizabeth Cady Stanton in the nineteenth, to Pauli Murray in the twentieth.

11. *New York Times*, "The Anniversaries: Important Session of the Anti-Slavery Society: Speeches of Wendell Phillips et al.," May 10, 1865, http://www.nytimes.com/1865/05/10/news/anniversaries-important-session-antislavery-society-speeches-wendell-phillips.html?pagewanted=1 (accessed July 28, 2013).

12. The slogan "This is the Negro's hour" was an allusion to Lincoln's phrase "one war at a time." Phillips' direct words do not seem so succinct, either at this meeting or two days later: "The question of all questions, to my mind, seems at this time to be, whether this question of race—this element of a[nti]pathy of different bloods—shall be forever eliminated from our history. There are doubtless other great and important questions, financial, social moral and political; but, as Abraham Lincoln once said, 'One war at a time,' so I too say 'One question at a time,'" he was reported to say. "To-day it is a question of race. To my mind, the question which presses to-day on the conscience and duty of the anti-slavery movement in this country is the wiping out forever the word 'white' from our statute-books," *New York Times*, "Negro Suffrage: Agitation of the Anti-Slavery Society," May 13, 1865, http://www.nytimes.com/1865/05/13/news/negro-suffrage-new-agitation-antislavery-societythe-plat form-announced.html?pagewanted=3 (accessed July 28, 2013). Phillips chose to ignore the fundamental contradiction of prioritizing equalities in his position. He also clearly defined the nation's other major problem in sex terms, and by including black males in the word "male" he ensured that the problem of sex inequalities, if purely because of population statistics even though women were in a minority in the population at that time, was the largest problem for the foreseeable future. His inability to include sex inequalities, of course, was not simply because of the number of women in the population, which would represent a much more fundamental shift than black male voting equality did. It was also because the problem of women was not the "discrete and insular" problem, to use the later legal jargon, that black males represented. As part of everyday life for all men, sex equality affected every hearth and was much more fundamental and dangerous.

13. Frederick Douglass, *Frederick Douglass, Selected Speeches and Writings*, ed. Philip S. Foner, abridged and adapted by Yuval Taylor (New York: Lawrence Hill Books, 1999), 600.

14. Stanton, Anthony and Gage, eds., *History of Woman Suffrage*, vol. 2, pp. 382–3; Ida

Husted Harper, *The Life and Work of Susan B. Anthony, Including Public Addresses, Her Own Letters and Many from Her Contemporaries During Fifty Years,* 2 vols. (Indianapolis and Kansas City: Bowen-Merrill, 1899), vol. 1, pp. 323–4.

15. See Kathleen Barry, *Susan B. Anthony: The Biography of a Singular Feminist* (New York: Ballantine, 1988), 192–3. Barry found that the official account of the *History of Woman Suffrage* excised key parts of Anthony's speeches at that 1869 meeting and this censorship has contributed to the continued characterization of Anthony as racist. Barry's observations deserve much more airing than they receive. See also Sally G. McMillen, *Seneca Falls and the Origins of the Women's Rights Movement* (Oxford: Oxford University Press, 2008), 168, 282–3, n. 45.

16. Contrary to frequent perception, not all women of the South were racist. Clara McDiarmid of Arkansas, who helped establish the Arkansas Equal Rights Association in 1878 and brought Susan B. Anthony to the South for the first time in 1879, was well known in Little Rock circles for "believ[ing] in equality for all people, regardless of sex or color" (see Wassell, "History of Equal Suffrage in Arkansas"; Bernadette Cahill, "Clara McDiarmid at Home: Suffrage and Society in *Fin de Siècle* Little Rock, Arkansas," unpublished, 2011).

17. Weimann, *The Fair Women,* chapter 6.

18. Helen A. Cook, "A Letter to Miss Anthony," *Washington Post,* 19 February 1898, in *Papers of Elizabeth Cady Stanton and Susan B. Anthony,* ed. Patricia G. Holland and Ann D. Gordon (Wilmington, DE: Scholarly Resources, 1991), microfilm, reel 38, frame 276, in Ann D. Gordon, ed. *African American Women and the Vote, 1937–1965* (Amherst: University of Massachusetts Press, 1997), 5. See also Bettina Aptheker, *Woman's Legacy: Essays on Race, Sex and Class in American History* (Amherst: University of Massachusetts Press, 1982) and Patricia A. Schechter, *Ida B. Wells-Barnett and American Reform, 1880–1930* (Chapel Hill: University of North Carolina Press, 2001).

19. Barry, *Susan B. Anthony,* 194.

20. Dorothy Sterling, *Ahead of Her Time: Abby Kelley and the Politics of Antislavery* (New York: Norton, 1994), 275.

21. For the complexity of the temper of that specific time in Washington, D.C., which included the rape of a white woman by a black man, see Walton, *A Woman's Crusade,* 63–64.

22. United States Congress, Record for the Senate, June 3, 1919, pp. 556–558, 561–571, and June 4, 1919, pp. 615–635. See also United States Congress, Record for the Senate, February 10, 1919, pp. 3052–3062.

Chapter 10

1. "Campbell Leading in Constable Race," *Arkansas Gazette,* November 3, 1920, p. 14.

2. "Negro Women in South Rushing to Register," *New York Times,* September 20, 1920.

3. Schuyler, *The Weight of Their Votes,* 24–26, 52.

4. "Negro Women Refused Suffrage in Georgia," *Indianapolis Star,* November 3, 1920, p. 11.

5. This was not necessarily racism. There was a total ban on female voting in Georgia in the 1920 election because enforcement of the law demanded registration months before an election (see Walton, *A Woman's Crusade,* 244).

6. One factor that would have affected white and black women unequally was the Democratic Party's southern white primaries (see Keyssar, *The Right to Vote,* 247). This raises further questions. How much of a disincentive did they represent to the registration of black women? If they were a disincentive, how did these 50 black women register to vote and why? Had they registered, in spite of the white primaries, in anticipation of ratification? How could the women afford the poll tax when blacks were supposedly extremely poor?

7. "Blount's Name to Appear on Ballot," *Arkansas Gazette,* September 15, 1920, p. 1.

8. "Negroes Organize to Elect Blount: Lethargy of Democrats May Cause Surprise at General Election," *Arkansas Gazette,* September 27, 1920, p. 7.

9. *Minor v. Happersett,* 88 U.S. 162 (1875).

10. "Address Prior to Trial," in Anthony, *The Trial,* 170.

11. Schuyler, *The Weight of Their Votes,* 32.

12. Christine Lunardini (*From Equal Suffrage to Equal Rights: Alice Paul and the National Woman's Party, 1910–1928* (New York: New York University, 1986) at 161–2) tackles this issue in a manner that gives the complexities their due.

13. Adams and Keene (*Alice Paul and the Suffrage Campaign,* xviii, n. 1) demonstrate how the NWP suffrage campaign and Alice Paul in particular have been ignored in histories of non-violence.

14. Walton, *A Woman's Crusade*, 26; Adams and Keene, *Alice Paul and the Suffrage Campaign*, 25–28.

Chapter 11

1. For Garvey's full story, see Colin Grant, *Negro with a Hat: The Rise and Fall of Marcus Garvey and His Dream of a Mother Africa* (London: Jonathan Cape, 2008).

2. See photograph at the Web site of the Decatur House Museum, Lafayette Square, Washington, D.C., http://www.whitehousehistory.org/decatur-house/african-american-tour/Default.aspx (accessed June 14, 2012).

3. For a concise summary of the history of the black civil rights movement, see Mark Newman, *The Civil Rights Movement* (Westport, CT: Praeger, 2004).

4. For the history of the development of the Mall's modern form, see National Park Service, United States Department of the Interior, National Register of Historic Places Inventory—Nomination, *National Mall*, March 23, 1981, http://pdfhost.focus.nps.gov/docs/NRHP/Text/66000031.pdf (accessed August 1, 2014); Scott W. Berg, *Grand Avenues: The Story of the French Visionary Who Designed Washington, D.C.* (New York: Pantheon Books, 2007), 263–274. Thomas J. Carrier (*Washington, D.C.: A Historical Walking Tour* [Charleston, SC: Arcadia, 1999]) tells of the development of modern D.C. after L'Enfant.

5. "The Seneca Falls Convention," *Equal Rights*, August 4, 1923, p. 195; "Memorial Pageant in the Garden of the Gods," *Equal Rights*, September 8, 1923, pp. 237–8; "Party Renews Its Faith at Belmont Bier," *Equal Rights*, February 18, 1933, pp. 19–20; "Great and Good Women Honored in Impressive Pageant," *Equal Rights*, July 15, 1933, p. 187.

6. For example, *Wiley v. District of Columbia*, 47 App. D.C. 412 (1918) and *Hunter v. District of Columbia*, 47 App. D.C. 406 (1918).

Chapter 12

1. Adams and Keene, *Alice Paul and the Suffrage Campaign*, 247. The authors use the words "social change," which may reflect reluctance to describe women's rights as a civil rights movement in the United States today due to its current narrow meaning.

2. For brief histories of many prominent black women, see Darryl Lyman, *Great African-American Women* (New York: Gramercy Books, 1999).

3. "Negro Women Join in Suffrage Fight: Many Accept Mrs. Belmont's Invitation to Become Members of Her Organization; Meet in Colored Church; Mrs. Villard Tells the Congregation That This Struggle Is Like That of Her Father for Emancipation," *New York Times*, February 7, 1910.

4. Patricia Bernstein (*The First Waco Horror: The Lynching of Jesse Washington and the Rise of the NAACP* (College Station: Texas A&M University Press, 2006) features Elisabeth Freeman's investigation of this notorious lynching. See http://www.elizabethfreeman.org/ and http://www.elizabethfreeman.org/exhibit.php (both accessed April 9, 2014). The author thanks Freeman's relative Margaret Johnson, curator of the Freeman exhibition, for this information.

5. For further information on Kelley's campaign against lynching, see Louis L. Athey, "Florence Kelley and the Quest for Negro Equality," *Journal of Negro History* 56, no. 4 (October 1971): 249–261. This article is also invaluable for insight regarding the difficult conflict women encountered when the question of women's rights versus black rights arose within the same general issue. As even Kelley experienced, the resolution of the conflict could be all but impossible, sometimes forcing a choice. In such circumstances, the individual's perception of priorities determined the outcome, not necessarily racism.

6. Bernadette Cahill, "Stepping Outside the Bounds of Convention: Adolphine Fletcher Terry and Radical Suffragism in Little Rock, 1911–1920," *Pulaski County Historical Review* 60 (Winter 2012): 122–129. See also, Bayless, *Obliged to Help*, 81–83.

7. Wilkerson-Freeman, in "The Second Battle," deals with the actual facts of the disproportionate disfranchisement of white women due to the poll tax and their campaign against it in Alabama; Podolefsky, "Illusion of Suffrage"; Schuyler, *The Weight of Their Votes*, 32; Keyssar, *The Right to Vote*, 236–7.

8. Schuyler, *The Weight of Their Votes*, 199.

9. Lyman, *Great African-American Women*, 22–24.

10. See Vicki L. Crawford, Jacqueline Anne Rouse and Barbara Woods, eds., *Women in the Civil Rights Movement: Trailblazers and Torchbearers, 1941–1965* (Bloomington and Indianapolis: Indiana University Press, 1990, 1993).

11. *Browder v. Gayle*, 352 U.S. 903 (1956).

12. Lyman, *Great African-American Women*, 178–180.

13. Grif Stockley, *Daisy Bates: Civil Rights Crusader from Arkansas* (Jackson: University of Mississippi Press, 2005).

14. Bernadette Cahill, "Terry and Radical Suffragism," *Pulaski County Historical Review* 60 (Winter 2012): 122–129; Bayless, *Obliged to Help,* 81–83.

15. Koehler, "Pioneers Recall."

16. Nelle Morton, *The Journey Is Home* (Boston: Beacon, 1985), 176–198, at 188–191 and 247–8, n. 16. See also Don Donahue, "Prophets of a New Social Order: Presbyterians and the Fellowship of Southern Churchmen, 1934–1963," *American Presbyterians* 74, no. 3 (Fall 1996), 209–221 at 214–218, http://www.jstor.org/stable/23333336 (accessed August 26, 2013). Quotation of Dr. Benjamin Mays, at 216, quoted from *Prophetic Religion* 7 (Spring 1946): 1.

17. Mike Marshall, "Her Times Shaped a Lifelong Activist," *Huntsville Times*, December 18, 2011, p. A3.

Chapter 13

1. For a summary of the sex discrimination within black civil rights see Stockley, *Daisy Bates,* 3–11.

2. Sara Evans, *Personal Politics: The Roots of Women's Liberation in the Civil Rights Movement and the New Left* (New York: Vintage, 1979).

3. See the 1890s controversy in the NAWSA over Stanton's "Woman's Bible."

4. For one interpretation of the failure of the ERA, see Jane L. Mansbridge, *Why We Lost the ERA* (Chicago: University of Chicago Press, 1986). See also Rymph, *Republican Women,* and Bernadette Cahill, "Pinky Hayden's Life in Politics," *High Country* (Boone, North Carolina), August 2008.

5. Voting age figures derived from Kennedy, *Population of the United States in 1860,* pp. 592–597. The white male population in the eighth census was 13,844,537. The 21-and-over white male population was 6,971,106.

6. Douglass, Foner, ed., *Frederick Douglass,* 600.

7. Lindsay Van Gelder, "Four Days That Changed the World," *Ms.,* March 1978, in Suzanne Levine and Harriet Lyons, eds., *The Decade of Women: A Ms. History of the Seventies in Words and Pictures* (New York: Paragon, 1980), 168.

8. See "Non-Hispanic Non-Men," in Bernadette Cahill, *Women in the High Country*

(Boone, NC: Unpublished Press, 2009), 96–110.

9. Laura Bates, *Everyday Sexism* (London: Simon & Schuster, 2014), http://everydaysexism.com/ (accessed July 31, 2014).

10. Eva Figes, *Patriarchal Attitudes: The Case for Women in Revolt* (New York: Fawcett Premier, 1970).

11. Nelle Morton, "Towards a Whole Theology," in *Sexism in the 1970s: Discrimination Against Women; A Report of the World Council of Churches Consultation, West Berlin, 1974* (Geneva: World Council of Churches, 1975), 56–65. Morton uses the word "pain" in this address in this general meaning, but not as in the quotation. The author heard her use the specific statement repeatedly in groups at the World Council of Churches consultation in Berlin and in later meetings in Dublin, Ireland, and in Claremont, California. Morton always spoke these words when partisan individuals were arguing that the oppression of women, especially in the Western world and in the United States in particular, was not as bad as the oppression of race and class.

12. Journalist Katie Breen of *Marie Claire* pointed out to me the rift in the World Council of Churches' Sexism Conference, held in West Berlin in June of 1974. Third World women held that poverty in undeveloped nations was much more important than sexism to deal with, deeming Western women self-indulgent when the latter complained about discrimination. The issue of poverty had to be tackled and conquered before the issue of discrimination against women (see Bernadette Cahill, "Sexism in the 1970s," *Irish Times,* June 26, 1974). This rift paralleled an experience I had the year before when an Irish journalist dismissed my protests about discrimination against women in the Ireland of that time in the presence of a visitor from South Africa. The journalist held that discrimination against women was nothing compared with racism and apartheid. Interestingly for the journalist, the young South African black man and I understood each other. It was essentially what Nelle Morton had said: no matter the details of respective oppressions, the pain is the same. Later in 1974, in a youth conference about women's equality, socialist youth group members put the inequality of women behind economic revolution, with women's equality a natural result of Marxist revolution. No matter the context, therefore, except with women concerned about women's inequality, women's equality always comes last, while

advocates of every other movement jockey for position ahead of women's equality.

Chapter 14

1. http://www.nwhm.org/education-re sources/activities/womans-suffrage-tours/ (accessed May 2, 2014). Since the original visit to Washington, D.C., another brochure of walking tours on women's history has surfaced, produced by tailoredtours.com, that is not linked on the Web site.

2. Louisiana, for example, was the only southern state to record by race and sex (Schuyler, *The Weight of Their Votes*, 230 and Table A4).

3. This history was related by a speaker at the 2010 Equal Rights Amendment rally outside the White House.

4. The brochure is no longer available at the original link. A new edition has since been issued and this, if anything, is worse in terms of woman suffrage history. See http://www. culturaltourismdc.org/portal/c/document_ library/get_file?uuid=c0f25a0f-cefa-48a3- 969d-782904380b40&groupId=701982 (accessed May 2, 2014).

5. The NAWSA had forty-four state auxiliaries and more than two million members when Carrie Chapman Catt took over late in 1915 (Graham, *Woman Suffrage*, 86).

6. Adams and Keene, *Alice Paul and the Suffrage Campaign*, 35, citing Hannah Geffen Josephson, *Jeannette Rankin, First Lady in Congress: A Biography*, (New York: Bobbs-Merrill, 1974). The membership declined by about 20,000 during the worst of the picketing controversy.

7. *Women Who Made History: A Guide to Women's History Sites in Washington, D.C.* (Washington, D.C.: The President's Commission on the Celebration of Women In American History, U.S. General Services Administration, Department of Communications, 2000).

8. *Capitol Hill Historic District* (Washington, D.C.: D.C. Historic Preservation Office, District of Columbia Government, 2003), 5.

9. "President's Park /Citizen's Soapbox: A History of Protest at the White House Walking Tour," http://www.whitehousehistory.org/wh ha_tours/citizens_soapbox/index.html (accessed March 2, 2013).

10. National Park Service, *Civil Rights in America: A Framework for Identifying Significant Sites* (Washington, D.C.: U.S. Department of the Interior, 2002, revised 2008).

11. *General Population Statistics, 1960,* Table 44, at 1–145. See also Michael R. Haines and Richard H. Steckel, *A Population History of North America* (New York: Cambridge University Press, 2000), Table A-4, 702–704, derived from U.S. Bureau of the Census (1975) data.

12. National Park Service, *Civil Rights in America*, table of contents, ii, 3.

13. Stanton, Anthony and Gage, eds., *History of Woman Suffrage,* vol. 2, p. 266.

Chapter 15

1. Caroline Katzenstein, *Lifting the Curtain: The State and National Woman Suffrage Campaigns in Pennsylvania as I Saw Them,* (Philadelphia: Dorrance, 1955), 306–7, 308–9. See also "Suffragists Burn Wilson in Effigy; Many Locked Up," *New York Times,* February 10, 1919.

2. "Colby Proclaims Woman Suffrage; Signs Certificate of Ratification at His Home Without Women Witnesses," *New York Times,* August 27, 1920, p. 1.

3. Newsreel: *President Johnson Signing Civil Rights Act,* https://www.youtube.com/ watch?v=U1rovPJid4Q (accessed August 1, 2014). President Johnson's remarks that day stand out for not referring to women and his exclusively male language ("President Lyndon B. Johnson's Radio and Television Remarks Upon Signing the Civil Rights Bill," broadcast from the East Room at the White House at 6:45 p.m., July 2, 1964, in *Public Papers of the Presidents of the United States: Lyndon B. Johnson, 1963–64,* vol.2, entry 446, pp. 842–844 (Washington, D.C.: Government Printing Office, 1965). The Civil Rights Act of 1964 is Public Law 88–352 (78 Stat. 241).

4. "National Woman's Party Moves Across Lafayette Square," *Suffragist,* January 5, 1918, p. 6. For further information on the history and notoriety of the building, see *Suffragist,* February 16, 1918, p. 5.

5. Information in an e-mail dated August 5, 2014, from collections and facilities manager, Sewall-Belmont House and Museum, home of the historic National Woman's Party, 144 Constitution Avenue NE, Washington, D.C.

6. See the advertisement for the restaurant in *Suffragist,* October 1920, p. 257, and Frederick O'Brien, "An Impression of a Suffrage Tea Room," *Suffragist,* September 21, 1918, p. 8.

7. The masthead of the *Suffragist* of December 27, 1913, gives the two different addresses for the different departments of the CU.

8. "The Suffrage Ball," *Suffragist*, March 21, 1914, p. 7.

9. Ida Husted Harper, *History of Woman Suffrage, 1900–1920*, vol. 5 (New York: National American Woman Suffrage Association, 1922), 439.

10. "Open Meeting at Mrs. Kent's Home," *Suffragist*, January 3, 1914, p. 2; "Appeal for Collection to Be Taken January 11," *Suffragist*, January 3, 1914, p. 3; "Official Program of the NWP 1921 Convention," *Suffragist*, January–February 1921, pp. 342.

11. Irwin, *The Story of Alice Paul*, 228, 336–7.

12. Walton, *A Woman's Crusade*, 130–1; Adams and Keene, *Alice Paul and the Suffrage Campaign*, 111.

13. Walton, *A Woman's Crusade*, 70–71

14. Irwin, *The Story of Alice Paul*, 183–4.

15. Walton, *A Woman's Crusade*, 144.

16. For the legislative proposals, see Thomas C. Pardo, ed., *The National Woman's Party Papers, 1913–1974: A Guide to the Microfilm Edition* (Sanford, NC: Microfilming Corporation of America, 1979).

Bibliography

Newspapers

Equal Rights
Glasgow Herald
Huntsville (AL) Times
Indianapolis Star
Irish Times
(Little Rock) Arkansas Democrat
(Little Rock) Arkansas Gazette

New York Evening Journal
New York Times
New York World
Philadelphia Inquirer
Suffragist
Woman Citizen
The Vote

Secondary Works and Primary Sources

Adams, Katherine H., and Michael L. Keene. *After the Vote Was Won: The Later Achievements of Fifteen Suffragists.* Jefferson, NC: McFarland, 2010.
_____. *Alice Paul and the American Suffrage Campaign.* Urbana: University of Illinois Press, 2008.
American Women. http://memory.loc.gov/ammem/awhhtml/awlaw3/property_law.html (accessed June 27, 2013).
American Women: Report of the President's Commission on the Status of Women. Washington, D.C.: Women's Bureau of the Department of Labor, 1963.
The Anniversaries: Important Sessions of the AntiSlavery Society; Speeches of Wendell Phillips et al. May 10, 1865. http://www.nytimes.com/1865/05/10/news/anniversaries-import ant-session-antislavery-society-speeches-wendell-phillips html?pagewanted=1 (accessed July 28, 2013).
Anthony, Susan B. *The Trial of Susan B. Anthony.* Classics in Women's Studies. Amherst, NY: Humanity Books, 2003.
Aptheker, Bettina, *Woman's Legacy. Essays on Race, Sex, and Class in American History.* Amherst: University of Massachusetts Press, 1982.
Archivist, United States. "Memorandum Opinion for the Counsel to the President." May 13, 1992.
Asian American Democracy Project. http://aaldef.org/programs/voting-rights/ (accessed October 24, 2013).
Athey, Louis L. "Florence Kelley and the Quest for Negro Equality." *Journal of Negro History* 56, no. 4 (October 1971): 249–261.
Baker, Jean H. *Sisters: The Lives of America's Suffragists.* New York: Hill & Wang, 2005.
Barber, Lucy G. *Marching on Washington: The Forging of an American Political Tradition.* Berkeley: University of California Press, 2002.

Barry, Kathleen. *Susan B. Anthony: A Biography of a Singular Feminist.* New York: Ballantine, 1988.

Bates, Laura. *Everyday Sexism.* London: Simon & Shuster, 2014.

Bayless, Stephanie. *Obliged to Help: Adolphine Fletcher Terry and the Progressive South.* Little Rock: Butler Center Books, 2011.

_____. *A Southern Paradox: The Social Activism of Adolphine Fletcher Terry.* M.A. Thesis, University of Arkansas at Little Rock, 2006.

Beard, Mary R. *Woman as Force in History: A Study in Traditions and Realities.* New York: Collier Books, 1971.

Becker, Mary. "The Sixties Shift to Formal Equality and the Courts: An Argument for Pragmatism and Politics." *William and Mary Law Review* 40, no. 1 (1998): 209–277.

Becker, Susan D. *The Origins of the Equal Rights Amendment: American Feminism Between the Wars.* Westport, CT; London, England: Greenwood Press, 1981.

Bendat, Jim. *Democracy's Big Day, 1789–2013.* iUniverse Star, 2012.

Berg, Scott W. *Grand Avenues: The Story of the French Visionary Who Designed Washington, D.C.* New York: Pantheon Books, 2007.

Bernstein, Patricia. *The First Waco Horror: The Lynching of Jesse Washington and the Rise of the NAACP.* College Station: Texas A&M University Press, 2006.

Biggs, Michael. *The Rationality of Self-Inflicted Sufferings: Hunger Strikes by Irish Republicans, 1916–1923.* University of Oxford, England, Department of Sociology. http://users.ox.ac.uk/~sfos0060/SWP2007-03.pdf (accessed November 22, 2013).

Bland, Sidney Roderick. *Techniques of Persuasion: The National Woman's Party and Woman Suffrage, 1913–1919.* Washington, D.C.: George Washington University, 1972.

Bly, Nellie. "Suffragists Are Men's Superiors." *New York Evening Journal,* March 3, 1913.

Boller, Paul F. *Presidential Inaugurations.* Orlando, FL: Harcourt, 2001.

Boyd, Mary Summer. "Jury Service—By Sufferance or by Law." *Woman Citizen* (1920): 1330–1.

Breedlove v. Suttles. U.S. Supreme Court, 1937.

Browder v. Gayle. U.S. Supreme Court, 1956.

Brown, Dorothy M. *Setting a Course: American Women in the 1920s.* Boston: Twayne, 1987.

Butler, Amy Eilene. "The Search for Women's Equality: Alice Paul and Ethel Smith in the ERA Debate, 1921–1923." Ph.D. diss., State University of New York at Binghamton, 1998.

Cahill, Bernadette. "Clara McDiarmid at Home: Suffrage and Society in *Fin de Siècle* Little Rock." Unpublished, 2011.

_____. "Congressional Medal for World War Two Granite Falls Woman Pilot." *High Country Press,* March 11, 2010.

_____. "Pinky Hayden's Life in Politics." *High Country Magazine,* August 2008.

_____. "Some Women 'Out of Touch' as U.S. Congress Breaks Again on Fairness and Equal Pay." *Women's News Network,* June 2012.

_____. "Stepping Outside the Bounds of Convention: Adolphine Fletcher Terry and Radical Suffragism in Little Rock, 1911–1920." *Pulaski County Historical Review* 60 (2012): 122–129.

_____. *Women in the High Country.* Boone, NC: Unpublished Press, 2009.

_____. "'Young people think women always had the right to vote': Josephine Miller and the Arkansas Woman Suffrage Campaign." *Pulaski County Historical Review* 61 (2013): 11–15.

Cannon, Carl M. *Youth Vote: Dems' Secret Weapon 40 Years in the Making?,* March 2011. http://www.realclearpolitics.com/articles/2011/03/25/youth_vote_dems_delayed_time_release_capsule.html#ixzz30eoWYl1v (accessed May 3, 2014).

Capitol Hill Historic District. Washington, D.C.: Historic Preservation Office, District of Columbia Government, 2003.

Carrier, Thomas J. *Washington, D.C: A Historical Walking Tour.* Charleston, SC: Arcadia, 1999.

Carroll, Peter. *The Free and the Unfree: A New History of the United States.* New York: Penguin, 1988.

Catt, Carrie Chapman, and Nettie Rogers Shuler. *Woman Suffrage and Politics: The Inner Story of the Suffrage Movement.* New York: Scribner's, 1923. Seattle: University of Washington Press Americana Library, 1969.

Censer, Jane Turner. *The Reconstruction of White Southern Womanhood, 1865–1895.* Baton Rouge: Louisiana State University, 2003.

Chenery, William L. "One in Three Women Vote." *New York Times,* December 19, 1920.

Civil Rights Act. Public Law 88-352 (78 Stat. 241). 1964.

Clinton, Catherine. *The Other Civil War: American Women in the Nineteenth Century.* New York: Hill and Wang, 1984.

Collins, Gail. *America's Women: 400 Years of Dolls, Drudges, Helpmates and Heroines.* New York: William Morrow/HarperCollins, 2003.

Constitution of the Women's Freedom League. London: Women's Freedom League, 1909.

Cooney, Robert P.J. *Winning the Vote: The Triumph of the American Woman Suffrage Movement.* Santa Cruz, CA: American Graphic Press, 2005.

Cotnam, Mrs. T.T. *History of Woman Suffrage in Arkansas.* 1919. http://www.arkansasties.com/Special/HistoryofWomensSuffrage.htm (accessed November 14, 2013).

Crawford, Elizabeth. *The Women's Suffrage Movement: A Reference Guide, 1866–1928.* London: Routledge, 1999, 2001.

Crawford, Vicki L., Jacqueline Anne Rouse and Barbara Woods. *Women in the Civil Rights Movement: Trailblazers and Torchbearers, 1941–1965.* Bloomington: University of Indiana Press, 1990, 1993.

CU/NWP Documents Which Chronicle Division Between NAWSA and CU/NWP. http://www.oocities.org/emilyc_25/cunwp_split.html (accessed April 24, 2014).

Dennis, Robert N. *Robert N. Dennis Collection of Stereoscopic Views.* http://digitalgallery.nypl.org/nypldigital/dgkeysearchdetail.cfm?strucID=624181&imageID=g91f182_006f (accessed November 3, 2013).

Dodd, Lynda G. "Parades, Pickets and Prison: Alice Paul and the Virtues of Unruly Constitutional Citizenship." *Journal of Law and Politics* (Fall 2008).

Donahue, Don. "Prophets of a New Social Order: Presbyterians and the Fellowship of Southern Churchmen, 1934–1963." *American Presbyterians* 74, no. 3 (1996): 209–221.

Dougan, Michael B. "The Arkansas Married Woman's Property Law." *Arkansas Historical Quarterly* 46, no. 1 (Spring 1987): 3–26.

Douglass, Frederick. *Frederick Douglass: Selected Speeches and Writings.* Edited by Philip S. Foner. Abridged and adapted by Yuval Taylor. New York: Lawrence Hill Books, 1999.

_____. *The Life and Times of Frederick Douglass.* Hartford, CT: Park, 1881.

DuBois, Ellen Carol. *Feminism and Suffrage: The Emergence of an Independent Women's Movement in America 1848–69.* Ithaca and London: Cornell University Press, 1978.

_____. *Harriot Stanton Blatch and the Winning of Woman Suffrage.* New Haven and London: Yale University Press, 1997.

_____. "Outgrowing the Compact of the Fathers: Equal Rights, Woman Suffrage, and the United States Constitution, 1820–1878." *Journal of American History: The Constitution and American Life* (1988): 176–202.

Dudden, Faye E. *Fighting Chance: The Struggle Over Woman Suffrage and Black Suffrage in Reconstruction America.* New York: Oxford University Press, 2011.

Dykeman, Therese Boos. *American Woman Philosophers, 1650–1930: Six Exemplary Thinkers.* Lewiston, NY/Queenston/Lampeter: Edwin Mellen, 1993.

Eastland, Terry. *Counting by Race: Equality from the Founding Fathers to Bakke and Weber.* New York: Basic Books, 1979.

"ERA Campaign." Opinion Research Corporation Caravan Services.

Evans, Sara. *Personal Politics: The Roots of Women's Liberation in the Civil Rights Movement and the New Left.* New York: Alfred A. Knopf, 1979.

Figes, Eva. *Patriarchal Attitudes: The Case for Women in Revolt.* New York: Fawcett Premier, 1970.

Flexner, Eleanor. *Century of Struggle: The Women's Rights Movement in the United States.* Cambridge, MA: Belknap Press of Harvard University, 1959; revised 1975.

Foner, Philip S. *Frederick Douglass on Women's Rights.* New York: Da Capo Press, 1992.

Ford, Linda G. *Iron-Jawed Angels: The Suffrage Militancy of the National Woman's Party, 1912–1920.* Lanham, NY; London: University Press of America, 1991.

Freeman, Jo. *The Politics of Women's Liberation.* New York: David McKay, 1975.

Frost, Catherine. *Women's Suffrage in America: An Eyewitness History.* New York: Facts on File, 1992.

Iron Jawed Angels. Movie directed by Katja Von Garner. 2004.

General Population Statistics, 1960: United States Summary. Washington, D.C: U.S. Census Bureau, 1961.

Ginzberg, Lori D. *Elizabeth Cady Stanton.* New York: Hill and Wang, 2009.

Gleason, Caroline J. *Report of the Social Survey Committee of the Consumers' League of Oregon on the Wages, Hours, and Conditions of Work and Cost and Standard of Living of Women Wage Earners in Oregon with Special Reference to Portland.* Portland, OR: Keystone Press, 1913.

Gordon, Ann D., and Bettye Collier-Thomas. *African American Women and the Vote, 1837–1965.* Edited by Ann D. Gordon with Bettye Collier-Thomas. Amherst: University of Massachusetts Press, 1997.

Gordon, Ann D., ed. *The Selected Papers of Elizabeth Cady Stanton and Susan B. Anthony.* 5 vols. Brunswick, NJ: Rutgers University Press, 1997.

Graham, Sara Hunter. *Woman Suffrage and the New Democracy.* New Haven and London: Yale University Press, 1996.

Grant, Colin. *Negro with a Hat: The Rise and Fall of Marcus Garvey and His Dream of a Mother Africa.* London: Jonathan Cape, 2008.

Grant, Kevin. "British Suffragettes and the Russian Method of Hunger Strike." *Comparative Studies in Society and History* 53, no. 1 (2011): 113–143.

Green, Elna C. *Southern Strategies: Southern Women and the Woman Suffrage Question.* Chapel Hill: University of North Carolina Press, 1997.

Greenberg, Hazel, and Anita Miller. *The Equal Rights Amendment: A Bibliographic Study.* Westport, CT: Greenwood Press, 1976.

Gruberg, Martin. *Women in American Politics: An Assessment and Sourcebook.* Oshkosh, WI: Academia, 1968.

Haines, Michael R., and Richard H. Steckel. *A Population History of North America.* New York: Cambridge University Press, 2000.

Hall, Fred Smith, and Elisabeth W. Brooke. *American Marriage Laws in Their Social Aspects: A Digest.* Russell Sage Foundation, 1919.

Hansen, Stephen A. "All in the Family: The Cutts-Madison and Benjamin Ogle Tayloe Houses on Lafayette Square." http://intowner.com/2013/12/16/all-in-the-family-the-cutts-madison-and-benjamin-ogle-tayloe-houses-on-lafayette-square/ (accessed May 17, 2014).

Harper, Ida Husted. *History of Woman Suffrage, 1900–1920.* Vol. 5. New York: National American Woman Suffrage Association, 1922.

_____. *History of Woman Suffrage, 1900–1920.* Vol. 6. National American Woman Suffrage Association, 1922.

_____. *The Life and Work of Susan B. Anthony, Including Public Addresses, Her Own Letters and Many from Her Contemporaries During Fifty Years.* Indianapolis and Kansas City: Bowen-Merrill, 1899.

Harper v. Virginia Board of Elections. U.S. Supreme Court, 1966.

Harrison, Cynthia Ellen. *On Account of Sex: The Politics of Women's Issues, 1945–1968*. Berkeley: University of California Press, 1988.

_____. "Prelude to Feminism: Women's Organizations, the Federal Government and the Rise of the Women's Movement, 1942–68." 2 vols. New York, Columbia University (Unpublished), 1970.

Harrison, Patricia Greenwood. *Connecting Links: The British and American Woman Suffrage Movements, 1900–1914*. Westport, CT: Greenwood Press, 2000.

Haynsworth, Leslie. *Amelia Earhart's Daughters: The Wild and Glorious Story of American Women Aviators from World War II to the Dawn of the Space Age*. New York: Perennial, 1998.

Heckscher, August. *The Politics of Woodrow Wilson*. New York: Harper, 1956.

Heintze, James R. *The First Celebrations*. http://www1.american.edu/heintze/fourth.htm#Beginning (accessed November 3, 2013).

_____. *Fourth of July Celebrations Database*. http://www1.american.edu/heintze/fourth.htm#Beginning (accessed November 3, 2013).

Held, Allison L., Sheryl L. Herndon, and Danielle M. Stager. "The Equal Rights Amendment: Why the ERA Remains Legally Viable and Properly Before the States." *William and Mary Journal of Women and the Law* 3, no. 1 (1997): 113–136.

Hersh, Blanche. *The Slavery of Sex: Feminist-Abolitionists in America*. Chicago: University of Illinois Press, 1978.

Hillsdale College Political Faculty. *The U.S. Constitutional Reader*. Hillsdale, MI: Hillsdale College Press, 2012.

Hoffert, Sylvia D. *Alva Vanderbilt Belmont: Unlikely Champion of Women's Rights*. Bloomington and Indianapolis: Indiana University Press, 2012.

Hunter v. District of Columbia. Washington, D.C., Appeals Court, 1918.

In Their Footsteps: Woman Suffrage Historic Sites in Washington, D.C. National Women's History Museum. http://www.nwhm.org/education-resources/activities/womans-suffrage-tours/ (accessed May 2, 2014).

Irwin, Inez Hayes. *Angels and Amazons: A Hundred Years of American Women*. Garden City, NY: Doubleday, Doran/National Council of Women, 1933.

_____. *The Story of Alice Paul and the National Woman's Party*. Washington, D.C.: National Woman's Party, 1964, 1977.

Jacobs, Donald M., Arvarh E. Strickland, and F.C. Bartone. *The Rise and Struggles of American Civil Rights*. Chicago: United States History Society, 1970.

Joint Congressional Committee on Inaugural Celebrations. http://www.inaugural.senate.gov/about/history (accessed May 3, 2014).

Jorgensen-Earp, Cheryl R. "The Picketing Campaign Nears Victory." National Advisory Council Conference (7 December 1917). http://archive.vod.umd.edu/citizen/vernon1917int.htm (accessed May 13, 2014).

Josephson, Hanna Geffen. *Jeannette Rankin, First Lady in Congress: A Biography*. New York: Bobbs-Merrill, 1974.

Katzenstein, Caroline. *Lifting the Curtain: The State and National Woman Suffrage Campaigns in Pennsylvania as I Saw Them*. Philadelphia: Dorrance, 1955.

Kennedy, Joseph C.G. *Population of the United States in 1860: Compiled from the Original Returns of the Eighth Census Under the Direction of the Secretary of the Interior*. Washington, D.C.: Government Printing Office, 1864.

Keyssar, Alexander. *The Right to Vote: The Contested History of Democracy in the United States*. New York: Basic Books, 2000.

Klarman, Michael J. *From Jim Crow to Civil Rights*. New York: Oxford University Press, 2004.

Klein, Herbert S. *A Population History of the United States*. Cambridge and New York: Cambridge University Press, 2004.

Koehler, Kay. "Woman Suffrage: Pioneers Recall the Early Days—and Look Ahead." *Arkansas Gazette*, June 22, 1969, p. 5 D.

Kousser, Morgan J. "Poll Tax." Edited by Richard Rose. 2000. http://www.hss.caltech.edu/~kousser/dictionary%20entries/poll%20tax.pdf.

Kraditor, Aileen S. *The Ideas of the Woman Suffrage Movement, 1890–1920.* New York: Anchor, 1971.

Lanctot, Catherine J. "'We Are at War and You Should Not Bother the President': The Suffrage Pickets and Freedom of Speech During World War I." Villanova Law/Public Policy Research Paper No. 2008-16. http://dx.doi.org/10.2139/ssrn.1126806 (accessed November 19, 2013).

Lapidus, Lenora, et al. *The Rights of Women: The Authoritative ACLU Guide to Women's Rights*, 4th ed. New York: New York University Press, 2009.

Ledbetter v. Goodyear Tire & Rubber Co. U.S. Supreme Court, 2007.

Lemons, J. Stanley. *The Woman Citizen: Social Feminism in the 1920s.* Urbana: University of Illinois Press, 1973.

Leneman, Leah. *A Guid Cause: The Women's Suffrage Movement in Scotland.* Aberdeen: Aberdeen University Press, 1991.

Levine, Suzanne, and Harriet Lyons. *The Decade of Women: A Ms. History of the Seventies in Words and Pictures.* New York: Paragon, 1980.

Lobel, Jules. *Success Without Victory: The Lost Legal Battles and the Long Road to Justice in America.* New York and London: New York University Press, 2003.

Lumsden, Linda J. *Inez: The Life and Times of Inez Milholland.* Bloomington: Indiana University Press, 2004.

_____. *Rampant Women: Suffragists and the Right of Assembly.* Knoxville: University of Tennessee Press, 1997.

Lunardini, Christine. *From Equal Suffrage to Equal Rights: Alice Paul and the National Woman's Party, 1910–1928.* New York: New York University, 1986, 2000.

Lyman, Darryl. *Great African-American Women.* New York: Gramercy Books, 1999.

Mansbridge, Jane J. *Why We Lost the ERA.* Chicago: University of Chicago Press, 1986.

Marlow, Joyce. *Votes for Women: The Virago Book of Suffragettes.* Virago Press: London, 2001.

Marshall, Mike. "Her Times Shaped a Lifelong Activist." *Huntsville (AL) Times*, December 18, 2011, p. A3.

Mastilio, Christine. *Boone Parade: Women's Suffrage in Iowa.* University of Iowa Exhibits. http://sdrc.lib.uiowa.edu/exhibits/suffrage/1890parade.html (accessed November 13, 2013).

Mathews, Donald G. *Sex, Gender and the Politics of ERA: A State and the Nation.* New York/Oxford: Oxford University Press, 1990.

Matthews, Burnita Shelton. "The Woman Juror." *Women Lawyers' Journal* 15, no. 2 (January 1927).

Mayer, Henry. *All on Fire: William Lloyd Garrison and the Abolition of Slavery.* New York: St. Martin's Press, 1998.

Mayeri, Serena. "'A Common Fate of Discrimination': Race-Gender Analogies in Legal and Historical Perspective." *Yale Law Journal* 110 (March 2001): 1045–1087.

_____. "Constitutional Choices: Legal Feminism and the Historical Dynamics of Change." *California Law Review* 92, no. 3 (May 2004): 755–839.

Mayhall, Laura E. Nym. *The Militant Suffrage Movement: Citizenship and Resistance in Britain, 1860–1930.* Oxford: Oxford University Press, 2003.

McCammon, Holly J. "Out of the Parlors and into the Streets: The Changing Tactical Repertoire of the U.S. Women's Suffrage Movements." *Social Forces* 81, no. 3 (March 2003): 787–818.

_____. *The U.S. Women's Jury Movements and Strategic Adaptation: A More Just Verdict.* New York: Cambridge University Press, 2012.

McFadden, Margaret H. *Golden Cables of Sympathy: The Transatlantic Sources of Nineteenth-Century Feminism.* Lexington: University Press of Kentucky, 1999.

McGuire, John Thomas. "The Most Unjust Piece of Legislation: Section 213 of the Economy Act of 1932 and Feminism During the New Deal." *Journal of Policy History* 20, no. 4 (2008): 516–541.

McMillen, Sally G. *Seneca Falls and the Origins of the Women's Rights Movement.* Oxford: Oxford University Press, 2008.

Meier, August, and Elliott Rudwick. *Along the Color Line: Explorations in the Black Experience.* Champaign: University of Illinois Press, 1976, 2002.

Merryman, Molly. *Clipped Wings: The Rise and Fall of the Women Airforce Service Pilots (WASPs) of World War II.* New York: New York University Press, 1998.

Minor v. Happersett. U.S. Supreme Court, 1875.

Morgan, Francesca. *Women and Patriotism in Jim Crow America.* Chapel Hill: University of North Carolina Press, 2005.

Morton, Nelle. *The Journey Is Home.* Boston: Beacon Press, 1985.

Nash, Gary B. *The Unknown American Revolution: The Unruly Birth of Democracy and the Struggle to Create America.* New York: Penguin, 2005.

National Industrial Conference Board. "Changes in Wages During and Since the War, September 1914–March 1920." New York, 1920.

"National Mall." National Register of History Places, Nomination Form. March 23, 1981. http://pdfhost.focus.nps.gov/docs/NRHP/Text/66000031.pdf (accessed August 1, 2014).

National Park Service. *Civil Rights in America: A Framework for Identifying Significant Sites.* Washington, D.C.: U.S. Department of the Interior, 2002; revised 2008.

Negro Suffrage: Agitation of the AntiSlavery Society. May 13, 1865. http://www.nytimes.com/1865/05/13/news/negro-suffrage-new-agitation-antislavery-societythe-platform-announced.html?pagewanted=3 (accessed July 28, 2013).

Newman, Mark. *The Civil Rights Movement.* Westport, CT: Praeger, 2004.

Norton, Mary Beth. *Major Problems in American Women's History,* 3d ed. Boston: New York: Houghton Mifflin, 2003.

O'Connor, Sandra Day. *The Majesty of the Law: Reflections of a Supreme Court Justice.* New York: Random House, 2003.

Ohio History Central. http://www.ohiohistorycentral.org/w/Temperance_Movement?rec=560.

Oregon Public Television. *The Suffragists.* 2012.

Originalist. "Justice Antonin Scalia." *California Lawyer,* January 2011.

Pardo, Thomas C. *The National Woman's Party Papers, 1913–1974: A Guide to the Microfilm Edition.* Sanford, NC: Microfilming Corporation of America, 1979.

Peck, Mary Gray. *Carrie Chapman Catt: A Biography.* New York: H.W. Wilson, 1944.

Phillips, Melanie. *The Ascent of Woman: A History of the Suffragette Movement and the Ideas Behind It.* London: Abacus, 2003.

Podolefsky, Ronnie L. "The Illusion of Suffrage: Female Voting Rights and the Women's Poll Tax Repeal Movement After the Nineteenth Amendment." *Columbia Journal of Gender and Law* 7 (1997): 185–237.

President Johnson Signing of Civil Rights Act. Newsreel, 1964.

"President Lyndon B. Johnson's Civil Rights Bill Remarks." LBJ Presidential Library. July 2, 1964. http://www.lbjlib.utexas.edu/johnson/archives.hom/speeches.hom/640702.asp (accessed August 1, 2014).

President's Commission on the Celebration of Women in American History. *Women Who Made History: A Guide to Women's History Sites in Washington, D.C.* Washington, D.C.: U.S. General Services Administration, Department of Communications, 2000.

"President's Park/Citizens' Soapbox: A History of Protest at the White House Walking Tour."

http://www.whitehousehistory.org/whha_tours/citizens_soapbox/index.html (accessed March 2, 2014).

Reed v. Reed. U.S. Supreme Court, 1971.

Rutgers University. The Elizabeth Cady Stanton and Susan B. Anthony Papers Project. http://ecssba.rutgers.edu/resources/wompolls.html (accessed November 14, 2013).

Rymph, Catherine E. *Republican Women: Feminism and Conservatism from Suffrage Through the Rise of the New Right.* Chapel Hill: University of North Carolina Press, 2006.

Scharf, Lois. *To Work and to Wed: Female Employment, Feminism and the Great Depression.* Westport, CT: Greenwood Press, 1980.

Schechter, Patricia A. *Ida B. Wells-Barnett and American Reform, 1880–1930.* Chapel Hill: University of North Carolina Press, 2001.

Schneir, Miriam. *Feminism: The Essential Historical Writings.* New York: Vintage, 1972.

Schuyler, Lorriane Gates. *The Weight of Their Votes: Southern Women and Political Leverage in the 1920s.* Chapel Hill: University of North Carolina Press, 2006.

Sealander, Judith. *As Minority Becomes Majority: Federal Reaction to the Phenomenon of Women in the Work Force, 1920–1963.* Westport, CT: Greenwood Press, 1983.

Sexism in the 1970s: Discrimination Against Women; A Report of the World Council of Churches Consultation, West Berlin, 1974. Geneva: World Council of Churches, 1975.

Shammas, Carole. "Reassessing the Married Women's Property Acts." *Journal of Women's History* 6, no. 1 (Spring 1994): 9–30.

Somers, Christina. *Who Stole Feminism: How Women Have Betrayed Women.* New York: Simon & Schuster, 1994.

Southard, Belinda A. Stillion. *Militant Citizenship: Rhetorical Strategies of the National Woman's Party, 1913–1920.* College Station: Texas A&M University Press, 2011.

Spears, Raymond S. "What Does the Militant Movement Mean?" *Designer,* September 1914, pp. 10, 47.

Sperling, Liz. *Women, Political Philosophy and Politics.* Edinburgh: Edinburgh University Press, 2001.

Stanton, Elizabeth Cady. *Eighty Years and More (1815–1897): Reminiscences of Elizabeth Cady Stanton.* New York: European, 1898.

Stanton, Elizabeth Cady, Susan B. Anthony, and Matilda Jocelyn Gage. *History of Woman Suffrage, 1876–885.* Vol. 3. Rochester, NY: Susan B. Anthony, 1886.

_____. *History of Woman Suffrage, 1861–76.* Vol. 2. New York: Fowler & Wells, 1882.

Sterling, Dorothy. *Ahead of Her Time: Abby Kelley and the Politics of Antislavery.* New York: Norton, 1994.

Stevens, Doris. *Jailed for Freedom.* New York: Schocken Books, 1976.

Stockley, Grif. *Daisy Bates: Civil Rights Crusader from Arkansas.* Jackson: University Press of Mississippi, 2005.

Suffrage Parade: Hearing Before a Subcommittee of the Committee on the District of Columbia, United States Senate, Sixty-third Congress. Washington, D.C: Government Printing Office, 1913.

Summerlin, Elizabeth Stephens. "Not Ratified but Hereby Rejected: The Women's Suffrage Movement in Georgia, 1895–1925." MA thesis, Georgia College and State University, 2007.

Taylor, Barbara. *Eve and the New Jerusalem: Socialism and Feminism in the Nineteenth Century.* New York: Pantheon, 1983.

Terborg-Penn, Rosalyn. *African American Women in the Struggle for the Vote, 1850–1920.* Bloomington and Indianapolis: Indiana University Press, 1998.

Thaw, Deborah M. "The Feminization of the Office of Notary Public: From *Femme Covert* to *Notaire Covert.*" *John Marshall Law Review* 31, no. 3 (Spring 1998): 703–723.

Thomas, Mary Martha. *The New Woman in Alabama: Social Reforms and Suffrage, 1890–1920.* Tuscaloosa: University of Alabama Press, 1992.

Thomas, Tracy A., and Tracey Jean Boisseau. *Feminist Legal History: Essays in Woman and Law*. New York and London: New York University Press, 2011.

Thompson, Amanda. "Scientific Racism: The Justification of Slavery and Segregated Education in America." Texas A&M University. pat.tamu.edu/journal/vol-1/thompson.pdf.

Tilly, Louise A. *Women, Politics and Change*. New York: Russell Sage Foundation, 1990.

Turning Point Suffragists Memorial. http://www.suffragistmemorial.org/Home_Page.html (accessed May 23, 2014).

Unidentified. "Miss Paul Tells of Tube Feeding in English Prison." http://sites.bergen.org/our story/resources/Suffrage/newsclips/Tube_Feeding_2_1910.pdf (accessed November 21, 2013).

United States Congress. *Record for the Senate*. June 1919.

_____. *Record for the Senate*. February 1919.

United States Presidential Inauguration. http://en.wikipedia.org/wiki/United_States_presi dential_inauguration (accessed November 3, 2013).

United States v. Virginia. United States Supreme Court, 1996.

Wagner, Sally Roesch. *A Time of Protest: Suffragists Challenge the Republic, 1870–1887*. Aberdeen, SD: Sky Carrier, 1992.

Walton, Mary. *A Woman's Crusade: Alice Paul and the Battle for the Ballot*. New York: Palgrave Macmillan, 2010.

Wassell, S.S. "History of Equal Suffrage Movement in Arkansas: An Account of the Patient, Persistent Efforts for the Emancipation of Women, from Pioneer Days to the Present." *Arkansas Gazette*, February 1919, p. 30.

Wayne, Tiffany K. *Women's Roles in Nineteenth Century America*. 2007: Greenwood, 2007.

Weimann, Jeanne Madeline. *The Fair Women: The Story of the Woman's Building, World's Columbian Exposition, Chicago 1893*. Chicago: Academy Chicago, 1981.

Wellman, Judith. *The Road to Seneca Falls: Elizabeth Cady Stanton and the First Woman's Rights Convention*. Urbana: University of Illinois Press, 2004.

Whalen, Charles, and Barbara Whalen. *The Longest Debate: A Legislative History of the 1964 Civil Rights Act*. Cabin John, MD: Seven Locks Press, 1985.

Wheeler, Marjorie Spruill. *New Women of the New South: The Leaders of the Woman Suffrage Movement in the Southern States*. New York; Oxford: Oxford University Press, 1993.

_____. *One Woman, One Vote: Rediscovering the Woman Suffrage Movement*. Troutdale, AZ: New Sage Press, 1995.

_____. *Votes for Women! The Woman Suffrage Movement in Tennessee, the South, and the Nation*. Knoxville: University of Tennessee Press, 1995.

Whittell, Giles. *Spitfire Women of World War II*. London: Harper Perennial, 2008.

Wiley v. District of Columbia. Washington, D.C. Appeals Court, 1918.

Wilkerson-Freeman, Sarah. "The Second Battle for Woman Suffrage: Alabama White Women, the Poll Tax, and V.O. Key's Master Narrative of Southern Politics." *Journal of Southern History* 68, no. 2 (May 2002): 333–374.

Winsor, Mary. "The Militant Suffrage Movement." *Annals of the American Academy of Political and Social Science* 56 (November 1914): 134–142.

"A Woman's Place Is in the Sewall-Belmont House: Alice Paul and Women's Rights." *Teaching with Historic Places Lesson Plans*. National Park Service. http://www.nps.gov/nr/twhp/wwwlps/lessons/148sewallbelmont/148sewallbelmont.htm (accessed May 18, 2014).

Women's Bureau. Women's Bureau of the Department of Labor. http://www.dol.gov/dol/aboutdol/history/dolchp01.htm (accessed March 8, 2014).

Woodward, C. Vann. *The Origins of the New South, 1877–1913*. Baton Rouge: Louisiana State University Press, 1971.

World Digital Library. http://www.wdl.org/en/item/4051/ (accessed November 3, 2013).

Zagarri, Rosemarie. "The Rights of Man and Woman in Post-Revolutionary America." *William and Mary Quarterly* 55, no. 2 (April 1998): 203–230 (Omohundro Institute of Early American History and Culture).

Index

Numbers in **bold italics** indicate pages with photographs.

215